4 Longman Academic Reading Series

READING SKILLS FOR COLLEGE

Robert F. Cohen

Judy L. Miller

Dedication

In loving memory of my mother, Lillian Kumock Cohen, and my uncle, Julian Kumock.
Robert F. Cohen

To my daughter, Ariana Miller, with love.
Judy L. Miller

Longman Academic Reading Series 4: Reading Skills for College

Copyright © 2014 by Pearson Education, Inc.
All rights reserved.

No part of this publication may be reproduced, stored in a retrieval system, or transmitted in any form or by any means, electronic, mechanical, photocopying, recording, or otherwise, without the prior permission of the publisher.

Pearson Education, 10 Bank Street, White Plains, NY 10606

Staff Credits: The people who made up the *Longman Academic Reading Series 4* team, representing editorial, production, design, and manufacturing, are Pietro Alongi, Margaret Antonini, Rosa Chapinal, Aerin Csigay, Ann France, Françoise Leffler, Amy McCormick, Liza Pleva, Massimo Rubini, and Robert Ruvo.

Cover image: The Loupe Project/Shutterstock
Text Composition: TSI Graphics

Library of Congress Cataloging-in-Publication Data
Böttcher, Elizabeth.
 Longman Academic Reading Series / Elizabeth Bottcher.
  volumes cm
 Includes index.
 ISBN 978-0-13-278664-5 (Level 1)—ISBN 978-0-13-278582-2 (Level 2)—
ISBN 978-0-13-276059-1 (Level 3)—ISBN 978-0-13-276061-4 (Level 4)—
ISBN 978-0-13-276067-6 (Level 5)
 1. English language—Textbooks for foreign speakers. 2. Reading
comprehension—Problems, exercises, etc. 3. College readers. I. Title.
 PE1128.B637 2013
 428.6'4—dc23
                                    2013007701

ISBN 10: 0-13-276061-4
ISBN 13: 978-0-13-276061-4

Printed in the United States of America
2 3 4 5 6 7 8 9 10—V082—18 17 16 15 14 13

CONTENTS

TO THE TEACHER

Welcome to the *Longman Academic Reading Series*, a five-level series that prepares English language learners for academic work. The aim of the series is to make students more effective and confident readers by providing **high-interest readings on academic subjects** and teaching them **skills and strategies** for

- effective reading
- vocabulary building
- note-taking
- critical thinking

Last but not least, the series encourages students to **discuss and write** about the ideas they have discovered in the readings, making them better speakers and writers of English as well.

High-Interest Readings On Academic Subjects

Research shows that if students are not motivated to read, if reading is not in some sense enjoyable, the reading process becomes mechanical drudgery and the potential for improvement is minimal. That is why high-interest readings are the main feature in the *Longman Academic Reading Series*.

Varied High-Interest Texts

Each chapter of each book in the series focuses on an engaging theme from a wide range of academic subjects such as art history, nutrition studies, American literature, and forensics. The reading selections in each chapter (two readings in Level 1 and three in Levels 2–5) are chosen to provide different and intriguing perspectives on the theme. These readings come from a variety of sources or genres — books, textbooks, academic journals, newspapers, magazines, online articles — and are written by a variety of authors from widely different fields. The Level 4 book, for instance, offers a memoir by anthropologist Margaret Mead, a case history by neurologist Oliver Sacks, an essay by writer Susan Sontag, a conversation with novelist Leo Tolstoy, an interview with movie director James Cameron, a speech by social reformer Frederick Douglass, and a book excerpt from political scientist Niccolò Machiavelli — all challenging reading selections that spark students' interest and motivate them to read and discuss what they read.

Academic Work

The work done in response to these selections provides students with a reading and discussion experience that mirrors the in-depth treatment of texts in academic coursework. Although the readings may be adapted for the lower levels and excerpted for the upper levels, the authentic reading experience has been preserved. The series sustains students' interest and gives a sample of the types of content and reasoning that are the hallmark of academic work.

Skills and Strategies

To help students read and understand its challenging readings, the *Longman Academic Reading Series* provides a battery of skills and strategies for effective reading, vocabulary building, note-taking, and critical thinking.

Effective Reading

The series provides students with strategies that will help them learn to skim, scan, predict, preview, map, and formulate questions before they begin to read. After they read, students are routinely asked to identify main ideas as well as supporting details, progressing through the chapter from the "literal" to the "inferential." Students using this series learn to uncover what is beneath the surface of a reading passage and are led to interpret the many layers of meaning in a text. Each text is an invitation to dig deeper.

Vocabulary Building

In all chapters students are given the opportunity to see and use vocabulary in many ways: guessing words in context (an essential skill, without which fluent reading is impossible), identifying synonyms, recognizing idioms, practicing word forms as well as using new words in their own spoken and written sentences. At the same time, students learn the best strategies for using the dictionary effectively, and have ample practice in identifying roots and parts of words, recognizing collocations, understanding connotations, and communicating in the discourse specific to certain disciplines. The intentional "recycling" of vocabulary in both speaking and writing activities provides students with an opportunity to use the vocabulary they have acquired.

Note-Taking

As students learn ways to increase their reading comprehension and retention, they are encouraged to practice and master a variety of note-taking skills, such as highlighting, annotating, paraphrasing, summarizing, and outlining. The skills that form the focus of each chapter have been systematically aligned with the skills practiced in other chapters, so that scaffolding improves overall reading competence within each level.

Critical Thinking

At all levels of proficiency, students become more skilled in the process of analysis as they learn to read between the lines, make inferences, draw conclusions, make connections, evaluate, and synthesize information from various sources. The aim of this reflective journey is the development of students' critical thinking ability, which is achieved in different ways in each chapter.

In addition to these skills and strategies, **Level 4** and **Level 5** of the series include a **Grammar for Reading** activity in each chapter. Grammar for Reading presents a short review and practice of a grammar structure often encountered in academic texts, such as the passive or parallel forms. This activity helps students realize how their understanding of a particular grammar point will enhance their general reading comprehension ability.

Speaking and Writing

The speaking activities that frame and contribute to the development of each chapter tap students' strengths, allow them to synthesize information from several sources, and give them a sense of community in the reading experience. In addition, because good readers make good writers, students are given the opportunity to express themselves in a writing activity in each chapter.

The aim of the *Longman Academic Reading Series* is to provide "teachable" books that allow instructors to recognize the flow of ideas in each lesson and to choose from many types of exercises to get the students interested and to maintain their active participation throughout. By showing students how to appreciate the ideas that make the readings memorable, the series encourages students to become more effective, confident, and independent readers.

The Online Teacher's Manual

The Teacher's Manual is available at www.pearsonelt.com/tmkeys. It includes general teaching notes, chapter teaching notes, answer keys, and reproducible chapter quizzes.

CHAPTER OVERVIEW

All chapters in the *Longman Academic Reading Series, Level 4* have the same basic structure.

Objectives

BEFORE YOU READ

A. Consider These Questions/Facts/etc.

B. Your Opinion *[varies; sometimes only Consider activity]*

READING ONE: [+ *reading title*]

A. Warm-Up

B. Reading Strategy

[Reading One]

COMPREHENSION

A. Main Ideas

B. Close Reading

VOCABULARY *[not necessarily in this order; other activities possible]*

A. Guessing from Context

B. Synonyms

C. Using the Dictionary

NOTE-TAKING *[in two reading sections per chapter]*

CRITICAL THINKING

READING TWO: [+ *reading title*]

A. Warm-Up

B. Reading Strategy

[Reading Two]

COMPREHENSION

A. Main Ideas

B. Close Reading

VOCABULARY *[not necessarily in this order; other activities possible]*

A. Guessing from Context

B. Synonyms

C. Using the Dictionary

CRITICAL THINKING

LINKING READINGS ONE AND TWO

READING THREE: [+ *reading title*]

A. Warm-Up

B. Reading Strategy

[Reading Three]

COMPREHENSION

A. Main Ideas

B. Close Reading

VOCABULARY *[not necessarily in this order; other activities possible]*

A. Guessing from Context

B. Synonyms

C. Using the Dictionary

D. Word Forms

GRAMMAR FOR READING *[in one reading section per chapter]*

NOTE-TAKING *[in two reading sections per chapter]*

CRITICAL THINKING

AFTER YOU READ

BRINGING IT ALL TOGETHER

WRITING ACTIVITY

DISCUSSION AND WRITING TOPICS

Vocabulary

Self-Assessment

Each chapter starts with a definition of the chapter's academic subject matter, objectives, and a Before You Read section.

A short **definition of the academic subject** mentioned in the chapter title describes the general area of knowledge explored in the chapter.

PSYCHOLOGY: Aggression and Violence

PSYCHOLOGY: the systematic, scientific study of behavior and mental processes

OBJECTIVES

To read academic texts, you need to master certain skills.

In this chapter, you will:

- Predict the content of a text from the title or the first paragraph
- Understand the most important idea of a text from the first and last paragraphs
- Guess the meaning of words from the context
- Use dictionary entries to learn the meanings of words
- Understand and use synonyms, phrases and idioms, collocations, and different word forms
- Identify adjective clauses and the reasons for their use
- Take notes to identify the author's assertions and supporting explanations
- Complete outlines to focus on the sequence of events and main discoveries

In psychology and other social sciences, "aggression" refers to behavior between members of the same species that is intended to cause pain or harm.

195

Chapter objectives provide clear goals for students by listing the skills they will practice in the chapter.

The **Before You Read** activities introduce the subject matter of the chapter, using a mix of information and questions to stimulate students' interest.

BEFORE YOU READ

A Consider These Questions

Discuss the questions with a partner.

1. Is aggressive behavior sometimes necessary in a society? In what situations?
2. When is aggression dangerous for society?
3. Do you ever feel that you would like to do violence to something or someone? In what situations? What makes you control yourself?
4. What helps society control violence?
5. Are people naturally violent, or is violence learned through culture?
6. What is the difference between being aggressive and being assertive?

B Consider These Quotes

Read the following quotes about aggression and violence. With a partner, discuss what each one means. Which one expresses your feelings on the matter?

1. "If it's natural to kill, how come men have to go into training to learn how?"

   —*Joan Baez*, American folk singer and political activist, born 1941

2. "Violence, naked force has settled more issues in history than has any other factor."

   —*Robert Heinlein*, American science fiction writer, 1907–1988

3. "If we don't end war, war will end us."

   —*H.G. Wells*, English science fiction writer, 1866–1946

4. "I am a violent man who has learned not to be violent and regrets his violence."

   —*John Lennon*, English singer and songwriter, member of the Beatles, 1940–1980

5. "In each of us there is a Mr. Hyde.[1] The point is to prevent the conditions that would allow the monster to emerge."

   —*Amin Maalouf*, Lebanese-born French author, born 1949

Poster of the 1931 movie based on Robert Louis Stevenson's novel

---

[1] *Mr Hyde:* the embodiment of the dark side of the good Dr. Jekyll; Mr. Hyde is released as an experiment and gradually takes over in Robert Louis Stevenson's *Dr. Jekyll and Mr. Hyde.*

196 CHAPTER 8

Chapter Overview **ix**

Each of the three reading sections in a chapter starts with a Warm-Up activity and a Reading Strategy presentation and practice, followed by the reading itself.

The **Warm-Up** activity presents discussion questions that activate students' prior knowledge and help them develop a personal connection with the topic of the reading.

Reading One sets the theme and presents the basic ideas that will be explored in the chapter. Like all the readings in the series, it is an example of a genre of writing (here, a book excerpt).

READING ONE: Civilization and Its Discontents

A   Warm-Up

Sigmund Freud (1856–1939) was an Austrian medical doctor and neurologist who began seeing patients with emotional problems. He wrote about his patients and about his theory of the unconscious mind, where passions and hidden desires fought for expression. His work in psychoanalysis with the "talking cure" began the modern movement to understand our mind and behavior.

In the years before the outbreak of World War II, Freud wrote *Civilization and Its Discontents*.

Discuss the question with a partner.

Do you think we always make rational and reasonable decisions, or do we sometimes wonder why we do things? Can you give examples of this? Are we often influenced by unconscious desires?

B   Reading Strategy

Predicting Content from First Paragraph

Reading the **first paragraph** of a text can help you to **understand the most important idea** of the passage before you read the entire reading.

Read the first paragraph of "Civilization and Its Discontents." Then read each statement and check (✓) *Yes* or *No*.

	YES	No
1. The reading will say that violence is inborn in human beings.	☐	☐
2. The reading will be optimistic about man's fate in the future.	☐	☐

Now read the text and decide if your answers were correct.

Psychology: Aggression and Violence   **197**

The **Reading Strategy** box gives a general description of a reading strategy, such as predicting content from first paragraph, and the reasons for using it. The **activity** below the box shows students how to apply that strategy to the reading.

Civilization and Its Discontents
By Sigmund Freud

1   *Homo homini lupus.* [Man is a wolf to man.] Who, in the face of all his experience of life and of history, will have the courage to dispute this assertion? As a rule, this cruel aggressiveness waits for some provocation or puts itself at the service of some higher purpose, whose goal might have been reached by milder measures. Anyone who calls to mind the atrocities committed during the invasions of the Huns,[1] or by the people known as the Mongols[2] under Genghis Khan and Tamerlane, or at the capture of Jerusalem by the pious Crusaders,[3] or even the horrors of the recent World War — anyone who calls these things to mind will have to accept the truth of this view.

2   The existence of this inclination to aggression, which we can detect in ourselves and justly assume to be present in others, is the factor which disturbs our relations with our neighbor and which forces civilization into such a high expenditure of energy. . . . Civilization has to use its utmost efforts in order to set limits to man's aggressive instincts.

3   The meaning of the evolution of civilization is no longer obscure to us. It must present the struggle between Eros and Thanatos,[4] between the instinct of life and the instinct of destruction, as it works itself out in the human species. This struggle is what all life essentially consists of, and the evolution of civilization may therefore be simply described as the struggle for the life of the human species.

4   The fateful question for the human species seems to me to be whether and to what extent their cultural development will succeed in mastering the disturbance of their communal life by the human instinct of aggression and self-destruction. It may be that in this respect precisely the present time deserves a special interest. Men have gained control over the forces of nature to such an extent that with their help they would have no difficulty in exterminating one another to the last man. They know this, and from this comes a large part of their current unrest, their unhappiness and their mood of anxiety. And now it is to be expected that the other of the two "Heavenly Powers," eternal Eros, will make an effort to assert himself in the struggle with his equally immortal adversary. But who can foresee with what success and with what result?

---

[1] *Huns:* a group of nomadic people from central Asia who attacked and controlled parts of Europe during the 4th and 5th centuries A.D.

[2] *Mongols:* a group of nomadic people from northeast and central Asia who conquered Asia, the Middle East, and eastern Europe in the 13th and 14th centuries, resulting in a vast Mongol empire under Genghis Khan and a descendant known as Tamerlane.

[3] *Crusaders:* people who took part in the wars fought in the 11th, 12th, and 13th centuries by Christian armies trying to take Palestine from the Muslims; the crusaders' conquest of Jerusalem in 1099 was accompanied by massacres of Muslims and Jews

[4] *Eros* and *Thanatos* were Greek gods — Eros was the god of love, Thanatos the god of death.

198   CHAPTER 8

Reflections on Natural History

By Stephen Jay Gould

Stephen Jay Gould (1941–2002) was a respected American paleontologist, evolutionary biologist, and historian of science. He taught at Harvard University and New York University and also worked at the American Museum of Natural History. He contributed articles to many academic journals and also wrote, among other books, The Mismeasure of Man, Bully for Brontosaurus, and Dinosaur in a Haystack.

1   How often have we been told that man is, by nature, aggressive and selfishly **acquisitive**? Such claims make no sense to me — in a purely empirical way, not as a statement about hope or preferred morality. What do we see on any ordinary day on the streets or in the homes of any American city — even in the subways of New York? Thousands of tiny and insignificant acts of kindness and consideration. We step aside to let someone pass, smile at a child, chat aimlessly with an acquaintance, or even with a stranger. At most moments, on most days, in most places, what do you ever see of the dark side — perhaps a parent slapping a child or a teenager on a skateboard cutting off an old lady? Look, I'm no ivory-tower[1] Pollyanna,[2] and I did grow up on the streets of New York. I understand the unpleasantness and danger of crowded cities. I'm only trying to make a statistical point.

2   Many people are under the impression that daily life is an unending series of unpleasantnesses — that 50 percent or more of human encounters are stressful or aggressive. But think about it seriously for a moment. Such levels of **nastiness** cannot possibly be **sustained**. Society would **devolve** to anarchy in an instant if half our **overtures** to another human being were met with a punch in the nose.

3   No, nearly every encounter with another person is at least neutral and usually pleasant enough. *Homo sapiens*[3] is a remarkably **genial** species. Ethnologists consider other animals relatively peaceful if they see one or two aggressive encounters while observing an organism for, say, tens of hours. But think of how many millions of hours we can log for most people on most days without noting anything more threatening than a raised third finger[4] once a week or so.

4   Why, then, do most of us have the impression that people are so aggressive, and **intrinsically** so? Unfortunately, one incident of violence can undo a thousand acts

(continued on next page)

---
[1] *ivory tower:* Universities are sometimes referred to as "ivory towers," meaning places that are insulated from the difficulties of ordinary life and therefore, unable to understand them.

[2] *Pollyanna:* an excessively or blindly optimistic person, based on the novel *Pollyanna* by Eleanor Hodgman Porter

[3] *Homo sapiens:* the Latin scientific name for the human species

[4] *raised third finger:* an insulting gesture in many cultures

Psychology: Aggression and Violence   **203**

Reading Two addresses the same theme as Reading One, but from a completely different perspective. In most cases, it is also an example of a different genre of writing (here, a magazine article).

Reading Three addresses the same theme as Readings One and Two, but again from a different perspective from the first two. And in most cases, it is also an example of a different genre of writing (here, an online article).

Most readings have **glosses** and **footnotes** to help students understand difficult words and names.

All readings have **numbered paragraphs** (with the exception of literary readings that have numbered lines) for easy reference. The **target vocabulary** that students need to know in order to read academic texts is set in boldface blue for easy recognition. Target vocabulary is recycled through the chapter and the level.

A Neuroscientist Uncovers a Dark Secret
By Barbara Bradley

1   The criminal brain has always held a fascination for James Fallon. For nearly 20 years, the neuroscientist at the University of California-Irvine has studied the brains of psychopaths.[1] He studies the biological basis for behavior, and one of his specialties is to try to figure out how a killer's brain differs from yours and mine.

2   About four years ago, Fallon made a **startling** discovery. It happened during a conversation with his then 88-year-old mother, Jenny, at a family barbecue. "I said, 'Jim, why don't you find out about your father's relatives?'" Jenny Fallon recalls. "I think there were some cuckoos[2] back there." Fallon investigated. "There's a whole **lineage** of very violent people — killers," he says. One of his direct great-grandfathers, Thomas Cornell, was hanged in 1667 for murdering his mother. That line of Cornells produced seven other alleged murderers, including Lizzy Borden. "Cousin Lizzy," as Fallon wryly calls her, was accused (and controversially acquitted) of killing her father and stepmother with an axe in Fall River, Massachusetts, in 1882.

3   A little spooked[3] by his ancestry, Fallon set out to see whether anyone in his family possesses the brain of a serial killer. Because he has studied the brains of dozens of psychopaths, he knew precisely what to look for. To demonstrate, he opened his laptop and called up an image of a brain on his computer.

4   "Here is a brain that's not normal," he says. Then he points to another section of the brain, in the front part of the brain, just behind the eyes. "Look at that — there's almost nothing here," Fallon says. This is the orbital cortex, the area that Fallon and other scientists believe is involved with ethical behavior, moral decision-making and impulse control. "People with low activity [in the orbital cortex] are either **free-wheeling** types or psychopaths," he says.

5   He's clearly oversimplifying, but Fallon says the orbital cortex **puts a brake on** another part of the brain called the amygdala, which is involved with aggression and appetites. But in some people, there's an imbalance — the orbital cortex isn't doing its job — perhaps because the person had a brain injury or was born that way. "What's left? What takes over?" he asks. "The area of the brain that drives your id-type behaviors,[4] which are rage, violence, eating, sex, drinking."

(continued on next page)

---
[1] *psychopath:* someone who has a personality disorder characterized by a lack of empathy and remorse, shallow emotion, and extremely violent behavior

[2] *cuckoo:* (informal) someone who is mentally ill; crazy or silly

[3] *spooked:* (informal) frightened

[4] *id-type behaviors:* In Freud's theory of the mind, the *id* represents the uncontrolled instincts, the *ego* is the organized, realistic part, and the *superego* is the critical and moralizing part.

Psychology: Aggression and Violence   **211**

Each reading in the chapter is followed by Comprehension and Vocabulary activities.

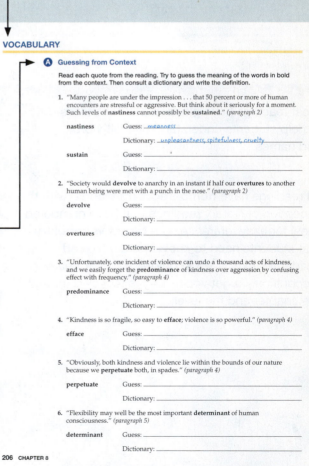

COMPREHENSION

Ⓐ Main Ideas

Read each statement. Decide if it is *True* or *False* according to the reading. Check (✓) the appropriate box. If it is false, change it to make it true. Discuss your answers with a partner.

	TRUE	FALSE
1. The author cannot understand how the oppressed can resign themselves to their fate.	☐	☐
2. The author sees nothing good about violence.	☐	☐
3. Nonviolence allows the oppressed minority to appeal to the majority's moral conscience.	☐	☐
4. Violence leaves a chance for the oppressors to change their minds and see the error of their ways.	☐	☐
5. According to the author, hatred is part of the struggle to change society.	☐	☐

Ⓑ Close Reading

Read the quotes from the reading. Circle the statement that best explains each quote. Share your answers with a partner.

1. "A few years ago in the slum areas of Atlanta, a Negro guitarist used to sing almost daily: 'Been down so long that down don't bother me.'" *(paragraph 2)*

   The guitarist could have said these words:

   a. "I've become so used to my poverty that it doesn't upset me anymore."

   b. "My poverty is not as bad as it seems."

2. "The oppressed must never allow the conscience of the oppressor to slumber." *(paragraph 3)*

   a. The oppressed must not let the oppressors trouble their conscience.

   b. The oppressed must make the oppressors ashamed of what is being done.

3. "[Violence] leaves society in monologue rather than dialogue." *(paragraph 5)*

   a. With violence, there is no discussion or exchange of ideas.

   b. No one listens when violence speaks.

4. "Nonviolent resistance is not aimed against oppressors but against oppression. Under its banner consciences, not racial groups, are enlisted." *(paragraph 7)*

   a. With nonviolent resistance, there is a moral outcome.

   b. Racial consciousness remains strongest with nonviolence.

244 CHAPTER 9

The **Comprehension** activities help students identify and understand the main ideas of the reading and their supporting details.

The **Vocabulary** activities focus on the target vocabulary in the reading, presenting and practicing skills such as guessing meaning from context or from synonyms, understanding word forms, and using a dictionary.

VOCABULARY

Ⓐ Guessing from Context

Read each quote from the reading. Try to guess the meaning of the words in bold from the context. Then consult a dictionary and write the definition.

1. "Many people are under the impression . . . that 50 percent or more of human encounters are stressful or aggressive. But think about it seriously for a moment. Such levels of **nastiness** cannot possibly be **sustained**." *(paragraph 2)*

   nastiness   Guess: *meanness*

               Dictionary: *unpleasantness, spitefulness, cruelty*

   sustain   Guess: _____

               Dictionary: _____

2. "Society would **devolve** to anarchy in an instant if half our **overtures** to another human being were met with a punch in the nose." *(paragraph 2)*

   devolve   Guess: _____

               Dictionary: _____

   overtures   Guess: _____

               Dictionary: _____

3. "Unfortunately, one incident of violence can undo a thousand acts of kindness, and we easily forget the **predominance** of kindness over aggression by confusing effect with frequency." *(paragraph 4)*

   predominance   Guess: _____

               Dictionary: _____

4. "Kindness is so fragile, so easy to **efface**; violence is so powerful." *(paragraph 4)*

   efface   Guess: _____

               Dictionary: _____

5. "Obviously, both kindness and violence lie within the bounds of our nature because we **perpetuate** both, in spades." *(paragraph 4)*

   perpetuate   Guess: _____

               Dictionary: _____

6. "Flexibility may well be the most important **determinant** of human consciousness." *(paragraph 5)*

   determinant   Guess: _____

               Dictionary: _____

206 CHAPTER 8

Guessing from Context helps students guess the meaning of the target vocabulary by encouraging them to go back to the reading to find clues in the context and base their guesses on these clues.

C Synonyms

Complete the essay with the words or phrases from the box. Use the synonym in parentheses to help you select the correct word. Compare answers with a partner.

abstract	binding	in retrospect	sever	ultimate
afflicted	coherent	luminous	transmitted	
bewildering	humiliating	persists	traumatic	

Freud's theory of mind was a _____*luminous*_____ milestone
1. (brilliant)
in the history of science because it provided a way to understand the

_____ hidden processes of the brain. Despite their faults,
2. (confusing)
Freud's theories offered a humane way to treat people _____
3. (tormented)
by mental problems or suffering from _____ memories.
4. (painful)
Freud felt that by appealing to the rational mind, unconscious fears and

_____ obsessions would diminish in intensity. If people could
5. (demeaning)
be brave and _____ their emotional ties to painful memories
6. (cut)
of the past, they could form a _____ and realistic picture of
7. (understandable)
their future.

_____, many of Freud's insights aimed at linking
8. (Looking backward)
psychology to physiology — _____ the workings
9. (connecting)
of the mind to the workings of the brain — have proven fruitful. Only an

interdisciplinary approach linking psychology to biology can answer the

_____ questions about the meaning of consciousness.
10. (theoretical)
In the 1980s, cognitive neuroscience made enormous progress with the invention

of brain imaging, a technology that allows scientists to realize their dream of looking

into the human brain. The activity of different parts of the brain is measured and

_____ to a computer screen. As people perceive a visual
11. (communicated)
image, think about a spatial route, or start a voluntary action, scientists can see the

activity that _____ in various parts of the brain. Eventually,
12. (continues)
scientists hope to address the _____ questions of how we
13. (final)
think, feel, learn, and remember.

Synonyms also helps students understand the meaning of the target vocabulary in the reading, but here for each target word students are given synonyms to match or choose from.

B Word Forms

1 Fill in the chart with the correct word forms. Some categories can have more than one form. Use a dictionary if necessary. An *X* indicates there is no form in that category.

	NOUN	VERB	ADJECTIVE	ADVERB
1.	charity	X	*charitable*	
2.	compassion	X		
3.	deception / *deceiver*	deceive		
4.	hypocrite /	X		
5.	manipulator /	manipulate		

2 Complete the sentences with the correct form of the words from the chart. Each item follows the order in which the words appear in the chart.

1. People who live in loving communities treat each other with

   _____*charity*_____ and respect. Such _____*charitable*_____

   behavior cultivates feelings of loyalty and trust in the society.

2. Sometimes it is dangerous to show too much _____

   toward others. _____ people do not always understand

   that their kind actions may make the people they are helping forget that they

   must learn how to help themselves. Treating people _____

   may therefore have unexpected negative consequences.

3. _____ may be useful for a while, but sooner or later

   the _____ is revealed for who he or she is. We can only

   _____ people for so long before we get caught.

4. A _____ is someone who pretends to do one thing

   and does the other. This _____ attitude is often seen in

   politicians, who are often criticized for their _____.

5. Some people _____ others in order to get what

   they want. Their _____ behavior may hide their

   selfishness for a while, but eventually those who are the victims of their

   _____ learn to see them for who they are.

Word Forms helps students expand their vocabulary by encouraging them to guess or find out the different forms some of the target words can have. Then students are challenged to use the forms correctly.

G Using the Dictionary

Read the dictionary entry for *faculty*.

> **faculty** *n. plural* **faculties** **1** all the teachers in a particular school or college, or in a particular department of a school or college: *Both students and faculty have protested.* / *faculty members* / *the Faculty of Social Sciences* **2** a particular skill that someone has + **for** *She has a great faculty for absorbing information.* **3** a natural ability, such as the ability to see, hear, or think clearly: *the patient's mental faculties* / + **of** *the faculty of hearing* / *Mrs. Darwin is no longer in full possession of all her faculties.*

1 Now read each sentence. Decide which meaning of *faculty* is being used. Write the number of the appropriate definition.

_____ **a.** The **faculty** of the women's studies program encourage both men and women to take their courses.

_____ **b.** Learning that there are women with an inborn **faculty** of thinking mathematically and men with an inborn **faculty** of writing poetically is an important lesson.

_____ **c.** Our individual **faculties** should not be defined according to gender stereotypes.

_____ **d.** The ninety-five-year-old man was still in the possession of all his **faculties**, and it was fascinating to hear his detailed accounts of his childhood in the segregated South.

_____ **e.** The **faculty** of the history department invited him to come speak at its seminar on the civil rights movement.

_____ **f.** A young student with a **faculty** for looking at a reading passage once and remembering everything in it was one of the few students who was able to keep up with the heavy reading load.

2 Complete the sentences with the words *faculty* or *faculties*.

1. Freedom cannot be fully enjoyed in a society unless the majority of people are given the opportunity to develop their _____.

2. That is why the _____ of our college are so special.

3. Only teachers with a great _____ for inspiring students will succeed in this college.

4. The interdisciplinary focus of the first-year curriculum allows students to take a variety of courses in the _____ of liberal arts, education, and engineering.

Using the Dictionary shows students how to understand a dictionary entry for one of the target words. Students choose the appropriate meaning of the word as it is used in the reading and in other contexts.

G Phrasal Verbs with *crack* and *step*

Read the dictionary entries of phrasal verbs with *crack* and *step*.

> **crack down** *phr. v.* to become more strict in dealing with a problem and punishing the people involved: *We have to crack down on software pirates.*
>
> **crack up** *phr. v. INFORMAL* **1 crack sb up** to laugh a lot at something or to make someone laugh a lot: *That joke still cracks me up.* **2** to have a mental breakdown: *If I don't get some time off soon, I'll crack up.* **3 sth's not all it's cracked up to be** something is not as good as people say it is: *The movie was OK, but it's not all it's cracked up to be.*

> **step down** *phr. v.* to leave your job or official position, to resign: + **as** *Arnez is stepping down as chairman.* / + **from** *She's stepping down from the committee.*
>
> **step in** *phr. v.* to become involved in a discussion, disagreement, etc., especially in order to stop trouble: *The police stepped in to break up the fight.*
>
> **step up** *phr. v.* **1 step sth up** to increase the amount of an activity or the speed of a process in order to improve a situation: *They have stepped up security at the airport.* **2 step up (to the plate)** to agree to help someone or to be responsible for doing something: *Residents will have to step up if they want to rid this area of crime.*

Now complete each sentence with the correct form of the appropriate phrasal verb.

1. The women _____ the pressure on the White House during World War I because they hoped they would finally get the vote.

2. Many men _____ at the ridiculous idea that women would ever be able to participate in the political process.

3. However, some men _____ and did what they could to support women's rights.

4. Carrie Chapman Catt _____ as president of the National American Woman Suffrage Association before the war but resumed its leadership in 1917.

5. She _____ to resolve the arguments about tactics.

6. The police _____ on the demonstrators and arrested them because they wouldn't move.

7. Although the demonstrations were always peaceful, the police _____ security at future events.

8. In order for the women's rights movement to be successful, men as well as women needed to _____ and show their support.

Phrasal Verbs shows students how phrasal verbs are formed and how to check their meanings in a dictionary. Then students are challenged to use the correct forms of the appropriate phrasal verbs.

Each chapter has a Grammar for Reading activity and two Note-Taking activities. These can be in any of the three reading sections.

The **Grammar for Reading** activity leads students through a short review and practice of a grammar structure often encountered in academic texts, such as the passive, parallel forms, and adjective clauses. Understanding this type of grammar point enhances students' general reading comprehension ability.

The **Note-Taking** activity teaches students to use skills such as circling, underlining, writing margin notes, categorizing, completing an outline, and summarizing information to increase their reading comprehension.

GRAMMAR FOR READING: Adjective Clauses

An **adjective clause** tells you something about the **noun** or **pronoun** it follows. An adjective clause begins with a word like who, whom, whose, that, which, when, where, why.

In academic English, sentences can become long and complicated. It's important to remember that an **adjective clause** describes the noun or pronoun that **comes right before** it.

EXAMPLE:
- He's clearly oversimplifying, but Fallon says the orbital cortex puts a brake on another

          noun   adjective clause
part of the brain called the **amygdala**, *which* **is involved with aggression and appetites.**

The word *which* and the entire adjective clause that follows refer to the noun "amygdala." The amygdala is involved with aggression and appetites.

Work with a partner. Read each sentence and identify which noun the adjective clause refers to. Circle the correct answer.

1. "[It is] the area of the brain that drives your id-type behaviors, *which* are rage, violence, eating, sex, drinking." *(paragraph 5)*

   a. id-type behaviors   **b.** brain

2. "Along with brain scans, Fallon also tested each family member's DNA for genes *that* are associated with violence." *(paragraph 8)*

   a. DNA   **b.** genes

3. "As for the psychopaths he studies, Fallon feels some compassion for these people *who*, he says, got 'a bad roll of the dice.'" *(paragraph 11)*

   a. people (psychopaths)   **b.** Fallon

4. "As a rule, this cruel aggressiveness waits for some provocation or puts itself at the service of some higher purpose, *whose* goal might have been reached by milder measures." *(Reading One, paragraph 1)*

   a. aggressiveness   **b.** purpose

5. "The existence of this inclination to aggression, *which* we can detect in ourselves and justly assume to be present in others, is the factor *which* disturbs our relations with our neighbor and *which* forces civilization into such a high expenditure of energy." *(Reading One, paragraph 2)*

   a. inclination   **b.** existence

   a. others   **b.** factor

   a. neighbor   **b.** factor

NOTE-TAKING: Completing an Outline with the Necessary Details

Go back to the reading and read it again. Using the cues given here, fill in the necessary details of the outline with notes in your own words.

   I. Argument about Bonobos' Language Ability

      A. Chomsky and some linguists

         1. humans: *language is spoken only by humans*

         2. chimps/other relatives: *do not have the brain structure to create language*

      B. Rumbaugh-Savage and other researchers

         1. few apes: _____

         2. modern research and bias: _____

   II. Research with Apes and Language

      A. Lab experiments

         1. sign language: _____

         2. keyboard: _____

         3. Kanzi: _____

      B. Experiments with apes in the wild

         1. difficulties for researchers: _____

         2. predators/marking of trails: _____

      C. Skeptics

         1. Skeptics' argument: _____

         2. Rumbaugh's response: _____

All three reading sections end with a Critical Thinking activity. The Linking Readings One and Two activity comes at the very end of the Reading Two section.

The **Critical Thinking** activity encourages students to analyze and evaluate the information in the reading. This activity develops students' critical thinking skills and their ability to express their opinions coherently.

The **Linking Readings One and Two** activity leads students to compare and contrast the ideas expressed in the first two readings. It helps students make connections and find correlations between the two texts.

CRITICAL THINKING

1 Agree or Disagree

Read each statement. Decide if you *Agree* or *Disagree*. Check (✓) the appropriate box. Discuss your answers with a partner.

	AGREE	DISAGREE
1. Machiavelli is immoral.	☐	☐
2. When Machiavelli says a ruler should be a "fox," he means the ruler should be an intellectual.	☐	☐
3. Machiavelli is an optimist.	☐	☐
4. According to Machiavelli, men are born to be subjects of a ruler, not citizens of a republic.	☐	☐

2 What Would Machiavelli Say?

Machiavelli has been assigned reading in some U.S. business schools. Books such as Antony Jay's *Management and Machiavelli* and Stanley Bing's *What Would Machiavelli Do?* apply Machiavelli's writings to a business context.

Here is a list of business decisions. Work with a small group. Decide whether Machiavelli would "probably agree" (*Yes*) or "probably disagree" (*No*) with these decisions. If there is not enough information to decide, write *Can't tell*. Explain your answers by referring to the reading.

_____ 1. The head of a company decides to put a new business plan to a vote among employees.

_____ 2. The directors of an insurance company saved from bankruptcy by taxpayers' bailout dollars decide to give millions of dollars in bonuses to their managers.

_____ 3. Businesses use advertising to encourage people to buy their products regardless of the usefulness of these products.

_____ 4. The head of the company involves all workers in discussion sessions to solve a company problem.

_____ 5. The company director decides to increase production.

_____ 6. A company decides to recall consumer products that have proven to be unsafe even though it costs them a lot of money.

_____ 7. Companies contribute a small percentage of their profits to support a charity for poor children and use this fact in their publicity.

174 CHAPTER 7

LINKING READINGS ONE AND TWO

Work with a partner. Fill in the chart with notes comparing the robber barons' practices with the progressives' proposals to get rid of these practices.

	READING ONE ROBBER BARONS' PRACTICES	READING TWO PROGRESSIVES' PROPOSALS
1.	kept wages very low	pass minimum wage laws
2.		institute regulation for workplace safety and respect for workers
3.	created monopolies	
4.		
5.		create cooperation and more opportunities for small business growth
6.	prevented freedom in the workplace	
7.		

READING THREE: Message to Wall Street

Ⓐ **Warm-Up**

1 Wall Street Today

Discuss the questions with a partner.

"Occupy Wall Street" became an international movement after the financial crisis of 2008.

1. Why did people want to "occupy" Wall Street?
2. What was the purpose of the demonstrations?

42 CHAPTER 2

Each chapter ends with an After You Read section, a Vocabulary chart, and a Self-Assessment checklist.

The **After You Read** activities go back to the theme of the chapter, encouraging students to discuss and write about related topics using the target vocabulary of the chapter.

AFTER YOU READ

BRINGING IT ALL TOGETHER

Work in groups of four. Role-play an interview with Sigmund Freud, Stephen Jay Gould, and James Fallon about men's aggressiveness and violence. The journalist will ask questions of the others. Freud, Gould, and Fallon will express their opinions. Use some of the vocabulary you studied in the chapter (for a complete list, go to page 220).

Topic: Men's aggressiveness and violence

ROLES:
- Journalist
- Stephen Jay Gould
- Sigmund Freud
- James Fallon

QUESTIONS:
- Are humans a very violent species?
- Is violence in our genes?
- How can we control and prevent the expression of violence?

WRITING ACTIVITY

Write a three-paragraph essay about how an important event or lesson in childhood shaped your ethical behavior and moral sense. Use more than five of the words or idioms you studied in the chapter.
- **Introduction:** Tell the reader about yourself as a child.
- **Body Paragraph:** Describe the situation and the lesson you learned.
- **Conclusion:** Discuss how it affected your later life.

DISCUSSION AND WRITING TOPICS

Discuss these topics in a small group. Choose one of them and write a paragraph or two about it. Use the vocabulary from the chapter.

1. Why do you think people, even scientists and writers of popular entertainment for movies and TV, are so interested in serial killers: their lack of empathy, fear, or remorse? Is it that they are a lot like us or very much unlike us?
2. What are some ways we can reduce aggression in today's society?
3. Do you think violent movies and video games contribute to violence among young people?
4. "The fault is not in our stars but in ourselves." — *William Shakespeare*

   Do you think the fault is in our genes or in our environment? Is aggression the result of "nature" (inborn qualities) or "nurture" (the result of experience)?
5. How can a belief in biological determinism affect our future and our concept of freedom? Does biological determinism excuse a violent criminal?

Psychology: Aggression and Violence **219**

The **Vocabulary chart**, which lists all the target vocabulary words of the chapter under the appropriate parts of speech, provides students with a convenient reference.

VOCABULARY			
Nouns	**Verbs**	**Adjectives**	**Adverb**
adversary	caution	acquisitive *	intrinsically *
assertion	devolve	disturbing	
atrocities	efface	fateful	**Phrases and Idioms**
determinant	exterminate	genial	a bad roll of the dice
expenditure	master	pious	free-wheeling
inclination *	perpetuate	startling	put a brake on
lineage	predispose	utmost	tongue-in-cheek
nastiness	reiterate		
nurture	sustain *		
overtures			
predominance *	**Phrasal Verbs**		
	dote on		
	zero in on		

* = AWL (Academic Word List) item

SELF-ASSESSMENT

In this chapter you learned to:
- ○ Predict the content of a text from the title or the first paragraph
- ○ Understand the most important idea of a text from the first and last paragraphs
- ○ Guess the meaning of words from the context
- ○ Use dictionary entries to learn the meanings of words
- ○ Understand and use synonyms, phrases and idioms, collocations, and different word forms
- ○ Identify adjective clauses and the reasons for their use
- ○ Take notes to identify the author's assertions and supporting explanations
- ○ Complete outlines to focus on the sequence of events and main discoveries

What can you do well? ☑

What do you need to practice more? ☑

The **Self-Assessment** checklist encourages students to evaluate their own progress. Have they mastered the skills listed in the chapter objectives?

220 CHAPTER 8

SCOPE AND SEQUENCE

CHAPTER	READING	VOCABULARY/GRAMMAR
1 SOCIOLOGY: Home and the Homeless **Theme:** The meaning of home; what it means not to have one; our reactions to people who are homeless **Reading One:** *Home and Travel* (a book excerpt) **Reading Two:** *Homeless* (a magazine article) **Reading Three:** *Helping and Hating the Homeless* (an online article)	• Understand and practice different reading strategies • Think about the title of a text and predict its content • Predict the subject of a text and the author's motivation from the first two sentences • Make up your own questions based on the title of a text • Identify the main ideas of a text • Understand the details that support the main ideas	• Guess the meaning of words from the context • Use dictionary entries to learn the meanings of words • Understand and use synonyms, different word forms, and the suffix *-en* and prefix *en-* • Use the Vocabulary list at the end of the chapter to review the words, phrases, and idioms learned in the chapter • Use this vocabulary in the After You Read speaking and writing activities • GRAMMAR: Identify the passive and the reasons for its use
2 HISTORY: Robber Barons Then and Now **Theme:** The power of money and business in the Gilded Age and today; the popular movements against that power **Reading One:** *The Robber Barons* (a textbook excerpt) **Reading Two:** *The Politics of Progressivism* (a textbook excerpt) **Reading Three:** *Message to Wall Street* (an online article)	• Understand and practice different reading strategies • Scan a text to find specific information • Scan the first paragraph of a text for definitions and background information • Predict the content of a text from the first and last paragraphs • Identify or complete the main ideas of a text • Understand the details that support the main ideas	• Guess the meaning of words from the context • Understand and use synonyms, collocations, and different word forms and idioms • Use the Vocabulary list at the end of the chapter to review the words, phrases, and idioms learned in the chapter • Use this vocabulary in the After You Read speaking and writing activities • GRAMMAR: Identify parallel forms and the reasons for their use
3 FILM STUDIES: Is Cinema an Art or a Business? **Theme:** Is making movies an art, a business, or both? **Reading One:** *One Hundred Years of Cinema* (an essay) **Reading Two:** *A Conversation with Leo Tolstoy on Film* (a newspaper article) **Reading Three:** *An Interview with James Cameron* (a magazine article)	• Understand and practice different reading strategies • Find the thesis statement in an essay • Skim an interview for the general idea • Scan an interview for the interviewee's attitude towards the subject • Identify the main ideas of a text • Understand the details that support the main ideas	• Guess the meaning of words from the context • Use dictionary entries to learn the meanings of words • Understand and use synonyms, idioms, connotations, and increase/decrease verbs • Use the Vocabulary list at the end of the chapter to review the words, phrases, and idioms learned in the chapter • Use this vocabulary in the After You Read speaking and writing activities • GRAMMAR: Recognize and use parallel structure for emphasis and contrast

NOTE-TAKING	CRITICAL THINKING	SPEAKING/WRITING
• Fill out an organizer to review details to help you remember • Use questions as "organizers" for notes	• Express your opinions and support them with examples from a text or from your own experience and culture • Analyze and evaluate information • Infer information not explicit in a text • Draw conclusions • Hypothesize about someone else's point of view • Find correlations between two texts • Make connections between ideas • Synthesize information and ideas	• Role-play a discussion about the homeless between Margaret Mead, Anna Quindlen, Peter Marin, and a taxpayer • Write a three-paragraph essay explaining and illustrating a saying about home • Discuss in a small group a number of topics related to the homeless and homelessness • Choose one of the topics and write a paragraph or two about it
• Use an organizer to identify important biographical details • Use note-taking to summarize an argument	• Express your opinions and support them with examples from a text or from your own experience and culture • Analyze and evaluate information • Infer information not explicit in a text • Draw conclusions • Find correlations between two texts • Make connections between ideas • Synthesize information and ideas • Understand the use of irony for social criticism	• Role-play a discussion about Wall Street between Jeffrey Sachs, an old robber baron, a new one, and an "Occupy Wall Street" protester • Write a paragraph or two explaining the meaning of a quote and your opinion • Discuss in a small group a number of topics about the power of the mega-rich and whether protest movements do any good • Choose one of the topics and write a paragraph or two about it
• Take notes to identify the main ideas of a text and the supporting details • Take margin notes, organize the notes, and write a summary of the text	• Express your opinions and support them with examples from a text or from your own experience and culture • Analyze and evaluate information • Infer information not explicit in a text • Draw conclusions • Hypothesize about someone else's point of view • Identify the concerns of two authors — same or different? • Make connections between ideas • Synthesize information and ideas	• Role-play a discussion about cinema between a journalist, Susan Sontag, Leo Tolstoy, and James Cameron • Write a three-paragraph essay about your favorite movie • Discuss in a small group a number of topics about movies • Choose one of the topics and write a paragraph or two about it

CHAPTER	READING	VOCABULARY/GRAMMAR
4 MEDIA STUDIES: The Internet and Social Media **Theme:** Do the Internet and social media have positive or negative effects on people and society? **Reading One:** *Mind Control and the Internet* (a newspaper article) **Reading Two:** *The Positive Effects of Social Networking Sites* (a textbook excerpt) **Reading Three:** *The Use of Social Media In the Arab Spring* (an online article)	• Understand and practice different reading strategies • Predict the content of a text from the title • Skim the first paragraph of a text to preview the most important idea • Understand scholarly references (in-text citations, bibliography) • Identify or complete the main ideas of a text • Understand the details that support the main ideas	• Guess the meaning of words from the context • Use dictionary entries to learn the meanings of words • Understand and use synonyms, collocations, different word forms, and the prefix *anti-* • Use the Vocabulary list at the end of the chapter to review the words, phrases, and idioms learned in the chapter • Use this vocabulary in the After You Read speaking and writing activities • GRAMMAR: Identify imperatives used as illustrative devices and the reasons for their use
5 NEUROSCIENCE: The Brain and Memory **Theme:** The importance of memory; the different types of memory and how they relate to different parts of the brain **Reading One:** *In Search of Memory* (a book excerpt) **Reading Two:** *The Brain and Human Memory* (a textbook excerpt) **Reading Three:** *Music and the Brain* (a book excerpt)	• Understand and practice different reading strategies • Visualize the content of a text to understand it better • Scan a chart to find specific information • Skim the first two paragraphs of a text to get an idea of what it will discuss • Match the different types of memory with their functions and the parts of the brain directly involved • Identify or complete the main ideas of a text • Understand the details that support the main ideas	• Guess the meaning of words from the context • Use dictionary entries to learn the meanings of words • Understand and use synonyms, collocations, different word forms, and words of Greek or Latin origin • Identify and interpret figurative language • Use the Vocabulary list at the end of the chapter to review the words, phrases, and idioms learned in the chapter • Use this vocabulary in the After You Read speaking and writing activities • GRAMMAR: Recognize and use rhetorical questions
6 ZOOLOGY: Animals and Language **Theme:** Do animals have the capability of communicating with one another and with humans? Are there animal languages? **Reading One:** *Bridges to Human Language* (a book excerpt) **Reading Two:** *Speaking to the Relatives* (an online article) **Reading Three:** *Language and Morality* (a book excerpt)	• Understand and practice different reading strategies • Scan a text for specific information • Find the link between the title of a text and the first paragraph • Predict the author's point of view from the first paragraph of a text • Identify or complete the main ideas of a text • Understand the details that support the main ideas	• Guess the meaning of words from the context • Understand and use synonyms, collocations, phrasal verbs, and different word forms • Use the Vocabulary list at the end of the chapter to review the words, phrases, and idioms learned in the chapter • Use this vocabulary in the After You Read speaking and writing activities • GRAMMAR: Recognize and use hedging language

NOTE-TAKING	CRITICAL THINKING	SPEAKING/WRITING
• Complete an outline • Take notes to identify the details that support the main ideas of a text	• Express your opinions and support them with examples from a text or from your own experience and culture • Analyze and evaluate information • Infer information not explicit in a text • Draw conclusions • Hypothesize about someone else's point of view • Make connections between ideas • Synthesize information and ideas	• Organize a debate about government control of the Internet and social media (in groups of four: two students are for, two are against) • Write a three-paragraph essay on the Internet service or type of social media that is the most interesting or worrisome to you • Discuss in a small group a number of topics related to the Internet and social media • Choose one of the topics and write a paragraph or two about it
• Make lists • Use keywords as a study tool	• Express your opinions and support them with examples from a text or from your own experience and culture • Infer information not explicit in a text • Draw conclusions • Hypothesize about someone else's point of view • Find correlations between two texts • Make connections between ideas • Synthesize information and ideas	• Role-play an interview with Eric Kandel and Oliver Sacks about the different types of memory and memory loss • Write a three-paragraph essay about your most important memory • Discuss in a small group a number of topics about memory • Choose one of the topics and write a paragraph or two about it
• Take notes to identify the arguments for or against the author's thesis • Complete an outline with the necessary details	• Express your opinions and support them with examples from a text or from your own experience and culture • Analyze and evaluate information • Infer information not explicit in a text • Draw conclusions • Hypothesize about someone else's point of view • Find correlations between two texts • Make connections between ideas • Synthesize information and ideas	• Role-play a discussion between a skeptic and the four authors or researchers encountered in the chapter about the work they have done • Write a short essay about how you have experienced learning a second language • Discuss in a small group a number of topics related to animals and language • Choose one of the topics and write a paragraph or two about it

CHAPTER	READING	VOCABULARY/GRAMMAR
7 POLITICAL SCIENCE: The Rulers and the Ruled **Theme:** Monarchy vs. democracy; how and why they work; how to go from one to the other **Reading One:** *The Morals of the Prince* (a book excerpt) **Reading Two:** *The Declaration of Independence* (a historical document) **Reading Three:** *Two Cheers for Democracy* (a book excerpt)	• Understand and practice different reading strategies • Skim a text to identify the author's point of view • Highlight the important information in a text • Think about the title of a text and predict its content • Identify or complete the main ideas of a text • Understand the details that support the main ideas	• Guess the meaning of words from the context • Use dictionary entries to learn the meanings of words • Understand and use synonyms, different word forms, figurative language, and expressions of similarity and contrast • Match types of government vocabulary with their definitions • Use the Vocabulary list at the end of the chapter to review the words, phrases, and idioms learned in the chapter • Use this vocabulary in the After You Read speaking and writing activities • GRAMMAR: Use a dash or dashes to isolate and emphasize a point
8 PSYCHOLOGY: Aggression and Violence **Theme:** Is mankind doomed to destruction by its aggressive and violent nature or do human beings have a gentler side that can master these base instincts? **Reading One:** *Civilization and Its Discontents* (a book excerpt) **Reading Two:** *Reflections on Natural History* (a journal article) **Reading Three:** *A Neuroscientist Uncovers a Dark Secret* (an online article)	• Understand and practice different reading strategies • Predict the content of a text from the first paragraph • Understand the most important idea of a text from the first and last paragraphs • Predict the content of a text from the title • Identify or complete the main ideas of a text • Understand the details that support the main ideas	• Guess the meaning of words from the context • Use dictionary entries to learn the meanings of words • Understand and use synonyms, phrases and idioms, collocations, and different word forms • Use the Vocabulary list at the end of the chapter to review the words, phrases, and idioms learned in the chapter • Use this vocabulary in the After You Read speaking and writing activities • GRAMMAR: Identify adjective clauses and the reasons for their use

NOTE-TAKING	CRITICAL THINKING	SPEAKING/WRITING
• Take notes to identify what a prince should or shouldn't do and why • Take notes to compare and contrast the ideas of two thinkers	• Express your opinions and support them with examples from the text or from your own experience and culture • Analyze and evaluate information • Infer information not explicit in a text • Draw conclusions • Hypothesize about someone else's point of view • Find correlations between the ideas of two thinkers through the lens of another thinker • Synthesize information and ideas	• In a small group, explain one of the quotes from three famous political philosophers, and compare it with the main ideas of the readings • Write an essay explaining your opinion about one of the main ideas of the readings • Discuss in a small group a number of topics related to government • Choose one of the topics and write an essay about it
• Take notes to identify the author's assertions and supporting explanations • Complete outlines to focus on the sequence of events and main discoveries	• Express your opinions and support them with examples from the text or from your own experience and culture • Analyze and evaluate information • Infer information not explicit in a text • Draw conclusions • Find correlations between two texts • Hypothesize about someone else's point of view • Make connections between ideas • Synthesize information and ideas	• Role-play an interview with Sigmund Freud, Stephen Jay Gould, and James Fallon about men's aggressiveness and violence • Write a three-paragraph essay about how an important event or lesson in childhood shaped your ethical behavior and moral sense • Discuss in a small group a number of topics related to human aggression and violence • Choose one of the topics and write a paragraph or two about it

CHAPTER	READING	VOCABULARY/GRAMMAR
9 ETHICS: **Resistance to Evil** **in the 20th Century** **Theme:** Nonviolent civil disobedience movements in India, Denmark, and the United States in the 20th century **Reading One:** *The Ghosts of Mrs. Gandhi* (a magazine article) **Reading Two:** *Denmark in World War II* (a book excerpt) **Reading Three:** *Three Ways to Meet Oppression* (a book excerpt)	• Understand and practice different reading strategies • Predict the content of a text from the subheadings • Preview a text using an Editor's Insert • Predict the content of a text from the title • Identify the main ideas of a text • Understand the details that support the main ideas	• Guess the meaning of words from the context • Use dictionary entries to learn the meanings of words • Understand and use synonyms, collocations, and different word forms • Use the Vocabulary list at the end of the chapter to review the words, phrases, and idioms learned in the chapter • Use this vocabulary in the After You Read speaking and writing activities • GRAMMAR: Identify noun clauses and the reasons for their use
10 WOMEN'S STUDIES: **Reaching for Equality** **Theme:** The history of women's rights and their struggle to achieve equality in the United States **Reading One:** *The Declaration of Sentiments (1848)* (a speech) **Reading Two:** *Speech on Women's Rights (1888)* (a speech) **Reading Three:** *The Day the Women Got the Vote* (a book excerpt)	• Understand and practice different reading strategies • Predict the content of a text from the first two paragraphs • Use paraphrasing to identify the main ideas of a text • Scan a text for dates to understand the sequence of events • Identify or complete the main ideas of a text • Understand the details that support the main ideas	• Guess the meaning of words from the context • Use dictionary entries to learn the meanings of words • Understand and use synonyms, collocations, phrasal verbs, and different word forms • Use the Vocabulary list at the end of the chapter to review the words, phrases, and idioms learned in the chapter • Use this vocabulary in the After You Read speaking and writing activities • GRAMMAR: Recognize the use of repetition for emphasis in speeches

NOTE-TAKING	CRITICAL THINKING	SPEAKING/WRITING
• Take notes to identify the main details of the actions • Complete a chart to identify the main points of the author's arguments	• Express your opinions and support them with examples from a text or from your own experience and culture • Infer information not explicit in a text • Draw conclusions • Hypothesize about someone else's point of view • Find correlations between two texts • Make connections between ideas • Synthesize information and ideas	• Role-play an interview with Amitav Ghosh, Hannah Arendt, and Martin Luther King, Jr. about resisting evil • Write a three-paragraph essay about a time when you or your family were caught up in a political or historical event of some importance • Discuss in a small group a number of topics related to nonviolent resistance • Choose one of the topics and write a paragraph or two about it
• Fill out an organizer with notes describing supporting details and your reaction • Fill out a timeline detailing the events for each date	• Express your opinions and support them with examples from a text or from your own experience and culture • Analyze and evaluate information • Infer information not explicit in a text • Draw conclusions • Hypothesize about someone else's point of view • Find correlations between two texts • Make connections between ideas • Synthesize information and ideas	• Role-play a discussion about women's rights between Elizabeth Cady Stanton, Frederick Douglass, someone living in 1919, and someone living today • Write a three-paragraph essay about something you had to fight for — a time you had to struggle to gain recognition for yourself and your abilities • Discuss in a small group a number of topics related to women's rights and equality • Choose one of the topics and write a paragraph or two about it

ACKNOWLEDGMENTS

Our heartfelt thanks go first and foremost to Massimo Rubini. Without his vision, this project would never have gotten off the ground. Not only did we have the advantage of his insight and directives as a fellow "architect" of the series, but we also benefited from his warmth and kindness in every way.

We owe another great debt of gratitude to our editor *extraordinaire,* Françoise Leffler. We gained immeasurably from her broad understanding of the project, her professional expertise, and her keen sense of precision in all stages of the writing process. Having such a creative editor and patient collaborator was a great gift.

Our sincere thanks also go to Amy McCormick, for her support and executive decision-making during many trying moments; to Rosa Chapinal, for her patience and devoted efforts throughout the permissions process; to Jill Krupnik, for her work in negotiating complex permissions contracts; and to Jane Lieberth, for her very thorough and close reading of our manuscript in the production phase.

We thank our colleagues at the American Language Program at Columbia University and the Department of Language and Cognition at Eugenio María de Hostos Community College for their enduring professional support and friendship.

Finally, we remember our students, from whom we continue to learn every day and who remain in our hearts our true teachers.

Robert F. Cohen and *Judy L. Miller*

Reviewers

The publisher would like to thank the following reviewers for their many helpful comments.

Jeff Bette, Naugatuck Valley Community College, Waterbury, Connecticut; **Kevin Knight**, Japan; **Melissa Parisi**, Westchester Community College, Valhalla, New York; **Jason Tannenbaum**, Pace University, Bronx, New York; **Christine Tierney**, Houston Community College, Stafford, Texas; **Kerry Vrabel**, GateWay Community College, Phoenix, Arizona.

CHAPTER 1

SOCIOLOGY:
Home and the Homeless

SOCIOLOGY: the scientific study of societies and the behavior of people in groups

OBJECTIVES

To read academic texts, you need to master certain skills.

In this chapter, you will:

- Think about the title of a text and predict its content

- Predict the subject of a text and the author's motivation from the first two sentences

- Make up your own questions based on the title of a text

- Guess the meaning of words from the context

- Use dictionary entries to learn the meanings of words

- Understand and use synonyms, different word forms, and the prefix *en-* and the suffix *-en*

- Identify the passive and the reasons for its use

- Fill out an organizer and use questions as "organizers" for notes

A **Consider These Sayings**

Read the sayings. What do they mean? Discuss with a partner. Be ready to report to the whole class on your insights. Add any other sayings from other languages that deal with the definition of "home."

1. "A house is not a home."

2. "Anywhere I hang my hat is home."

3. "You can't go home again."

4. "Home is where the heart is."

5. "To go forward, we must keep leaving home."

Others: _____

_____

B **Your Personal Experience**

Discuss the questions with a partner.

1. Which saying(s) do you agree with?

2. What is your definition of "home"?

3. Is "home" the place where you live or the place where you were born? Is it your "hometown" or a personal place?

4. What would you do if you lost your home and could never go back?

READING ONE: Home and Travel

A **Warm-Up**

Discuss the question in a small group. Share your answers with the class.

Do you think our idea of home changes at different times of our lives and in different cultures?

B **Reading Strategy**

Thinking about the Title and Predicting Content

To understand academic texts, you may have to read them more than once. You can prepare for your first reading by **looking at the title**.

The **title of a text** is the **first "contact" we have with the author**. It can inspire us to enter into a **dialogue with the author** even before reading one word of the text. It can also help us **predict** (guess) the content of the text.

Answer the questions about the title of the reading: *Home and Travel.*

1. Are these two ideas contradictory? In what way? Can they be combined: a home while traveling?

2. What do you think this reading will be about?

Now read the text to find out if your guess was correct.

Home and Travel

By Margaret Mead

Anthropologist Margaret Mead on a field trip in New Guinea

1   The need to define who you are by the place in which you live remains **intact**, even when that place is defined by a single object, like the small blue vase that used to mean home to one of my friends, the daughter of a widowed trained nurse who continually moved from one place to another. The Bushmen of the Kalahari Desert in Africa often build no walls when they camp in the desert. They simply hollow out a small space in the sand. But then they bend a slender young tree into an arch to make a doorway, an entrance to a **dwelling** as protected from invasion as the walled **estates** of the wealthy are or as Makati[1] in Manila is, where watchmen guard the rich against the poor.

2   I realized how few things are needed to make a "home" when I took my seven-year-old daughter on her first sea voyage. The ship — a **converted** troop ship — was crowded with over a thousand students. They were bunked below where the troops had slept, while Cathy and I shared one cabin with six other members of the staff. Cathy climbed into her upper berth, opened the little packages that had been given to her as going-away presents, and arranged them in a circle around her. Then she leaned over the side of the berth and said, "Now I am ready to see the ship."

3   Home, I learned, can be anywhere you make it. Home is also the place to which you come back again and again. The really **poignant** parting is the one that may be forever.

4   In all my years of **fieldwork**, each place where I have lived has become home. Each small object I have brought with me, each arrangement on a shelf of tin cans holding beads or salt for trade or crayons for the children becomes the **mark** of home. When it is **dismantled** on the last morning — a morning that is marked by the greed of those who have little and hope for a share of whatever is left behind, as well as by the **grief** of feeling that someone is leaving forever — on that morning I weep. I, too, know that this departure, unlike my **forays** from home as a child, is likely to be forever.

---

[1] *Makati:* a district in metropolitan Manila; the financial center of the Philippines

COMPREHENSION

 Main Ideas

Check (✓) the statements that best express the main ideas in the reading. Discuss your answers with a partner.

☐ **1.** Making a home is a way of marking off your private space.

☐ **2.** A home has to have a defense system.

☐ **3.** A home can be temporary.

☐ **4.** A home is a happy place.

☐ **5.** A very simple thing can symbolize home.

B **Close Reading**

Read the quotes from the reading. Circle the statement that best explains each quote. Share your answers with a partner.

1. "The need to define who you are by the place in which you live remains intact, even when that place is defined by a single object." *(paragraph 1)*

   a. Even an object can represent (or symbolize) home.

   b. When you have no home, you have no objects.

   c. Objects are essential to identity.

2. "But then [the people of the Kalahari] bend a slender young tree into an arch to make a doorway, an entrance to a dwelling as protected from invasion as the walled estates of the wealthy are . . . against the poor." *(paragraph 1)*

   a. Social customs protect privacy.

   b. The rich have more protection than the poor.

   c. Invasion often occurs in the desert.

3. "I, too, know that this departure, unlike my forays from home as a child, is likely to be forever." *(paragraph 4)*

   a. The author is sad about losing a home.

   b. The author never leaves home.

   c. The author is sad about childhood.

VOCABULARY

A **Guessing from Context**

> Looking up every word in the dictionary as you read is not an effective way to read. It is much better to **guess the meaning of unfamiliar words from the rest of the sentence or paragraph (the context)** and keep reading. You can use the dictionary after you get the main idea of the reading. No one guesses correctly all the time. But practice makes all the difference.

1 Read each quote from the reading. Try to guess the meaning of the words in bold from the context. Write your guess. Then consult a dictionary and write the definition.

1. "When [the arrangement of shelves and cans] is **dismantled** on the last morning . . . on that morning I weep." (*paragraph 4*)

   dismantle   Guess: *take apart — the pieces of the arrangement are no longer*

   together, but they remain and are distributed to friends

   Dictionary: *to take a machine or piece of equipment apart so*

   that it is in separate pieces

2. "They bend a slender young tree into an arch to make a doorway, an entrance to a **dwelling** as protected from invasion as the walled **estates** of the wealthy are." (*paragraph 1*)

   dwelling   Guess: _____

   Dictionary: _____

   estate   Guess: _____

   Dictionary: _____

3. "The really **poignant** parting is the one that may be forever." (*paragraph 3*)

   poignant   Guess: _____

   Dictionary: _____

2 Now answer the questions. Compare answers with a partner.

1. What is the difference between **dismantle** and **destroy**?

   When something is dismantled, the pieces are no longer together, but

   they remain. When something is destroyed, nothing may remain.

2. What is the difference between a **house** and a **dwelling**?

   _____

   _____

3. What is the difference between an **estate** and a **home**?

   _____

   _____

4. What is the difference between **sad** and **poignant**?

   _____

   _____

Read the dictionary entry for the noun *foray*.

> **foray** *n.* [C] **1** a short attempt at doing a particular job or activity, especially one that is very different from what you usually do **2** a short sudden attack by a group of soldiers, especially in order to get food or supplies **3** a short trip somewhere in order to get something or do something

Now read each sentence. Decide which meaning of *foray* is being used. Write the number of the appropriate meaning on the line.

_____ **a.** It was Mead's first foray into the village since she arrived.

_____ **b.** After an unsuccessful foray into theology, she decided to make her career in cultural anthropology.

_____ **c.** The raiding party made nightly forays into the enemy camp.

Which meaning is used in the reading?

C **Synonyms**

Complete the essay with the words from the box. Use the synonym in parentheses to help you select the correct word. Compare answers with a partner.

converted	dwellings	fieldwork	grief	mark
dismantle	estates	forays	intact	poignant

Margaret Mead was born into a family of educators in 1901. Her original major was theology, but her friend Ruth Benedict convinced her to change her major to anthropology. They both later became famous anthropologists.

Mead's _____*fieldwork*_____ was done in Samoa and New Guinea,
          1. (research)
where she often lived for years at a time doing research on culture. Although she

made frequent _____ to the South Pacific, her intellectual
                        2. (trips)
base was the Museum of Natural History in New York. In her autobiography,

Blackberry Winter, she writes about her tower office in a _____
                                                                        3. (modified)
attic of the museum. She kept this office for decades, unwilling to

_____ her files and displays to transport them elsewhere. She
      4. (take apart)
never cared much about money or _____; she lived in several
                                          5. (mansions)
modest _____ in New York City, where she taught at many
              6. (homes)
universities. Although some of her research findings have been challenged through

the years, her major insights remain _____: gender roles are

7. (unchanged)

influenced by culture and are not the unchangeable result of biological destiny. The

_____ of her success came when other scientists voted her

8. (symbol)

president of the American Association for the Advancement of Science in 1973.

Told as a young woman that she could never have children, Mead carried this

_____ for many years, but she and her third husband,

9. (mental suffering)

Gregory Bateson, had a daughter. Mary Catherine Bateson, also an educator, has

written a _____ memoir of life with her parents.

10. (nostalgic)

NOTE-TAKING: Filling Out an Organizer

Go back to the reading and read it again. Then fill out the organizer with the names of the people mentioned in the reading and a short description of their situation, the objects connected to these people, and what these objects meant to them.

	PEOPLE / SITUATION	OBJECT(S)	MEANING OF OBJECT(S) FOR PEOPLE
1.	Mead's friend / moved from place to place	a small blue vase	symbolized home and gave her a sense of belonging
2.			
3.			
4.			

CRITICAL THINKING

Discuss the questions in a small group. Be prepared to share your points of view with the class.

1. Look back at the sayings at the beginning of the chapter (page 2). Which one(s) would Mead agree with?

2. Why did gifts come to symbolize "home" for Mead's daughter? What other things came to symbolize home for other people in the reading?

3. How can people who must leave their homes to study or live in other countries build a new or temporary home for themselves?

A Warm-Up

Discuss the questions with a partner.

1. Are there homeless people where you live? Have you ever had a conversation with a homeless person?

2. What would you ask him or her if you had to write an article about the homeless?

B Reading Strategy

Predicting Content from First Two Sentences

The first two sentences of a text can help you **predict** (guess) what the **subject** of the text is and **what motivated the author** to explore this subject.

Look at the first two sentences in the reading. Answer the question on the line.

Do you think this will be a personal view of the homeless or a reading providing general information about this social problem?

_____

Now read the rest of the text to find out if your prediction was correct.

Homeless

By Anna Quindlen

1   Her name was Ann, and we met in the Port Authority Bus Terminal several Januaries ago. I was doing a story on homeless people. She said I was wasting my time talking to her; she was just **passing through**, although she'd been passing through for more than two weeks. To prove to me that this was true, she **rummaged** through a tote bag and a manila envelope and finally unfolded a sheet of typing paper and brought out her photographs.

2   They were not pictures of family, or friends, or even a dog or cat, its eyes brown-red in the flashbulb's light. They were pictures of a house. It was like a thousand houses in a hundred towns, not suburb, not city, but somewhere in between, with aluminum siding and a chain-link fence, a narrow driveway running up to a one-car garage and a **patch** of back yard. The house was yellow. I looked on the back for a date or a name, but neither was there. There was no need for discussion. I knew what she was trying to tell me, for it was something I had often felt. She was not **adrift**, alone, anonymous, although her bags and her raincoat with the **grime** shadowing its creases had made me believe she was. She had a house, or at least once upon a time had had one. Inside were curtains, a couch, a stove, potholders. You are where you live. She was somebody.

3   I've never been very good at looking at the big picture, taking the global view, and I've always been a person with an overactive sense of place, the **legacy** of an Irish grandfather. So, it is natural that the thing that seems most wrong with the world to me right now is that there are so many people with no homes. I'm not simply talking about **shelter** from the elements or three square meals a day or a mailing address to which the welfare people[1] can send the check — although I know that all these are important for survival. I'm talking about a home.

4   Home is where the heart is. There's no place like it. I love my home with a **ferocity** totally out of proportion to its appearance or location. I love dumb things about it: the hot-water heater, the plastic rack you drain dishes in, the roof over my head, which occasionally leaks. And yet it is precisely those dumb things that make it what it is — a place of certainty, stability, **predictability**, privacy, for me and for my family. It is where I live. What more can you say about a place than that? That is everything.

5   It has been customary to take people's pain and **lessen** our own participation in it by turning it into an issue, not a collection of human beings. We turn an adjective into a noun: the poor,[2] not poor people; the homeless, not Ann or the man who lives in the box or the woman who sleeps on the subway grate.

6   Sometimes I think we would be better off if we forgot about the broad strokes and concentrated on the details. Here is a woman without a bureau. There is a man with no mirror, no wall to hang it on. They are not the homeless. They are people who have no homes. No drawer that holds the spoons. No window to look out upon the world. My God. That is everything.

---

[1] *welfare people:* government agents who send aid to the poor to help them survive

[2] *the poor:* Some adjectives can be changed into nouns using "the": *the poor, the rich, the homeless.* These nouns are plurals: *The homeless have no shelter.* You can never say "a homeless." It should be "a homeless person."

COMPREHENSION

A Main Ideas

Check (✓) the statements that Anna Quindlen would agree with according to the reading. Compare answers with a partner. Explain your choices.

☐ **1.** We should see the homeless as individuals.

☐ **2.** We should build more homeless shelters.

☐ **3.** When we turn people into social "problems," we become indifferent to them.

☐ **4.** We should think about how we would feel if we lost our home.

B Close Reading

Read the quotes from the reading. Circle the statement that best explains each quote. Share your answers with a partner.

1. "[Ann] said I was wasting my time talking to her; she was just passing through, although she'd been passing through for more than two weeks." *(paragraph 1)*

   a. Ann was ashamed to admit that she lived in the bus station.

   b. Ann wanted to take a train to leave the city.

   c. Ann didn't want to waste her time talking to Quindlen.

2. "I've never been very good at looking at the big picture, taking the global view." *(paragraph 3)*

   a. There are a lot of things I don't understand.

   b. I see individual people and not abstract problems.

   c. I don't know how this problem appears elsewhere.

3. "I love my home with a ferocity totally out of proportion to its appearance or location." *(paragraph 4)*

   a. My home is beautiful, and I love it.

   b. My home is in a fashionable location, but I don't really love it

   c. My home is not beautiful or in a fashionable location, but I love it.

4. "We turn an adjective into a noun: the poor, not poor people; the homeless, not Ann or the man who lives in the box or the woman who sleeps on the subway grate." *(paragraph 5)*

   a. We use language to erase personal suffering and allow ourselves to become indifferent.

   b. A noun is more personal than an adjective.

   c. We use language to protect the homeless from suffering.

VOCABULARY

A **Guessing from Context**

1 Read each quote from the reading. Try to guess the meaning of the words in bold from the context. Write your guess. Then consult a dictionary and write the definition.

1. "She said I was wasting my time talking to her; she was just **passing through**, although she'd been passing through for more than two weeks." *(paragraph 1)*

   pass through   Guess: _on her way to another place_

   Dictionary: _to walk through a place on your way to another place_

2. "To prove to me that this was true, she **rummaged** through a tote bag and a manila envelope and finally unfolded a sheet of typing paper and brought out her photographs." *(paragraph 1)*

   rummage   Guess: _____

   Dictionary: _____

3. "It was like a thousand houses in a hundred towns, not suburb, not city, but somewhere in between, with aluminum siding and a chain-link fence, a narrow driveway running up to a one-car garage and a **patch** of back yard." *(paragraph 2)*

   patch   Guess: _____

   Dictionary: _____

4. "I love my home with a **ferocity** totally out of proportion to its appearance or location." *(paragraph 4)*

   ferocity   Guess: _____

   Dictionary: _____

2 Now answer the questions. Compare answers with a partner.

1. What is the difference between **passing through** and **traveling**?

   "Traveling" implies a destination while "passing through" could be aimless
   wandering.

2. Was she just **looking through** her bag in a leisurely manner? How does a person **rummage**?

   _____

3. How does a **patch** of backyard compare to **an acre** of land? Which is smaller?

   _____

(continued on next page)

4. How is **ferocity** different from **intensity**? Why do you think Quindlen uses such a word of violent passion?

_____

B Synonyms

Complete the essay with the words from the box. Use the synonym in parentheses to help you select the correct word. Compare answers with a partner.

adrift	grime	lessen	patch	rummage
ferocity	legacy	passing through	predictable	shelter

Losing a job, health problems, domestic violence, fire, and other problems can lead to

homelessness. The worldwide financial crisis did not _____ lessen _____ the
                 1. (diminish)

problem; on the contrary, it has made it much worse. Never has unemployment been so

high for so long in the United States. Many families are _____
               2. (floating out of control)

in the world, not knowing where to turn. Sometimes they double up with family

or friends; sometimes they lead a life of _____ homeless
              3. (moving through)

shelters trying to stay together. But what happens when the shelters are full? In

central Florida, unemployment is so acute that some families live in their cars. They

_____ through shopping bags and suitcases to find their clothes
      4. (search frantically)

every morning and wash off the _____ of the streets in gas station
                 5. (dirt)

bathrooms. This is the _____ of the great recession of 2008.
          6. (gift)

What should be done? The experience of recent years has led to the conclusion that

permanent housing is the key to a stable and _____ life for a
              7. (expected)

family. _____ is not enough; people need a home. Just a room
  8. (protection from the elements)

or a _____ of land is enough to make a difference. Without a
     9. (small piece)

home, families cannot do all the other things they need to do: reenter the job market, find

schooling, stabilize their health, and find other services. Some families and individuals will

need lifelong support to prevent future homelessness. The _____
                    10. (intensity)

of competition in our society means that many people will need help. Is it not more socially

productive to avoid masses of homeless people in our cities?

C Suffix -en and Prefix en-: Making Adjectives and Nouns into Verbs

> When the **suffix -en** is attached to certain adjectives and nouns, a **verb** is created.
>
> **less** *adj.*
> **lessen** *v.* to make something less
> **strength** *n.*
> **strengthen** *v.* to make strong
>
> **En-** can also be a **prefix**.
>
> **able** *adj.*
> **enable** *v.* to give someone what he/she needs in order to be able to do something
> **force** *n.*
> **enforce** *v.* to give power to something, as the law: **enforce** *the law*
>
> A word can have **en** as **a prefix or a suffix**, and sometimes **both** at the same time.
>
> **light** *adj.*
> **lighten** *v.* to make light
> **enlighten** *v.* to bring "light" or knowledge: *Education has* **enlightened** *the masses.*

1 Make these nouns and adjectives into verbs using the suffix *-en.*

	NOUN	VERB			ADJECTIVE	VERB
1.	black	blacken		6.	short	
2.	length			7.	wide	
3.	fright			8.	broad	
4.	height			9.	weak	
5.	light			10.	moist	

2 Make these nouns and adjectives into verbs using the prefix *en-.*

	NOUN	VERB			ADJECTIVE	VERB
1.	franchise	enfranchise		6.	large	
2.	danger			7.	rich	
3.	gender			8.	noble	
4.	joy			9.	feeble	
5.	rage			10.	dear	

CRITICAL THINKING

Discuss the questions in a small group. Be prepared to share your answers with the class.

1. The author and the main character in the reading have similar names. Do you think this is by accident? Why do you think the author chose to give the homeless woman a name close to her own? Native Americans have an expression: "Don't judge someone until you have walked a mile in his shoes." Do you think Anna Quindlen would agree?

2. Can you explain why Ann keeps a picture of the house she used to have and shows it to Quindlen?

3. Quindlen says that a lot of "dumb things" make up a home. What does she mean? Do you have dumb things that help make a place home for you? Are they really so foolish (dumb)?

4. Why does Quindlen say that losing a home means losing "everything"? Do you agree or disagree?

5. Why did Anna Quindlen write this article: To inform us about the homeless? To entertain us about the homeless? To persuade us to help the homeless? Does she say exactly what we should do? Why not?

LINKING READINGS ONE AND TWO

Your city is debating how to help the homeless. Some people want to build a shelter to give everyone a bed in a huge room overnight. Other people want to build a place where each person can have his or her own little room with a door and a window.

Use evidence from Reading One and Reading Two to support the idea that a person needs a private space in order to maintain his or her identity and mental stability.

	EVIDENCE TO SUPPORT A PERSON'S NEED FOR PRIVATE SPACE
Reading One	• The idea of home is so important that people will use symbols of home to give them that same warm and safe feeling (blue vase), but this is impossible in a shelter. • • •
Reading Two	• Giving shelter to a human being may be enough for survival, but it's not enough for a decent life. • • •

A **Warm-Up**

Discuss the questions with a partner.

1. The title of this reading is "Helping and Hating the Homeless." Why does the author think we are "helping" the homeless and "hating" them at the same time? What reason would we have for helping them? What reason would we have for hating them?

2. What does society owe the homeless in your opinion?

An advocate for the homeless talking to a homeless man about staying safe

B **Reading Strategy**

Making Up Questions Based on the Title

Making up your own questions about a text is the sign of an **active reader**. It puts you more **in charge of the reading process**. This strategy is possible when the title of the text is as provocative as the title of this reading.

Look at the title of the reading. Make up questions about information that you would like to know about the homeless. Here are some suggestions:

1. Who are the homeless?

2. Why are they homeless?

3. Whose fault is it?

4. Who should fix this?

Your Questions:

5. _____

6. _____

7. _____

8. _____

Now read the text and take notes on any information that might help you answer these questions.

Helping and Hating the Homeless
By Peter Marin

1 The trouble begins with the word "homeless." It has become such an abstraction, and is applied to so many different kinds of people, with so many different histories and problems, that it is almost meaningless.

2 Homelessness, in itself, is nothing more than a condition visited upon[1] men and women (and, increasingly, children) as the final stage of a variety of problems about which the word "homelessness" tells us almost nothing. Or, to put it another way, it is a catch basin into which pour all of the people **disenfranchised** or **marginalized** or scared off by processes beyond their control, those which lie close to the heart of American life. Here are the groups packed into the single category of "the homeless":

- Veterans, mainly from the war in Vietnam. In many American cities, vets make up close to 50 percent of all homeless males.
- The mentally ill. In some parts of the country, roughly a quarter of the homeless would, a couple of decades ago, have been **institutionalized**.[2]
- The physically disabled or chronically ill, who do not receive any benefits or whose benefits do not enable them to afford permanent shelter.
- The elderly on fixed incomes, whose funds are no longer sufficient for their needs.
- Men, women, and whole families pauperized by the loss of a job.
- Single parents, usually women, without the **resources** or skills to establish new lives.
- Runaway children, many of whom have been abused.
- Alcoholics and those in trouble with drugs (whose troubles often begin with one of the other conditions listed here).
- Immigrants, both legal and illegal, who often are not counted among the homeless.
- Traditional tramps, hobos, and transients, who have taken to the road or the streets for a variety of reasons and who prefer to be there.

3 You can quickly learn two things about the homeless from this list. First, you can learn that many of the homeless, before they were homeless, were people more or less like ourselves: members of the working or middle class. And you can learn that the world of the homeless has its roots in various **policies**, events, and ways of life for which some of us are responsible and from which some of us actually **prosper**.

4 We decide, as a people, to go to war, we ask our children to kill and to die, and the result, years later, is grown men homeless on the street.

5 We change, with the best intentions, the laws **pertaining to** the mentally ill, and then, without intention, neglect to provide them with services; and the result, in our streets, drives some of us crazy with rage.

---

[1] *visited upon:* inflicting on, as punishment

[2] When new drugs were developed to combat the symptoms of mental disease, most mental hospitals were closed to save tax money. Patients were sent out with their medications; however, if they do not have a family, they often get confused, stop taking the medications, and become homeless.

6 We cut taxes and **prune** budgets, we modernize industry and **shift** the balance of trade, and the result of all these actions and errors can be read, sleeping form by sleeping form, on our city streets.

7 The liberals cannot blame the conservatives. The conservatives cannot blame the liberals. Homelessness is the sum total of our dreams, policies, intentions, errors, omissions, cruelties, kindnesses, all of it recorded, in flesh, in the life of the streets.

8 The central question emerging from all this is, What does a society owe to its members in trouble, and how is that debt to be paid? A society owes its members whatever it takes for them to regain their places in the social order. And when it comes to specific **remedies**, one need only read backward the various processes which have created homelessness and then figure out where help is likely to do the most good. But the real point here is not the specific remedies required — affordable housing, say — but the basis upon which they must be offered, the necessary underlying ethical notion we seem in this nation unable to grasp: that those who are the inevitable **casualties** of modern industrial capitalism and the free market system are **entitled**, by right, and by the simple virtue of their participation in that system, to whatever help they need. They are entitled to help to find and hold their places in the society whose social contract they have, in effect, signed and observed.

9 Look at that for just a moment: the notion of a contract. The majority of homeless Americans have kept, insofar as they could, to the terms of that contract. In any shelter these days you can find men and women who have worked ten, twenty, forty years, and whose lives have nonetheless come to nothing. These are people who cannot afford a place in the world they helped create. And in return? Is it life on the street they have earned? Or the cruel charity we so **grudgingly** grant them?

COMPREHENSION

A Main Ideas

Read each statement. Decide if it is *True* or *False* according to the reading. Check (✓) the appropriate box. If it is false, change it to make it true. Discuss your answers with a partner.

According to the author:

	TRUE	FALSE
1. The homeless have been marginalized in society.	☐	☐
2. Homelessness probably increases with unemployment.	☐	☐
3. Conservatives are responsible for creating the homeless problem.	☐	☐
4. A society shaped by a free market economy has no ethical responsibility to help the homeless.	☐	☐

Read the quotes from the reading. Circle the statement that best explains each quote. Share your answers with a partner.

1. "Homelessness, in itself, is nothing more than a condition visited upon men and women (and, increasingly, children) as the final stage of a variety of problems about which the word 'homelessness' tells us almost nothing." *(paragraph 2)*

   a. Homelessness comes at the end of a long line of problems.

   b. Saying someone is homeless tells the whole story.

   c. Homelessness is a syndrome representing many conditions.

2. "And you can learn that the world of the homeless has its roots in various policies, events, and ways of life for which some of us are responsible and from which some of us actually prosper." *(paragraph 3)*

   a. Homelessness is like an act of God; no one is responsible.

   b. Many of us are responsible for the decisions that lead to homelessness, and some profit from the pain of others.

   c. The homeless people we see on the streets make us want to examine what responsibilities we have to make others more prosperous.

3. "Homelessness is the sum total of our dreams, policies, intentions, errors, omissions, cruelties, kindnesses, all of it recorded, in flesh, in the life of the streets." *(paragraph 7)*

   a. All the good and bad actions of modern society are reflected in the faces of the homeless.

   b. There is both good and bad in the life of homeless people on the streets.

   c. The reality of life on the streets is seen in its raw form in the flesh of homeless people.

4. "They are entitled to help to find and hold their places in the society whose social contract they have, in effect, signed and observed." *(paragraph 8)*

   a. The homeless will be worthy of respect only when they join society.

   b. The homeless need our charity.

   c. The homeless are people who helped build our country and have earned the right to our assistance.

5. "Is it life on the streets they have earned? Or the cruel charity we so grudgingly grant them?" *(paragraph 9)*

   a. The author is criticizing the homeless.

   b. The author is criticizing our heartlessness.

   c. The author is asking us to contribute to charity.

VOCABULARY

A Word Forms

1 Fill in the chart with the correct word forms. Use a dictionary if necessary. An **X** indicates there is no form in that category.

	NOUN	VERB	ADJECTIVE	ADVERB
1.	*disenfranchisement*		disenfranchised	X
2.			entitled	X
3.			institutionalized	X
4.			marginalized	X
5.		prosper		
6.	remedies			X
7.	resources	X		

2 Complete the essay with the correct form of the words from the chart. The first letter of each missing word has been given to you as a clue. Compare answers with a partner.

Peter Marin wants us to realize that the homeless are stripped of everything and

*disenfranchised*_____ in our society. He tells the story of Alice, a former
    1.

Chicago elementary school teacher, who suffered a nervous breakdown after being

attacked. As a result, she had to be **i**_____ for three months.
                                                2.

When she was released from the mental institution, all the modest signs of her former

middle-class **p**_____ had been taken away from her: Her
                   3.

landlord had sold all her belongings in order to cover the rent that she hadn't paid,

and the school had terminated her employment. Depressed and without any financial

r_____, she no longer wanted to be a burden to the friends
   4.

who had taken her in for a while. To **r**_____ the situation, she
                                     5.

decided to go to Los Angeles, where she has been a homeless person for years.

One tragic attack, resulting in a nervous breakdown, hospitalization, and

depression, led to a life on the streets for Alice, even though she should be

e_____ to help from the rest of society. The
   6.

m_____ of Alice is just one story among many.
   7.

B Synonyms

Complete the text with the words or phrases from the box. Use the synonym in parentheses to help you select the correct word or phrase. Compare answers with a partner.

casualties	grudgingly	pertaining to	policies	prune	shift

Homelessness involves all the problems _____*pertaining to*_____ the
                                              1. (relating to)

human condition. Human beings often give to charity _____,
                                                        2. (unwillingly)

especially during tough economic times. During economic crises, the government has

to _____ its budget. Sometimes, in so doing, it must choose to
      3. (trim)

_____ the direction of its social _____.
      4. (change)   **5. (programs)**

Those who are in great need of the government's help are less likely to receive it. The

homeless are without a doubt the _____ in such a situation.
                                        6. (ones who suffer)

GRAMMAR FOR READING: The Passive

When we use the **passive** instead of the active, we do so to **change the focus**:

- From the **action** to the **result of the action**

                 action
  ACTIVE: Society **has disenfranchised** the homeless.

                     result
  PASSIVE: The homeless **have** *been* **disenfranchised** by society.

- From the **agent** to the **receiver**

       agent   **receiver**
  ACTIVE: **Society** has disenfranchised **the homeless**.

       receiver   **agent**
  PASSIVE: **The homeless** have been disenfranchised *by* **society**.

In many cases, we do **not mention the agent**; the agent is just **implied**:

- When the agent is **not important** or **not known**

       [no agent mentioned]
  PASSIVE: The homeless **have** *been* **institutionalized**.

- When we want to **avoid blaming the agent**

       [no agent mentioned]
  PASSIVE: Mistakes **have** *been* **made** when dealing with the homeless.

1   Work with a partner. Discuss these passive sentences from the reading. Answer the
     questions that follow.

1.   "[The word homeless] is applied to so many different kinds of people, with so many
     different histories and problems, that it is almost meaningless." *(paragraph 1)*

     Q: Who is the implied agent? Why is it not mentioned?

     A: *The implied agent is all of us who use the word "homeless" without being*
        precise. The agent isn't mentioned because it is a universal practice.

2.   "Homelessness, in itself, is nothing more than a condition [that is] visited upon
     men and women." *(paragraph 2)*

     Q: Does this sentence imply that the homeless are to blame or that society is
     to blame?

     A: _____

3.   "They are entitled to help to find and hold their places in the society whose social
     contract they have, in effect, signed and observed." *(paragraph 8)*

     Q: According to Marin, they are entitled by what? What gives them the right to
     ask for help?

     A: _____

4.   "When it is dismantled on the last morning — a morning that is marked by the
     greed of those who have little and hope for a share of whatever is left behind, as
     well as by the grief of feeling that someone is leaving forever — on that morning
     I weep." *(Reading One, paragraph 4)*

     Q: Who is the agent here?

     A: _____

2   Put yourself into Peter Marin's shoes. Consider why he chose to use the passive
     voice in his essay. Check (✓) the statements that he might have made about his style.

☐ 1. I use the passive voice to show that the homeless have not been proactive
      enough to prevent these bad things from happening to them.

☐ 2. I don't always include an agent because I am afraid to blame anyone.

☐ 3. I don't always include an agent because my primary goal is to get everyone to
      join together and do something positive rather than just blame others.

☐ 4. I don't always include an agent because I want my readers to realize that we
      (that is, the whole society) are all at fault for many of the conditions that cause
      homelessness.

☐ 5. I use the passive voice to sound more formal.

NOTE-TAKING: Using Questions as "Organizers" for Notes

Go back to the questions on page 15. Read "Helping and Hating the Homeless" again, and take notes by writing answers to the questions suggested.

	QUESTIONS	ANSWERS
1.	Who are the homeless?	*The homeless can be veterans, the mentally ill, the physically disabled, the chronically ill, the elderly, substance abusers, single mothers and children, runaways, immigrants, and transients.*
2.	Why are they homeless?	
3.	Whose fault is it?	
4.	Who should fix this?	

CRITICAL THINKING

Discuss the questions in a small group. Be prepared to share your opinions with the class.

1. Marin writes: "The solution of [the homeless problem] depends on a drama occurring at the heart of the culture: the tension between the generosity we owe to life and the darker tendencies of the human psyche — our fear of strangeness, our hatred of deviance, our love of order and control. How we balance between those contrary forces will determine not only the destinies of the homeless but also something crucial about the nation, and perhaps — let me say it — about our own souls."

   • Why does Marin think we "hate" the homeless?
   • Can you think why he says it is essential not just for the homeless but for our own souls that we help these people?

2. Do you agree with Marin that we are responsible for the development of homelessness? Are we also responsible for substance abusers? Runaways? Is Marin making us responsible for too much?

3. How could cutting taxes contribute to homelessness?

BRINGING IT ALL TOGETHER

Work in groups of five. Role-play a discussion organized by Public Radio between people with different opinions about the homeless.

TOPIC: The meaning of home and the problem of being homeless

ROLES:

- Journalist from Public Radio
- Margaret Mead
- Anna Quindlen
- Peter Marin
- Taxpayer who disagrees with Quindlen and Marin

QUESTIONS:

- Can the idea of home ever be symbolized by just one thing?
- Why do people need a home? Why is home important to them?
- Who are the homeless?
- Why is society responsible for solving the homeless problem?

The journalist will ask questions of the others. Mead, Quindlen, Marin, and the taxpayer will express their opinions. Use some of the vocabulary you studied in the chapter (for a complete list, go to page 24).

WRITING ACTIVITY

Write a three-paragraph essay explaining and illustrating one of the sayings about home at the beginning of the chapter. Use more than five of the words or idioms you studied in the chapter.

- **Introduction:** Choose and explain the saying you chose. It can be a saying you agree with or one you disagree with. Say why you agree or disagree with it.
- **Body Paragraph:** Give examples that illustrate your opinion. The examples can come from your life or reading.
- **Conclusion:** Briefly discuss what it would be like to lose your home.

DISCUSSION AND WRITING TOPICS

Discuss these topics in a small group. Choose one of them and write a paragraph or two about it. Use the vocabulary from the chapter.

1. Describe homelessness in another country you may be familiar with. Are the causes of homelessness there similar to those in the United States?

2. The "Housing First" movement believes that the homeless need housing first of all. Do you agree or disagree? What other services do you think homeless people might need?

3. What can a local community do to help the homeless? Build homes like Habitat for Humanity? Provide services? What are the advantages and disadvantages of such programs?

VOCABULARY

Nouns
casualty
dwelling
estate *
ferocity
fieldwork
foray
grief
grime
legacy
mark
patch
policy *
predictability *
remedy
resource *
shelter

Verbs
disenfranchise
dismantle
institutionalize *
lessen
marginalize *
prosper
prune
rummage
shift *

Adjectives
adrift
converted *
entitled
intact
poignant

Adverb
grudgingly

Phrases and Idioms
pass through
pertain to

*= AWL (Academic Word List) item

SELF-ASSESSMENT

In this chapter you learned to:

○ Think about the title of a text and predict its content

○ Predict the subject of a text and the author's motivation from the first two sentences

○ Make up your own questions based on the title of a text

○ Guess the meaning of words from the context

○ Use dictionary entries to learn the meanings of words

○ Understand and use synonyms, different word forms, and the prefix **en-** and the suffix **-en**

○ Identify the passive and the reasons for its use

○ Fill out an organizer and use questions as "organizers" for notes

What can you do well? ✓

What do you need to practice more? ✓

CHAPTER 2

HISTORY: Robber Barons Then and Now

HISTORY: the study of all the things that happened in the past, including political, social, and economic developments

OBJECTIVES

To read academic texts, you need to master certain skills.

In this chapter, you will:

- Scan a text to find specific information

- Scan the first paragraph of a text for definitions and background information

- Predict the content of a text from the first and last paragraphs

- Guess the meaning of words from the context

- Understand and use synonyms, collocations, and different word forms and idioms

- Identify parallel forms and the reasons for their use

- Use an organizer to identify important biographical details

- Use note-taking to summarize an argument

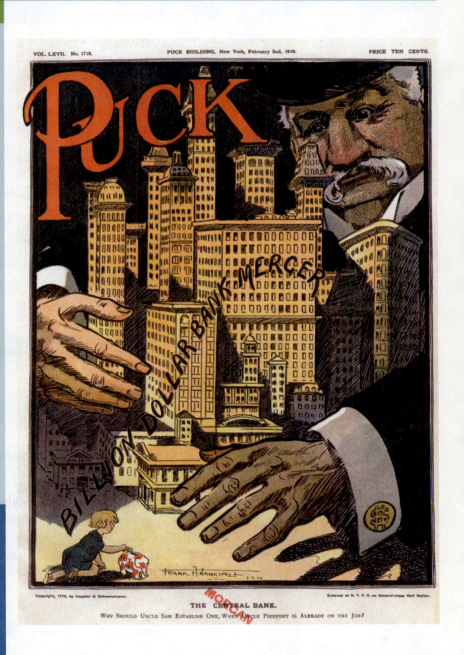

A Consider These Quotes

Read the quotes. What do they mean? Do you agree or disagree with them? Be ready to report to the whole class on your insights.

1. "History is philosophy taught by examples."

   —*Thucydides, Greek historian, probably lived between 460 and 400 B.C.*

2. "History is an account (mostly false) of events (mostly unimportant) which are brought about by rulers (mostly unscrupulous) and soldiers (mostly fools)."

   —*Ambrose Bierce, American author, 1842–1913*

3. "Those who cannot remember the past are condemned to repeat it."

   —*George Santayana, American writer born in Spain, 1863–1952*

B Your Opinion

Discuss the questions with a partner.

1. What is your favorite definition of history? Did you enjoy studying history in school?

2. Why is it important for history to be reliable?

3. Do governments try to "rewrite" history for their people? Do you know any examples of this?

4. If one of the purposes of history is to learn from the past, why do people and countries keep making the same mistakes?

READING ONE: The Robber Barons

A Warm-Up

1 Who were the "robber barons"?

Read this introduction and discuss the questions with a partner.

"Robber barons" is a term historians applied to businessmen who used questionable business practices to become wealthy at the end of the 19th century in America. The term combines the idea of a criminal (robber) and an illegitimate aristocracy (barons). Other historians argued that while Rockefeller and others may have engaged in unethical and illegal business practices, this should not overshadow their contributions to order and stability in competitive business. Called the Gilded Age by Mark Twain, the period from 1870 to 1898 was marked by the growth of industry, great wealth, and political corruption.

1. What would you agree to do in order to become rich?

2. Is there anything you wouldn't do?

2 Wall Street Vocabulary

To read about the "robber barons," you need to brush up on your Wall Street vocabulary. Work with a partner. Try to match the words or phrases with their definitions. Consult a dictionary if necessary.

__d__ 1. broker

_____ 2. dividends

_____ 3. financial convulsions

_____ 4. monopoly

_____ 5. stocks

_____ 6. stockholder

_____ 7. bonds

_____ 8. commission

a. profits you receive from your shares in a company

b. economic recessions and depressions

c. shares in the ownership of a company

d. someone who buys and sells stocks and bonds for someone else

e. exclusive control of the market so that prices can be manipulated in favor of one company and competition is eliminated

f. payment to an agent for buying or selling stocks or for other financial operations

g. owner of shares (stocks) in a company

h. official documents promising that a government or company will pay back money that it has borrowed, often with interest

B Reading Strategy

Scanning

Scanning a text means **looking quickly at the text to find specific information**. This can be useful on standardized tests when you may not have time to read everything. You just look quickly to find the answer to the question. Scanning can also help you when you have many pages to read; you can learn to look for the essential information.

From the title of the reading, it is clear that the text is going to discuss certain people. Scan the reading to find the names of the three people discussed. Circle them in the reading and write them on the lines.

1. _____

2. _____

3. _____

Do you know these people? Do you recognize their names?

Now read the text to find out more about these people.

The Robber Barons

By Howard Zinn

father had written to him that "a man may be a patriot without risking his own life or sacrificing his health. There are plenty of lives less valuable."

3   While making his fortune, Morgan brought rationality and organization to the national economy. He kept the system stable. He said, "We do not want financial **convulsions** and have one thing one day and another thing another day." He linked railroads to one another, all of them to banks, and banks to insurance companies. By 1900, he controlled 100,000 miles of railroad, half the country's mileage.

1   J. P. Morgan started his career before the Civil War,[1] as the son of a banker who began selling stocks for the railroad for good commissions. During the Civil War, he bought five thousand rifles for $3.50 each from an army arsenal,[2] and sold them to a general in the field for $22 each. The rifles were **defective** and would shoot off the thumbs of the soldiers using them. A congressional committee noted this in the small print of an **obscure** report, but a federal judge **upheld** the deal as the fulfillment of a valid legal contract.

2   Morgan had escaped military service in the Civil War by paying $300 to a substitute. So did other wealthy businessmen like John D. Rockefeller, Andrew Carnegie, Philip Armour, Jay Gould, and James Mellon. Mellon's

---

[1] *the Civil War:* the war that was fought from 1861 to 1865 in the United States between the northern and southern states over whether it was right to own slaves

[2] *arsenal:* a building where weapons are stored; an armory

4   John D. Rockefeller started as a bookkeeper in Cleveland, became a merchant, **accumulated** money, and decided that, in the new industry of oil, whoever controlled the oil refineries controlled the industry. He bought his first oil refinery in 1862, and by 1870 set up Standard Oil Company of Ohio, made secret agreements with railroads to ship his oil with them if they gave him rebates — discounts — on their prices, and thus drove competitors out of business.

5   By 1899, Standard Oil Company was a holding company,[3] which controlled the stock of many other companies. The capital was $110 million, the profit was $45 million a year, and John D. Rockefeller had **amassed** a fortune estimated at $200 million. Before long, he would move into iron, copper, coal, shipping, and banking (Chase Manhattan Bank).

6   Andrew Carnegie was a telegraph clerk at seventeen, then secretary to the head of the Pennsylvania Railroad, then broker in Wall Street selling railroad bonds for huge commissions, and was soon to be a millionaire. He went to London in 1872, saw the new Bessemer method of producing steel, and returned to the U.S. to build a million-dollar steel **plant**. Foreign competition was kept out by a high **tariff** conveniently set by Congress, and by 1880, Carnegie was producing 10,000 tons of steel a month making $1 ½ million a year in profit. In 1900, he agreed to sell his steel company to J. P. Morgan for $492 million.

7   Morgan then formed the U.S. Steel Corporation, combining Carnegie's corporation with others. He sold stocks and bonds for $1,300,000,000 ($400 million more than the combined worth of the two companies). How could dividends be paid to all those stockholders and bondholders? By making sure Congress passed tariffs keeping out foreign steel; by closing off competition and maintaining the price at $28 a ton; and by working 200,000 men twelve hours a day for wages that **barely** kept their families alive.

8   And so it went, in industry after industry — **shrewd**, efficient businessmen building empires, choking out competition, maintaining high prices, keeping wages low, using government subsidies. These industries were the first **beneficiaries** of the "welfare state."[4] By the turn of the century, American Telephone and Telegraph had a monopoly[5] of the nation's telephone system, International Harvester made 85% of all farm machinery, and in every other industry resources became concentrated and controlled. The banks had interests in so many of these monopolies as to create an interlocking network of powerful corporation directors, each of whom sat on the boards of many other corporations.

---

[3] **holding company:** a company that owns and controls other companies

[4] **welfare state:** the system by which the government provides money, free medical care, etc. for people who are old, do not have jobs, are sick, etc.

[5] **monopoly:** the control of all or most of a business activity by a single company. Later laws prohibited monopolies because they were "in restraint of trade" — an obstacle to competition and innovation.

COMPREHENSION

A Main Ideas

Read each statement. Decide if it is *True* or *False* according to the reading. Check (✓) the appropriate box. If it is false, change it to make it true. Discuss your answers with a partner.

	TRUE	FALSE
1. All the "robber barons" started off as poor or middle-class people.	☐	☐
2. The first beneficiaries of welfare were not poor people but large corporations.	☐	☐
3. The robber barons believed in competition.	☐	☐
4. These men made a great deal of money and took care of their workers.	☐	☐

B Close Reading

Read the quotes from the reading. Circle the statement that best explains each quote. Share your answers with a partner.

1. "A congressional committee noted [that the rifles were defective] in the small print of an obscure report, but a federal judge upheld the deal as the fulfillment of a valid legal contract." *(paragraph 1)*

   a. The federal courts considered that selling broken guns to the army was acceptable.

   b. The federal courts considered that selling broken guns to the army was illegal.

   c. J. P. Morgan was punished for what he did.

2. "There are plenty of lives less valuable." *(paragraph 2)*

   a. Let a poor man's son die in the place of a rich man's son.

   b. The lives of all soldiers are equally precious.

   c. Military service is a patriotic duty for every citizen.

3. "He bought his first oil refinery in 1862, and by 1870 set up Standard Oil Company of Ohio, made secret agreements with railroads to ship his oil with them if they gave him rebates — discounts — on their prices, and thus drove competitors out of business." *(paragraph 4)*

   a. These agreements were secret so that competitors would also sign up for rebates.

   b. These agreements were secret so that other businesses wouldn't know that Standard Oil was paying lower prices.

   c. Competitors didn't care about these secret agreements.

4. "[How could he make a profit?] By making sure Congress passed tariffs keeping out foreign steel; by closing off competition and maintaining the price at $28 a ton; and by working 200,000 men twelve hours a day for wages that barely kept their families alive." *(paragraph 7)*

   a. Profits came from free market competition.

   b. Profits came from keeping wages down and getting the government to stop competition.

   c. Profits came from producing excellent products.

5. "These industries were the first beneficiaries of the 'welfare state.'" *(paragraph 8)*

   a. Only poor people received welfare from the government.

   b. The robber barons' industries were able to function on their own.

   c. The robber barons' wealth was subsidized by the government.

6. "The banks had interests in so many of these monopolies as to create an interlocking network of powerful corporation directors, each of whom sat on the boards of many other corporations." *(paragraph 8)*

   a. Wealth was concentrated in very few hands.

   b. Banks, railroads, and corporations were all separate from each other.

   c. Government actually owned some companies.

VOCABULARY

A **Collocations**

> Remember that **collocations** are "word partners." They are words or phrases that are paired together frequently.
>
> **EXAMPLES:**
> - make a mistake
> - take a test
> - eradicate a disease
> - destroy someone's hopes

Check (✓) the words that are often paired together. Then answer the question below. Discuss your answers with a partner.

 1. accumulate possessions   ☐ 7. uphold an argument

☐ 2. accumulate people   ☐ 8. uphold a decision

☐ 3. amass a fortune   ☐ 9. a defective machine

☐ 4. amass an army   ☐ 10. a defective person

☐ 5. a steel factory   ☐ 11. defective reasoning

☐ 6. a steel plant

Which word — **accumulate** or **amass** — can be used with both things and people?

B Synonyms

Complete the essay with the words from the box. Use the synonym in parentheses to help you select the correct word. Compare answers with a partner.

accumulated	barely	convulsions	obscure	shrewd	upheld
amassed	beneficiary	defective	plant	tariffs	

Andrew Carnegie, an immigrant from Scotland, never passed up an opportunity to find a way to make money, even in bad times. He had the ____shrewd____
1. (calculating)
street smarts shared by most of the robber barons. However, when the American economy faced the _____ of an economic downturn, even the
2. (contractions)
vast fortune he had _____ was not immune.
3. (acquired)

Carnegie Steel was a huge company; it wasn't a complete monopoly, but it controlled most of the market. Carnegie had lobbied Congress to agree to _____ that would condemn foreign competitors. His
4. (import duties)
company was the _____ of government protection.
5. (recipient)
Carnegie's plan, carried out by general manager Henry C. Frick, was to use the recession to cut wages and break the union of skilled workers in Homestead, near Pittsburgh, Pennsylvania. In spring 1892, the union called a strike.

Frick refused to negotiate with the union, locked out the workers at the _____, and threw them out of company housing. He
6. (factory)
_____ a private army of security agents called the Pinkertons
7. (gathered)
to fight the workers. He and Carnegie thought the workers would just give in, but they clearly suffered from _____ reasoning. Three
8. (faulty)
thousand workers turned out to defend their jobs. The governor of Pennsylvania _____ Frick's decisions and sent the state militia into Homestead.
9. (supported)

Although the entire Strike Committee was arrested and accused of treason against the state, sympathetic juries refused to convict. Frick became the "most hated man in America." He was later the target of an assassination attempt by a previously _____ anarchist, Alexander Berkman. Frick
10. (unknown)
_____ survived. Carnegie's reputation never recovered.
11. (with difficulty)

NOTE-TAKING: Identifying Biographical Details

Go back to the reading and read it again. Then fill out this biographical organizer. Take notes on the three robber barons mentioned in the reading: how they began their careers, what industries they developed, and how they behaved as businessmen.

NAME	HOW DID HIS CAREER START?	WHAT INDUSTRIES DID HE DEVELOP?	HOW DID HE DO THIS?
J. P. Morgan			
John D. Rockefeller			
Andrew Carnegie			

CRITICAL THINKING

Discuss the questions in a small group. Be prepared to share your answers with the class.

1. "Congress conveniently enacted tariffs." What effect did tariffs have on competition? Did these early industrialists want to engage in competition or to build monopolies? What is the irony in the use of the word *conveniently*? Why do you think Congress did everything to help business? Why didn't they help workers at this time?

2. Is the author of the reading "neutral" about the industrialists he discusses? What do you think his opinion of them is? Refer back to the reading. Does the author say anything good about these leaders of industry?

3. Carnegie's life was a "rags-to-riches" story: his father was a factory worker, and his mother fixed shoes. He started with nothing and amassed a vast fortune. Do you think this is possible today? Can you think of some examples? What are the qualities needed for such a life?

4. Carnegie and Rockefeller controlled hundreds of millions of dollars in their day. Today Bill Gates and Warren Buffett control billions. Due to low tax rates for the rich, these businessmen get to decide what they want to do with vast sums of money that are sometimes greater than the GDP (Gross Domestic Product) of whole nations. Should this situation be allowed?

A Warm-Up

Read these quotes from Theodore Roosevelt. Discuss what they mean with a partner. What is President Roosevelt asking Americans to do? What is he warning against?

Theodore Roosevelt
(President from 1901–1909)

1. "Let the watchwords of all our people be the old familiar watchwords of honesty, decency, fair-dealing, and common sense. . . . We must treat each man on his worth and merits as a man. We must see that each is given a square deal, because he is entitled to no more and should receive no less. . . . The welfare of each of us is dependent fundamentally upon the welfare of all of us."

   — *Speech at New York State Fair, Syracuse, September 7, 1903*

2. "Our government, National and State, must be freed from the sinister influence or control of special interests. . . . The great special business interests too often control and corrupt the men and methods of government for their own profit. We must drive the special interests out of politics. . . . The Constitution guarantees protection to property, and we must make that promise good. But it does not give the right of suffrage to any corporation."

   — *Speech on the Square Deal, "The New Nationalism," August 31, 1910*

B Reading Strategy

Scanning First Paragraph for Definitions and Background Information

Scanning the first paragraph of a text for definitions and background information can give you an **understanding of the subject** and prepare you for the rest of the reading.

Work with a partner. Answer the questions.

1. Look at the title of the essay and read the first two sentences. What was

   progressivism a response to? _____

2. Then scan the rest of the first paragraph to find out the following:

   a. the time period involved: _____

   b. the different places where progressivism took root: _____

   _____

   c. the idea for a new "social economy": _____

THE POLITICS OF PROGRESSIVISM

By Eric Foner, from *Give Me Liberty: An American History*

The 1902 coal strike in Pennsylvania

1   Progressivism was an international movement. In the early 20th century, cities throughout the world experienced similar social **strains** arising from rapid industrialization and urban growth. In 1850, Paris and London were the only cities whose population **exceeded** 1 million. By 1900, there were twelve — New York, Chicago, and Philadelphia in the United States, and others in Europe, Latin America, and Asia. Facing similar social problems, reformers across the globe exchanged ideas and **envisioned** new social policies. Sun Yat-Sen, the Chinese leader, was influenced by the writings of Henry George and Edward Bellamy.[1] The mayor of Osaka, Japan, called for a new "social economy" that replaced competition with cooperation.

2   As governments in Britain, France, and Germany **instituted** old age pensions, minimum wage laws, unemployment insurance, and the regulation of workplace safety,

---

[1] *Henry George* (1839–1897), who wrote *Progress and Poverty,* and *Edward Bellamy* (1850–1898), who wrote *Looking Backward,* were two 19th-century critics of capitalism.

American reformers came to believe they had a lot to learn from the Old World. The term "social legislation," meaning governmental action to **address** urban problems and the insecurities of working-class life, originated in Germany but soon entered the political vocabulary of the United States.

3   Progressives believed that the modern era required a fundamental rethinking of the functions of political authority, whether the aim was to combat the power of giant corporations, protect consumers, civilize the marketplace, or guarantee industrial freedom at the workplace. Progressives sought to **reinvigorate** the idea of an activist, socially conscious government. Even in South Carolina, with its strong tradition of belief in local autonomy, Governor Richard I. Manning **urged** his **constituents** to modify their view of government as a "threat to individual liberty," to see it instead as "a means for solving the ills of the body politic."

4   Progressives could reject the traditional assumption that powerful government posed a threat to freedom because their understanding of freedom was itself **in flux**. "Effective freedom," wrote the philosopher John Dewey, was far different from the "highly formal and limited concept of liberty" as protection from outside **restraint**. Freedom was a positive, not a negative, concept — "the power to do specific things." "Freedom," wrote Dewey's brilliant young admirer, the writer Randolph Bourne, "means a democratic cooperation in determining the ideals and purposes and industrial and social institutions of a country."

COMPREHENSION

A Main Ideas

Complete this summary of the reading with some of the choices from the box. There are four extra choices. Compare answers with a partner.

Because of the _____ that industrialization caused,
            1.
reformers all over the world started to discuss policies that could benefit workers

and counterbalance the great power of corporations. The British, French, and German

workers were the first to be entitled to such benefits as old age pensions, minimum

wage regulations, and unemployment insurance because their governments had

passed laws that Germans were the first to call "_____."
                                              2.
Inspired by what was happening in Europe, progressives in the United States

called for a government that would be more _____. To
                                         3.
some extent, there was a fear that _____ would be lost.
                                  4.
But American educator and philosopher John Dewey responded to this concern

by _____ "effective freedom," which he said would exist
      5.
when government insured that all citizens would be able to live a decent life in a

democratic society.

a. legislation	**d.** coining the term	**g.** individual freedom
b. social legislation	**e.** socially conscious	**h.** social strains
c. cities	**f.** urban growth	**i.** social policies

B Close Reading

Read the quotes from the reading. Circle the statement that best explains each quote. Share your answers with a partner.

1. "As governments in Britain, France, and Germany instituted old age pensions, minimum wage laws, unemployment insurance, and the regulation of workplace safety, American reformers came to believe they had a lot to learn from the Old World." *(paragraph 2)*

   a. The New World always had something to teach the Old World.

   b. Britain, France, and Germany were the first countries to pass old age pensions, minimum wage laws, unemployment insurance, and the regulation of workplace safety.

   c. Social reform in the United States was inspired by policies that had first been established in Europe.

2. "Progressives believed that the modern era required a fundamental rethinking of the functions of political authority, whether the aim was to combat the power of giant corporations, protect consumers, civilize the marketplace, or guarantee industrial freedom at the workplace." *(paragraph 3)*

   a. Progressives wanted to help the workers and limit the corporations.

   b. Progressives wanted to help the workers and the corporations.

   c. Progressives wanted to help the corporations but not the workers.

3. "Even in South Carolina, with its strong tradition of belief in local autonomy, Governor Richard I. Manning urged his constituents to modify their view of government as a 'threat to individual liberty,' to see it instead as a 'means for solving the ills of the body politic.'" *(paragraph 3)*

   a. Even conservatives believed in individual liberty.

   b. Even conservatives saw it was necessary to give some rights to workers.

   c. Even conservatives thought everyone was free to be exploited.

VOCABULARY

A **Guessing from Context**

Read each quote from the reading. Try to guess the meaning of the words in bold from the context. Write your guess. Then consult a dictionary and write the definition.

1. "In 1850, Paris and London were the only cities whose population **exceeded** 1 million." *(paragraph 1)*

   exceed   Guess: _be over_

                  Dictionary: _to be more than a particular number, amount, etc._

2. "Facing similar social problems, reformers across the globe exchanged ideas and **envisioned** new social policies." *(paragraph 1)*

   envision   Guess: _____

                  Dictionary: _____

3. "As governments in Britain, France, and Germany **instituted** old age pensions, minimum wage laws, unemployment insurance, and the regulation of workplace safety . . ." *(paragraph 2)*

   institute Guess: _____

                  Dictionary: _____

4. "The term 'social legislation,' meaning governmental action to **address** urban problems and the insecurities of working-class life . . ." *(paragraph 2)*

   address   Guess: _____

                  Dictionary: _____

Complete the essay with the words or idioms from the box. Use the synonym in parentheses to help you select the correct word or idiom. Compare answers with a partner.

address	envisioned	in flux	reinvigorated	strains
constituents'	exceeded	institute	restraints	urged

Theodore Roosevelt and Trust-Busting

When Theodore Roosevelt, often known as the first of the progressive presidents, became president of the United States in 1901, he _____ *envisioned* _____

1. (imagined)

a "Square Deal" that would _____ "the three Cs": control

2. (do something about)

over corporations, consumer protection, and conservation. To deal with the first

concern, he would soon have to _____ more government

3. (establish)

regulation of conflicts between large corporations and their workers. Although

big business had played a key role in building America, particularly through the

creation of monopolies, Roosevelt believed these trusts had acquired too much

control over people's lives and even over the government itself with hardly any

_____. The growing _____ between

4. (limitations)   **5. (signs of tension)**

workers and corporations could no longer be ignored. Nor could the need for greater

competition to ensure innovation and change.

Roosevelt's first major challenge came in 1902, with the anthracite coal strike

in Pennsylvania, when he was able to activate his belief in "speak[ing] softly and

carry[ing] a big stick." At this time, 140,000 miners had gone on strike and demanded

a 20% pay increase and a reduction in the workday from 10 to 9 hours. When

winter approached, and the strike had still not been settled, Roosevelt intervened

because the greatly diminished coal supply had put the nation at risk. Taking the

side of the miners, he _____ the mine owners to negotiate

6. (strongly encouraged)

with the workers. But when they refused, he threatened to seize the mines and

operate them with federal troops. The result of this unprecedented government

intervention in a labor dispute, in which the executive power of the presidency had far _____ its normal limits, was a 10% increase in salary and
7. (gone beyond)
a reduction of the workday from 10 to 9 hours.

This victory for labor, which was engineered by a president who had sided with the unions, made Roosevelt more and more the "people's president" and reinforced his _____ confidence in him. Roosevelt's success
8. (voters')
here also _____ his belief in his mission as the country's first
9. (gave renewed energy to)
"trust-buster." He soon took on large corporations that had engaged in corrupt and unlawful business practices, such as J. P. Morgan's Northern Securities Company, J. D. Rockefeller's Standard Oil Trust, and James B. Duke's tobacco trust, by starting lawsuits against them.

The accepted definition of the relationship between government and business and government and the people is still _____ today.
10. (changing)
However, beginning with President Theodore Roosevelt and the other progressive presidents who followed him, Howard Taft and Woodrow Wilson, the office of the president assumed greater authority as people began to expect more from the executive branch.

Garment workers on strike,
New York City circa 1913

C Word Forms: Dictionary Work

1 Some words can be used either as a noun or as a verb. Read the different meanings for the noun and verb forms of *address*, *institute*, and *strain*.

	NOUN	VERB
address	1 the number of the building and the name of the street where someone lives or works 2 a formal and important speech made to a group of people 3 the title or name that you use for someone when you speak to him or her	1 to write on an envelope the name and address of the person you are sending it to 2 to make a speech to a large group of people 3 to use a particular title or name when speaking or writing to someone 4 if you address a problem, you start trying to solve it
institute	an organization that has a particular purpose such as scientific or educational work, or the building where this organization is based	to introduce or start a system, rule, legal process, etc.
strain	1 worry caused by having to deal with a problem or having to work hard over a long period of time 2 a problem or difficulty when something is used too much 3 an injury to a muscle or part of your body, caused by using it too much 4 problems that develop in relations between two people or groups; tension	1 to try very hard to do something, using all your physical or mental strength 2 to force something to be used too much 3 to injure a muscle or part of your body by making it work too hard 4 *strain relations:* to cause problems between people, countries, etc.

2 Complete the sentences with the correct word in the correct form. In parentheses, write whether it is a noun or a verb and the number of its meaning (if it has more than one meaning).

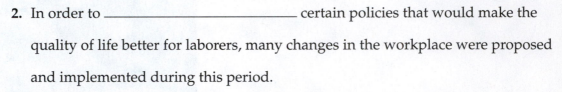

1. A _strain (noun, 4)_____ in the relationship between government and

   business leaders existed during Theodore Roosevelt's presidency.

2. In order to _____ certain policies that would make the

   quality of life better for laborers, many changes in the workplace were proposed

   and implemented during this period.

3. These policies were established after people with a conscience had started to

_____ conditions in the workplace that were totally

unacceptable.

4. For instance, it was surely unfair to see factory workers _____

to get a job done without being able to take a break.

5. In an _____ to veterans, President Roosevelt said: "A man

who is good enough to shed his blood for his country is good enough to be given

a square deal afterwards. More than that no man is entitled, and less than that no

man shall have."

6. Today, in a more global economy, there are many public and private

_____ that fund research projects on important topics such

as business ethics and finance.

Go back to the reading and see in what form (noun or verb) the words *address*, *strain*, and *institute* are used.

CRITICAL THINKING

Discuss the questions in a small group. Be prepared to share your points of view with the class.

1. Why did progressivism become an international movement? How was its presence in so many different cultures proof that people do have a lot in common with each other? What do they have in common?

2. The "social economy" proposed by the mayor of Osaka was meant to replace "competition with cooperation." Which one — competition or cooperation — do you think is more important? In what situations? Are competition and cooperation mutually exclusive? That is, are they separate, independent forces that have nothing to do with each other? Or, do competitors sometimes need to cooperate with the individuals that they are competing against?

3. Do you believe the progressives' hope for help from the government was realistic or unrealistic? Is that the role of government in your opinion?

4. The writer says that progressives' "understanding of freedom was . . . in flux." Some people felt that corporations should have the "freedom" to do as they wanted, and others thought the government should have the "freedom" to help workers. How can a definition of something as essential to life as freedom be "in flux"? Shouldn't this definition be the same for everybody? Why after all these centuries do we still not agree with one another on what freedom is?

Work with a partner. Fill in the chart with notes comparing the robber barons' practices with the progressives' proposals to get rid of these practices.

	READING ONE ROBBER BARONS' PRACTICES	READING TWO PROGRESSIVES' PROPOSALS
1.	kept wages very low	pass minimum wage laws
2.		institute regulation for workplace safety and respect for workers
3.	created monopolies	
4.		
5.		create cooperation and more opportunities for small business growth
6.	prevented freedom in the workplace	
7.		

READING THREE: Message to Wall Street

A **Warm-Up**

1 Wall Street Today

Discuss the questions with a partner.

"Occupy Wall Street" became an international movement after the financial crisis of 2008.

1. Why did people want to "occupy" Wall Street?

2. What was the purpose of the demonstrations?

2 More Wall Street Vocabulary

Work with a partner. Try to match the words and phrases with their definitions. Consult a dictionary if necessary.

__g__ 1. deregulation

_____ 2. hedge funds

_____ 3. mortgages

_____ 4. securities laws

_____ 5. shorting

_____ 6. toxic assets

_____ 7. fines

_____ 8. bailout money

a. investment funds now in excess of $2 billion and open only to certain institutions and very wealthy people

b. investments for which there is no longer any market because their value is so low

c. loans to buy houses

d. entering into a contract where the investor will profit from a fall in the value of an asset

e. money, usually from the government, to save a company from a difficult situation

f. government regulation of investments to insure legal activity

g. withdrawal of legislation by government that lets investors do what they want

h. financial penalties for wrongdoing

B Reading Strategy

Predicting Content from First and Last Paragraphs

Before you read a text, skim the first and last paragraphs to get a general idea of what will be discussed. In newspaper articles, the **first and last paragraphs often summarize the main points** of the text. Reading the first and last paragraphs of an article often allows you to **predict** (guess) the content of the article.

Read the first and last paragraphs of "Message to Wall Street." Answer the questions.

1. What is this reading going to explain?

_____

2. Is the reading a defense of Wall Street or a criticism?

_____

Now read the rest of the article to find out if your predictions were correct.

Message to Wall Street

By Jeffrey Sachs

Jeffrey Sachs is an American economist and the director of the Earth Institute at Columbia University. This article appeared in the Huffington Post online at the time of the Occupy Wall Street movement.

1   The Wall Street elite seems completely **befuddled** by the Occupy Wall Street movement. The demonstrators are called "unsophisticated" or "misguided," or much worse. Here's a short note to the Titans[1] of Wall Street to help them understand what's happening.

2   Let me start with the *Wall Street Journal*, which seems to be the most confused of all. In its Friday edition, the *Journal* editorial board couldn't understand why the protesters would want to protest JPMorgan[2] and hedge-fund manager John Paulson.

3   The protesters are annoyed with JPMorgan because it, like its fellow institutions on the street, helped to **bring** the world economy **to its knees** through unprincipled and illegal actions. The *Journal* editorial board apparently missed the news carried in the *Journal*'s own business pages that JPMorgan recently paid $153.6 million in fines for violating securities laws in the lead-up to the 2008 financial collapse. JPMorgan, like other Wall Street institutions, **connived** with hedge funds to **peddle** toxic assets to unsuspecting investors, allowing the hedge funds to **make a killing** at the expense of their "**mark**" and the world economy.

4   The protesters are not very fond of Mr. Paulson either, since he played this role together with Goldman Sachs.[3] Paulson made a fortune by **teaming up with** Goldman to bundle failed mortgages, which Goldman then peddled to its customers, in this case, some unsuspecting German banks. Paulson shorted these assets and thereby profited as the bank's investments collapsed. For this little maneuver, Goldman paid $560 million to the government Securities and Exchange Commission in fines. Of course this is a small amount compared to the profits that Goldman reaped for years playing in toxic assets. On Wall Street, misbehavior pays, at least up until now.

5   Mr. Paulson actually made some extraordinary statements in the *New York Times* on Friday (hard even to believe the nonsensical quotations are correct, but there they are, in the paper of record). He too expressed befuddlement about the protests against his business dealings. Didn't the protesters know he created 100 high-paying jobs in New York City? 100?

---

[1] ***Titans:*** a generation of Greek gods that ate their young. They were supplanted by a revolt of their children, the Olympians.

[2] ***JPMorgan:*** the bank, not the man

[3] ***Goldman Sachs:*** an investment bank

6   What the protesters do know is that Mr. Paulson's success in shorting toxic assets bundled for **gullible** investors has **netted** him billions. In 2007, he reportedly took home $3.7 billion by betting against the U.S. mortgage market. And the protesters can also do their arithmetic. Paulson's take-home pay was enough to cover not just 100 jobs at $50,000 a year but rather approximately 70,000 jobs at $50,000 a year. Nice try, Mr. Paulson, but the people at Liberty Plaza[4] don't think your hedge-fund play is really worth the **compensation** of 70,000 people. Nor do they understand why hedge-fund managers pay a top rate of 15% on their hedge-fund earnings.[5]

7   The *Wall Street Journal*, Paulson, and others who accuse the protesters of being "unsophisticated" somehow have forgotten a basic point. It's not just Paulson or Goldman or JPMorgan that **parlayed** their unethical behavior into vast fortunes at the expense of **hapless** investors. Just name any big name of Wall Street in the past decade, **scratch the surface**, and uncover a financial scandal. Bank of America, Goldman, JPMorgan, AIG, Merrill Lynch, Countrywide Finance, Lehman Brothers are only the start of the list.

8   The protesters are not envious of wealth, but sick of corporate lies, cheating, and unethical behavior. They are sick of corporate lobbying[6] that led to the **reckless** deregulation of financial markets; they are sick of Wall Street and the *Wall Street Journal* asking for trillions of dollars of near-zero interest loans and bailout money for the banks, but then fighting against unemployment insurance and health coverage for those drowning in the wake of the financial crisis. They are sick of absurdly low tax rates for hedge-fund managers.

9   Here then, Wall Street and Big Oil, is **what it comes down to**. The protesters are no longer **giving you a free ride**, in which you can set the regulations, set your mega-pay, hide your money in tax havens,[7] enjoy sweet tax rates at the hands of ever-willing politicians, and await your bailouts as needed. The days of lawlessness and greed are coming to an end. Just as the Gilded Age turned into the Progressive Era, just as the Roaring Twenties and its excesses turned into the New Deal,[8] be sure that the era of mega-greed is going to turn into an era of renewed **accountability**, lawfulness, modest compensation, honest taxation, and government by the people rather than by the banks.

10   That, in short, is why Wall Street is filled with protesters and why you should wake up, respect the law rather than try to write it, and pay your taxes to a government that is ruled by the people rather than by corporate power.

---

[4] *Liberty Plaza:* the crossroads on Wall Street where the demonstrations took place

[5] This refers to taxes. Compare this with the following: secretaries who earned $35,000 a year in 2011 paid 25% of their income in taxes; the highest income tax bracket is 35% for those who earn from $350,000 to a billion a year.

[6] *lobbying:* seeking to influence the decisions of government officials

[7] *tax haven:* a place, such as Switzerland or the Cayman Islands, where companies or individuals can secretly put their money while paying little or no taxes in the haven and none in their home countries

[8] *The Roaring Twenties* (the 1920s) were a time when great fortunes were made on the stock market with very little oversight by government regulations. This was followed by the 1929 crash and the Great Depression, when millions of people were plunged into desperate poverty. *The New Deal* policies of President Franklin Roosevelt gave relief to the poor, protected savings in banks, and regulated business to insure honesty.

COMPREHENSION

A Main Ideas

Check (✓) the main ideas of the reading. Discuss your answers with a partner.

_____ 1. Hedge-fund operations and other Wall Street practices must be changed.

_____ 2. Wall Street leaders are out of touch with what people think of them.

_____ 3. Wall Street must be protected because it is the heart of the economy.

_____ 4. Lawless financiers are undermining democracy.

B Close Reading

Read the quotes from the reading. Circle the statement that best explains each quote. Share your answers with a partner.

1. "JPMorgan, like other Wall Street institutions, connived with hedge funds to peddle toxic assets to unsuspecting investors, allowing the hedge funds to make a killing at the expense of their 'mark' and the world economy." *(paragraph 3)*

   a. JPMorgan sold worthless assets and then lost a lot of money while their clients and the economy gained.

   b. JPMorgan sold worthless assets and made a great deal of money while their clients and the economy lost.

   c. JPMorgan sold worthless stock and made a lot of money for their clients.

2. "On Wall Street, misbehavior pays, at least up until now." *(paragraph 4)*

   a. The law is too weak to punish Wall Street.

   b. Wall Street is going to behave now.

   c. Up to now, the laws have been effective.

3. "They are sick of Wall Street and the *Wall Street Journal* asking for trillions of dollars of near-zero interest loans and bailout money for the banks, but then fighting against unemployment insurance and health coverage for those drowning in the wake of the financial crisis." *(paragraph 8)*

   a. Banks would prefer that the government help the poor.

   b. Banks want zero-interest help from the government but refuse it to the poor.

   c. Banks don't want government help.

4. "Just as the Gilded Age turned into the Progressive Era, just as the Roaring Twenties and its excesses turned into the New Deal, be sure that the era of mega-greed is going to turn into an era of renewed accountability, lawfulness, modest compensation, honest taxation, and government by the people rather than by the banks." *(paragraph 9)*

   a. In the future, corporations will run the government.

   b. In the future, the government will agree with the banks.

   c. In the future, the people will force the government to control Wall Street's risky behavior.

VOCABULARY

A **Guessing from Context**

1 Read each quote from the reading. Try to guess the meaning of the words in bold from the context. Write your guess. Then consult a dictionary and write a short definition.

1. "JPMorgan . . . allow[ed] the hedge funds to make a killing at the expense of their '**mark**' and the world economy." *(paragraph 3)*

   mark   Guess: _victim_____

                Dictionary: _someone that a criminal has chosen to steal from or to trick_

2. "The Wall Street elite seems completely **befuddled** by the Occupy Wall Street movement." *(paragraph 1)*

   befuddled   Guess: _____

                Dictionary: _____

3. "JPMorgan, like other Wall Street institutions, **connived** with hedge funds to **peddle** toxic assets to unsuspecting investors." *(paragraph 3)*

   connive   Guess: _____

                Dictionary: _____

   peddle   Guess: _____

                Dictionary: _____

4. "What the protesters do know is that Mr. Paulson's success in shorting toxic assets bundled for **gullible** investors has **netted** him billions." *(paragraph 6)*

   gullible   Guess: _____

                Dictionary: _____

   net   Guess: _____

                Dictionary: _____

5. "It's not just Paulson or Goldman or JPMorgan that **parlayed** their unethical behavior into vast fortunes at the expense of **hapless** investors." *(paragraph 7)*

   parlay   Guess: _____

                Dictionary: _____

   hapless   Guess: _____

                Dictionary: _____

2 Now answer the questions. Compare answers with a partner.

1. What's the difference between **a mark** and a **victim**?

    A person can be a victim by accident or on purpose, but a mark is deliberately

    chosen for someone else's profit.

2. When you read the word **befuddled**, what is the image that comes to mind? How is it different from **confused**?

3. Peddlers sell cheap merchandise on the street. Why did the author use **peddle** rather than **sell**?

4. What kind of person is **gullible**? What word is similar in this reading?

5. When you earn something, you have worked for it. Why did the author use **netted** a lot of money rather than **earned** a lot of money?

6. Parlay is a gambler's term. Why is the word **parlay** used for shorting assets?

B Synonyms

Read the sentences. Match each word in bold with its synonym in the box below. Compare answers with a partner.

_____ 1. In a time of large-scale unemployment, **compensation** and bonuses for Wall Street managers can amount to millions of dollars.

_____ 2. Pity the **hapless** students who have to pay more than 6% interest on student loans while Wall Street bankers got free loans of billions of dollars.

_____ 3. The problems of Wall Street were brought on by their own **reckless** behavior.

_____ 4. Some people blame the lobbying tactics of bankers; they think investment bankers **connived** with legislators to make it legal to peddle toxic derivatives and encourage excessive risk-taking in world financial markets.

_____ 5. This makes people like Jeffrey Sachs hope that new legislation will bring some **accountability** to investment banking.

a. unlucky	**c.** risky	**e.** salaries
b. personal responsibility	**d.** plotted	

Read the expressions from the reading. Match them with their meanings.

<u>d</u> 1. **bring to its knees**

_____ 2. **give (someone) a free ride**

_____ 3. **make a killing**

_____ 4. **scratch the surface**

_____ 5. **team up with**

_____ 6. **what it comes down to**

a. the main point is

b. make it easy for someone to get away with something unethical or harmful

c. make a lot of money at someone else's expense

d. almost destroy

e. give something a superficial look

f. work with

GRAMMAR FOR READING: Parallel Forms

Jeffrey Sachs is a master stylist. He uses **parallel forms** (repetitive patterns) internally, within paragraphs, in order to make his point clearly as he summarizes and concludes.

EXAMPLE:

adjective + prep.   adj. + prep.
• The protesters are not **envious of** wealth, *but* **sick of** corporate lies . . .

Q: What grammatical structure is repeated?
A: **adjective + preposition** combination

Q: Why did the author use this repetition?
A: To focus on the feelings of the protesters

When you want **to connect ideas**, you **use parallel forms**. That is, you put all items in a series in the **same grammatical form** — matching nouns with nouns, verbs with verbs, adjectives with adjectives, and so on.

Work with a partner. Underline the parallel forms in each excerpt from the reading. Discuss and answer the questions that follow.

1. "They are sick of corporate lobbying that led to the reckless deregulation of financial markets; they are sick of Wall Street and the *Wall Street Journal* asking for trillions of dollars of near-zero interest loans and bailout money for the banks, but then fighting against unemployment insurance and health coverage for those drowning in the wake of the financial crisis." *(paragraph 8)*

Q: What grammatical structures are repeated?

A: _____

Q: Why did the author use these repetitions?

A: _____

(continued on next page)

2. "The protesters are no longer giving you a free ride, in which you can set the regulations, set your mega-pay, hide your money in tax havens, enjoy sweet tax rates at the hands of ever-willing politicians, and await your bailouts as needed." *(paragraph 9)*

Q: What part of speech is repeated? Noun? Verb? Adjective?

A: _____

Q: What does the author want to show with this repetition?

A: _____

3. "Just as the Gilded Age turned into the Progressive Era, just as the Roaring Twenties and its excesses turned into the New Deal, be sure that the era of mega-greed is going to turn into an era of renewed accountability, lawfulness, modest compensation, honest taxation, and government by the people rather than by the banks." *(paragraph 9)*

Q: There are three types of repetitions. What parts of speech are they?

A: _____

Q: What does the author want to emphasize with this repetition?

A: _____

NOTE-TAKING: Summarizing the Argument

1   Go back to the reading and read it again. Then fill out the organizer with short notes giving Professor Sachs's response to each point made by Wall Street. Use your own words; do not copy the text.

	WALL STREET'S POINT	PROFESSOR SACHS'S ARGUMENT
1.	We did nothing wrong.	*Their unethical actions almost crashed the world economy.*
2.	We don't understand the criticism.	
3.	We were just selling funds.	

	WALL STREET'S POINT	PROFESSOR SACHS'S ARGUMENT
4.	We created jobs.	
5.	It's just some bad apples.	Many, if not all, of the companies have financial scandals.
6.	The protesters are jealous because we're rich.	
7.	We are good citizens.	
8.	We don't have to learn from history.	

2 Write a brief summary of Sachs's argument. Then write another paragraph with your opinion of what he claims.

According to Professor Sachs in "Message to Wall Street," the leaders of Wall Street have acted in an unethical and illegal manner. The risky behavior of many Wall Street investment banks almost . . .

_____

_____

_____

[Your Opinion]

_____

_____

_____

_____

_____

_____

CRITICAL THINKING

> **Using Irony for Social Criticism**
>
> People who want to criticize the rich and powerful often use **irony:** They use language that normally signifies **the opposite of what they really mean**, typically for **humorous or dramatic effect**. Social criticism in the United States is often put in humorous form.

With a partner, discuss the irony in these statements from the reading. Answer the questions following each statement.

1. "The Wall Street elite seems completely befuddled by the Occupy Wall Street movement. . . . Here's a short note to the Titans of Wall Street to help them understand what's happening." *(paragraph 1)*

   - Do the leaders of Wall Street not understand criticism of their behavior, or do they simply refuse to accept it?
   - What is Sachs offering to do for them?
   - How is calling them "Titans" of Wall Street related to calling others "robber barons"?

2. "The *Journal* editorial board apparently missed the news carried in the *Journal*'s own business pages that JP Morgan recently paid $153.6 million in fines for violating securities laws in the lead-up to the 2008 financial collapse." *(paragraph 3)*

   - What did the *Journal* "miss"?
   - Did they really overlook these facts? Why doesn't the newspaper mention these facts?

3. "Didn't the protesters know he [Paulson] created 100 high-paying jobs in New York City? 100?" *(paragraph 5)*

   - Creating 100 jobs is a good thing, isn't it? So why is Sachs making fun of Paulson's "generosity"?
   - Why did Sachs choose this example? What was he trying to show?

4. "[The protesters] are sick of Wall Street and the *Wall Street Journal* asking for trillions of dollars of near-zero interest loans and bailout money for the banks, but then fighting against unemployment insurance and health coverage for those drowning in the wake of the financial crisis." *(paragraph 8)*

   - When does the *Journal* ask the government to give money? When does it ask the government not to give money?
   - What does the author want to show?

BRINGING IT ALL TOGETHER

Work in groups of four. Role-play a discussion about Wall Street between Jeffrey Sachs, two robber barons, and an "Occupy Wall Street" protester. Professor Sachs will ask questions of the others. He will also express his own opinions. Use some of the vocabulary you studied in the chapter (for a complete list, go to page 55).

TOPIC: The Wall Street of yesterday and of today

ROLES:

- Jeffrey Sachs
- An old robber baron (J. P. Morgan, John D. Rockefeller, or Andrew Carnegie)
- A new robber baron (JPMorgan CEO, Goldman Sachs CEO, or John Paulson)
- An "Occupy Wall Street" protester

QUESTIONS:

- How did you make your money?
- Do you believe your business practices were necessary? Ethical?
- Do you agree with the progressive era legislation?
- Why did you behave in such a risky manner with toxic assets?
- Why were you protesting Wall Street in the "Occupy" movement?
- What should be done to prevent this kind of situation from happening again? Higher taxes for the rich? Stricter laws governing Wall Street activities? Limiting massive profits for investment bankers?
- What do you think should be done to help the economy today? To help the unemployed?

WRITING ACTIVITY

Choose one of the quotes. Write a paragraph or two explaining the meaning of the quote. Do you agree or disagree? Give examples to illustrate your opinion of the quote. Use more than five of the words and idioms you studied in the chapter.

1. "The truth is we are all caught in a great economic system which is heartless."

    — *Woodrow Wilson, 28th president of the United States, 1856–1924*

2. "Moneymakers are the benefactors of humanity."

    — *P. T. Barnum, American showman, businessman, and entertainer, 1810–1891*

DISCUSSION AND WRITING TOPICS

Discuss these topics in a small group. Choose one of them and write a paragraph or two about it. Use the vocabulary from the chapter.

1. What were the errors of the Gilded Age? Have we repeated the mistakes of the past today? In what ways?

2. Do you agree or disagree with Sachs's condemnation of Wall Street hedge-fund managers? Why or why not?

3. Do the mega-rich help society with their philanthropy, or do they drain resources and create unemployment? Today, certain individuals have power over billions of dollars. They decide what charities to support and how to use their money. Is this positive for our society?

4. Do demonstrations like "Occupy Wall Street" do any good? Why do people join them?

5. In "The Deserted Village," 18th-century British poet Oliver Goldsmith wrote:

> Ill fares the land, to hastening ills a prey,
> Where wealth accumulates, and men decay:
> Princes and lords may flourish, or may fade;
> A breath can make them, as a breath has made;
> But a bold peasantry, their country's pride,
> When once destroyed, can never be supplied.

In Goldsmith's poem, princes and lords may come and go, but the nation's true stability comes from ordinary people, its hard-working and confident farmers. How could what the poet says be applied to the difficulties of capitalism today described in this chapter?

6. Go back to the quotes on pages 26 and 53 and discuss how the readings may have clarified or changed your point of view.

Nouns	Verbs	Adjectives	Adverb
accountability	accumulate*	befuddled	barely
beneficiary*	address	defective	
compensation*	amass	gullible	**Phrases and Idioms**
constituent*	connive	hapless	bring sb to their knees
convulsion	envision	obscure	give sb a free ride
mark	exceed*	reckless	in flux
plant	institute*	shrewd	make a killing
restraint*	net		scratch the surface
strain	parlay		team up with
tariff	peddle		what it comes down to
	reinvigorate		
	uphold		
	urge		

* = AWL (Academic Word List) item

SELF-ASSESSMENT

In this chapter you learned to:

○ Scan a text to find specific information

○ Scan the first paragraph of a text for definitions and background information

○ Predict the content of a text from the first and last paragraphs

○ Guess the meaning of words from the context

○ Understand and use synonyms, collocations, and different word forms and idioms

○ Identify parallel forms and the reasons for their use

○ Use an organizer to identify important biographical details

○ Use note-taking to summarize an argument

What can you do well? ✓

What do you need to practice more? ✓

CHAPTER 3

FILM STUDIES: Is Cinema an Art or a Business?

FILM STUDIES: an academic discipline that explores the economic, cultural, and artistic implications of the cinema

OBJECTIVES

To read academic texts, you need to master certain skills.

In this chapter, you will:

- Find the thesis statement in an essay

- Skim an interview for the general idea and scan for the interviewee's attitude towards his subject

- Guess the meaning of words from the context

- Use dictionary entries to learn the meanings of words

- Understand and use synonyms, idioms, connotations, and increase/decrease verbs

- Recognize and use parallel structure for emphasis and contrast

- Take notes to identify the main ideas of a text and the supporting details

- Take margin notes, organize the notes, and write a summary of the text

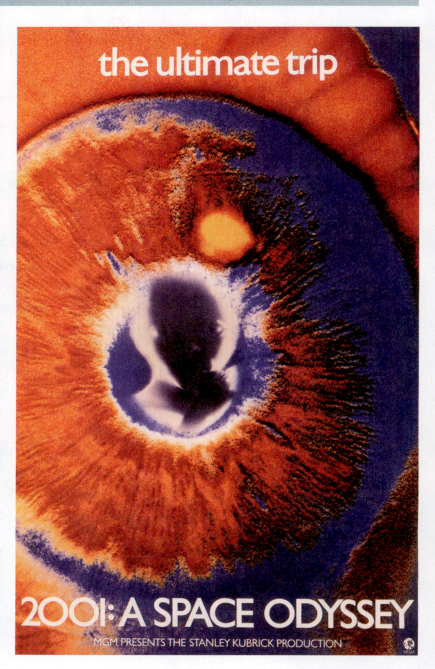

the ultimate trip

2001: A SPACE ODYSSEY

MGM PRESENTS THE STANLEY KUBRICK PRODUCTION

A Consider These Questions

Discuss the questions in a small group. Share your answers with the class.

1. What are your favorite types of movies: action films, romantic films, comedies, science fiction, fantasy? Why do they appeal to you?

2. Do you like to see old movies made many years ago? Do you like to see movies from other countries?

3. What are the characteristics of a good film?

4. What is your favorite movie? Why?

B What Are the World's Best Films?

Every decade the British magazine *Sight and Sound* publishes its best movies list. These are the best movies chosen by movie directors. Read the list. Then answer the questions. Discuss your answers with a partner.

The 2012 List from *Sight and Sound* — Directors' Choices

1. *Tokyo Story* (1953) Yasujiro Ozu (Japan)
2. *2001: A Space Odyssey* (1968) Stanley Kubrick (U.S.)
3. *Citizen Kane* (1941) Orson Welles (U.S.)
4. *8 1/2* (1963) Federico Fellini (Italy)
5. *Taxi Driver* (1976) Martin Scorsese (U.S.)
6. *Apocalypse Now* (1979) Francis Ford Coppola (U.S.)
7. *The Godfather* (1972) Francis Ford Coppola (U.S.)
8. *Vertigo* (1958) Alfred Hitchcock (U.S.)
9. *The Mirror* (1975) Andrei Tarkovsky (U.S.S.R.)
10. *Bicycle Thieves* (1948) Vittorio De Sica (Italy)

1. Have you seen any of these movies?

2. Are you interested in the history of cinema?

3. Do you think it is a good idea to have a "top ten" list? Why or why not?

4. Why do you think this list includes no film made in the last 30 years?

A   Warm-Up

Discuss the question in a small group. Share your answers with the class.

It has been said that movies combine all the other arts: photography, dance, music, theater, poetry, painting, and architecture. What do you think?

B   Reading Strategy

Finding the Thesis Statement of an Essay

An academic **essay** aims to **persuade readers of an idea** based on evidence. In academic essays, the **thesis statement** contains the **main idea** of the entire essay. It is usually found in the **last sentence of the first paragraph**.

Find the thesis statement in "One Hundred Years of Cinema." What is the main idea of this essay? Write it on the lines.

_____

Now read the whole essay. Were you right about the main idea?

One Hundred Years of Cinema

By Susan Sontag

Susan Sontag wrote novels, short stories, and essays, including Against Interpretation, On Photography, Illness as Metaphor, *and* Regarding the Pain of Others. *She was also an occasional filmmaker, playwright, and theater director. Her cultural studies were the voice of a generation.*

1   Cinema's history seems to have the shape of a life cycle: a birth, a steady accumulation of glories, and then the **irreversible** decline. It's not that you can't look forward to new films that you can admire. But such films are exceptions. Ordinary films, films made purely for entertainment (that is, commercial) purposes, are **astonishingly** foolish. Cinema, once **heralded** as the art of the 20th century, seems now to be a decadent[1] art.

---
[1] *decadent:* in a state of deterioration and decline

2   In the past, it was from a weekly visit to the cinema that you learned (or tried to learn) how to walk, to smoke, to kiss, to fight, to grieve. Movies gave you **tips** about how to be attractive. But whatever you took home was only a part of the larger experience of losing yourself in other people's lives and faces. You wanted to be kidnapped by the movie — and to be kidnapped was to be **overwhelmed** by the image. The experience of "going to the movies" was part of it. To see a great film only on television isn't to have really seen that film. It's not only a question of how big the image is. To be kidnapped, you have to be in a movie theater, seated in the dark among anonymous strangers.

3   In the mid-1950s, a **dazzling** number of original, passionate films of the highest seriousness got made. It was at this specific moment in the history of cinema that going to movies, thinking about movies, talking about movies became a passion among university students and other young people. You fell in love not just with actors but with cinema itself.

The 400 Blows (1959–France)

Cinephilia² had first become visible in the 1950s in France: its forum was the legendary film magazine *Cahiers du Cinéma* (followed by similarly **fervent** magazines in Germany, Italy, Great Britain, Sweden, the United States, and Canada). Its meeting places were the many *cinémathèques*³ and clubs specializing in films from the past. For some 15 years there were new **masterpieces** every month. How far away that **era** seems now.

4   To be sure, there was always a conflict between cinema as an industry and cinema as an art, cinema as routine and cinema as experiment. But the conflict was not such as to make impossible the making of wonderful films. Now the balance has **tipped** decisively in favor of cinema as an industry. The catastrophic rise in production costs meant the imposition of industry standards on a far more coercive, this time truly global scale. (**Soaring** production costs means that a film has to make a lot of money right away, in the first month of its release, if it is to be profitable at all — a **trend** that favors the blockbuster⁴ over the low-budget film. Movie theaters continued to close — many towns no longer have even one — as movies became, mainly, one of a variety of habit-forming home entertainments.)

5   Predictably, the love of cinema has **waned**. People still like going to the movies, and some people still care about and expect something special from a film. And wonderful films are still being made. But you hardly find anymore, at least among the young, the distinctive cinephilic love of movies that is **grounded** in an appetite for seeing and reseeing as much as possible of cinema's glorious past. If cinephilia is dead, then movies are dead too — no matter how many movies, even very good ones, go on being made. If cinema can be **resurrected**, it will only be through the birth of a new kind of cine-love.

² *cinephilia:* love of movies

³ *cinémathèque:* a film archive with small screening rooms showing cinema classics

⁴ *blockbuster:* a high-budget film with a massive advertising campaign aimed at achieving a great commercial success all over the world

COMPREHENSION

A **Main Ideas**

Check (✓) the main idea of each paragraph. Compare answers with a partner.

PARAGRAPH 1:

☐ **a.** Movies are better now than they used to be.

☐ **b.** Movies are worse now than they used to be.

☐ **c.** Some movies today can be admired.

PARAGRAPH 2:

☐ **a.** Movies are not able to teach us much about life anymore.

☐ **b.** Movies are in decline on home screens.

☐ **c.** Movies are no longer a social experience shared with others.

PARAGRAPH 3:

☐ **a.** Today there are hardly any great films being produced.

☐ **b.** The love of film, or cinephilia, first surfaced in France in the film magazine *Cahiers du Cinéma*.

☐ **c.** The 1950s in France and in other countries marked the beginning of a 15-year period in which the passion for great films was at its height.

PARAGRAPH 4:

☐ **a.** Because of the rising costs of producing a film, a major trend today is to pay more attention to the business side of films than to the artistic side.

☐ **b.** The saying, "Money talks," explains the reason why many towns in America no longer have even one movie theater.

☐ **c.** The movie industry has changed a great deal because there are no more low-budget films.

PARAGRAPH 5:

☐ **a.** Because young people no longer like going to the movies, cinema is in decline.

☐ **b.** Because cinephilia is dead, wonderful movies can never be made.

☐ **c.** Without a new kind of cine-love, the cinema cannot be revived.

Read the quotes from the reading. Circle the statement that best explains each quote. Share your answers with a partner.

1. "To be kidnapped, you have to be in a movie theater, seated in the dark among anonymous strangers." (*paragraph 2*)

   a. Seeing a film in the darkness of a movie theater helps you to be in a dreamlike state.

   b. Seated with strangers in the darkness of a movie theater is the best way to fully experience a film.

   c. Entering the world of a film is the only possible way to be kidnapped.

2. "For some 15 years there were new masterpieces every month. How far away that era seems now." (*paragraph 3*)

   a. There are no cinematic masterpieces being created today.

   b. Fifteen years ago the movie industry was very different from what it is now.

   c. There are fewer masterpieces today than in the fifteen years when cinema was at its height.

3. "The catastrophic rise in production costs meant the imposition of industry standards on a far more coercive, this time truly global scale." (*paragraph 4*)

   a. The pressures of production costs have determined the nature of films that are produced.

   b. The pressures of production costs have made industry standards rise dramatically.

   c. The pressures of the global economy on the movie industry have favored Hollywood.

4. "But you hardly find anymore, at least among the young, the distinctive cinephilic love of movies that is grounded in an appetite for seeing and reseeing as much as possible of cinema's glorious past." (*paragraph 5*)

   a. Most young people today are not cinephiles.

   b. Most cinephiles want to see and resee the films of the past.

   c. The cinephiles of the past are not like the cinephiles of the present.

VOCABULARY

A Synonyms

Complete each paragraph with the words from the box. Use the synonym in parentheses to help you select the correct word. Compare answers with a partner.

astonishingly	fervent	irreversible	overwhelmed
era	heralded	masterpieces	resurrected

The films of the silent _____era_____ are _____
                         1. (period)   **2. (surprisingly)**
moving, even today, with a visual beauty that time has not destroyed. Despite

the occasional overacting, *Metropolis, Potemkin, Napoleon,* and *Intolerance*

are _____ that still speak to our minds and hearts.
        3. (classics)
Movies freed from talk have the strange effect of making us even more

_____ by the visual images and the music. These films about
  4. (deeply affected)
revolution and change _____ the coming of a new art form
                   5. (proclaimed)
and still find _____ admirers today. In 2012, the French
       6. (passionate)
film *The Artist* won the Academy Award as a tribute to the great art of the past.

It _____ the silent film in modern form and showed for a
   7. (revived)
moment that in art the march of time is not _____.
                                            8. (unchangeable)

dazzling	grounded	soaring	tip	trend	waned

The need for _____ special effects in today's movies
               9. (awesome)
is _____ as always in the desire to tell stories in ever more
      10. (based)
exciting ways. But these special effects are a part of what has sent the production

costs of movies _____. The _____
             11. (skyrocketing)   **12. (tendency)**
is for studios to invest in blockbuster movies that appeal to the widest

possible audiences in order to cover their costs. Interest in small, intimate

films has _____. Screenwriters and directors give this
       13. (declined)
_____ to young people wanting to break into the business:
  14. (piece of advice)
Write what will be produced.

Read the dictionary entries for the word *tip*.

> **tip** *n.* **1** the end of something, especially something pointed **2** a small amount of additional money that you give to someone **3** a helpful piece of advice
>
> **tip** *v.* **1** to lean at an angle instead of being level or straight; to make something do this **2** to give an additional amount of money to someone **3** to give a slight but important advantage to someone or something

Read each sentence. Decide which word form is being used and what its specific meaning is. Write the name of the word form and the number of the appropriate definition.

noun (1)   **a.** The writer of the screenplay had the secrets of all future projects hidden in the **tip** of his pen.

_____ **b.** The publisher gave the budding writer a **tip** on the kinds of stories that would now sell in the mass market.

_____ **c.** In Hollywood these days, the balance is **tipping** in favor of the demands of the financiers.

_____ **d.** The tourist **tipped** the waiter in the restaurant very generously in order to help finance his acting lessons.

_____ **e.** Whenever he sat down, the heavy-set director made his chair **tip** backward.

C **Verbs Showing Increase or Decrease**

INCREASE	DECREASE	THINGS USED FOR	EXAMPLES
soar	plummet plunge	prices/costs/values	Sales **plummeted** last month. The company's profits **plunged** by 60%. It is hoped that, in the future, with an improved economy, both sales and profits will **soar**.
wax	wane	the moon	The moon **waxes and wanes** every month.*
		enthusiasm/passion/ love/power	The critic **waxed eloquent** about the director's genius.**

* *wax and wane:* usually used in connection with the moon: when the moon **waxes**, it grows larger; when the moon **wanes**, you gradually see less of it.

** *wax eloquent:* used when someone talks about something enthusiastically

(continued on next page)

Work with a partner. Complete each sentence with the correct form of one of the verbs in the chart.

1. Usually, as production costs _____, ticket prices rise.

2. When ticket prices rise, people's enthusiasm for buying movie tickets often

   _____.

3. Movie ticket sales may _____ dramatically

   when the economy is weak and prices for the basic necessities of life

   _____.

D **Idioms with *ground/grounded***

Read the sentences. Each one uses an idiom with *ground* or *grounded*. Match the idiom used in each sentence with one of the meanings from the box below. Use a dictionary if necessary. Compare answers with a partner.

___c___ 1. Movies can be **fertile ground** for breeding both tolerance and intolerance in our society.

_____ 2. Movies can also help opposing parties in a dispute find **common ground**.

_____ 3. Screenwriters who take **the moral high ground** and refuse to write violent blockbusters may not often be successful.

_____ 4. To **get** a film **off the ground**, its creative directors need to be assured of the producer's financial backing.

_____ 5. When a mega-hit is in the planning stages, potential investors immediately compete to **get in on the ground floor**.

_____ 6. In epic dramas that span many centuries, the story line **covers a lot of ground**.

_____ 7. Obviously, a film can be a success only when everyone involved in it — actors, directors, costume designers, and so on — **works himself into the ground**.

_____ 8. Their dedication to the task at hand is **grounded in** their belief in the value of cinema as an art form.

> **a.** an opinion that is regarded as morally better than others
> **b.** works too hard to the point of exhaustion
> **c.** a situation in which it is easy for something to develop
> **d.** includes a great deal of material in time and space
> **e.** start to be successful
> **f.** an area of opinion that two people or groups share
> **g.** be there at the beginning when something is created or started
> **h.** based on

GRAMMAR FOR READING: Parallel Structure for Emphasis and Contrast

> Most of the time, we try to avoid repeating words and phrases in writing. But sometimes an author's use of **parallel structure** (repetition of certain forms) is necessary and effective. The repetition keeps the reader **focused on the main points** of the argument and also contributes to a **pleasant rhythm** in the sentences.

Work with a partner. Examine the quotes from the reading. Underline the repeated forms in each. Answer the questions that follow.

1. "To be sure, there was always a conflict between cinema as an industry and cinema as an art, cinema as routine and cinema as experiment. . . . Now the balance has tipped decisively in favor of cinema as an industry." *(paragraph 4)*

   Q: Why did the author repeat the expressions you have underlined?

   A: _____

   Q: Do you think the repetition gives a pleasing rhythm to the sentences?

   A: _____

2. "Predictably, the love of cinema has waned. People still like going to the movies, and some people still care about and expect something special from a film. And wonderful films are still being made. But you hardly find anymore . . . the distinctive cinephilic love of movies . . . " *(paragraph 5)*

   Q: Why does the author repeat the word "still"?

   A: _____

   Q: What is the purpose of the word "but"?

   A: _____

3. "If cinephilia is dead, then movies are dead, too. . . . If cinema can be resurrected, it will only be through the birth of a new kind of cine-love." *(paragraph 5)*

   Q: How do the two "if" sentences at the very end of the essay permit the reader to focus on the author's main point?

   A: _____

   Q: How does the word "resurrected" justify the author's repetition of the word "dead" in the first "if" sentence?

   A: _____

NOTE-TAKING: Identifying Main Idea and Supporting Details

Go back to the reading and read it again. Then fill out the chart. For each paragraph, write the details that support the main idea. Share your answers with a partner.

Paragraph 1	**Main Idea:** *Movies are worse now than they used to be.* **Support:** *glorious past / some exceptions today / but mostly foolish junk*
Paragraph 2	**Main Idea:** *Movies are no longer a social experience shared by others.* **Support:**
Paragraph 3	**Main Idea:** *The 1950s in France and other countries marked the beginning of a 15-year period in which the passion for great films was at its height.* **Support:**
Paragraph 4	**Main Idea:** *Because of the rising costs of producing a film, a major trend today is to pay more attention to the business side of films than to the artistic side.* **Support:**
Paragraph 5	**Main Idea:** *Without a new kind of cine-love, the cinema cannot be revived.* **Support:**

CRITICAL THINKING

Discuss the questions in a small group. Be prepared to share your answers with the class.

1. Do you agree with Sontag's opinion that movies are in decline? Do you think she liked blockbusters? Do you? What would she think of Computer Generated Imagery (CGI)?

2. Would Sontag agree with showing her favorite films on a cell phone or tablet? Why or why not?

3. Do you prefer to see movies in a theater? Is there any advantage to being able to see movies at home when you can fast forward them and go back and forth at will? Are international movies more available today?

A **Warm-Up**

Leo Tolstoy

Discuss the question with a partner.

Leo Tolstoy (1828–1910) was the celebrated Russian author of *War and Peace* and *Anna Karenina*.

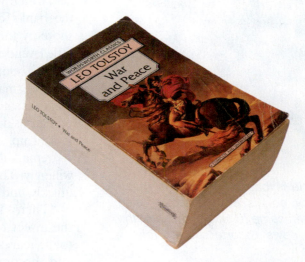

Tolstoy was a Russian aristocrat who, after a moral awakening, became a social reformer, opening a school for the children of serfs on his property, criticizing social privilege, and defending non-violence. His work inspired the ideas of Gandhi and Martin Luther King, Jr. Many of his novels have been repeatedly made into movies.

What do you think a great writer like Tolstoy thought of movies when he first saw them as an older person? Do you think he dismissed them as foolish popular entertainment, or recognized them as a new art form?

B **Reading Strategy**

Scanning for an Interviewee's Attitude toward His Subject

When a text is based on an interview, **scanning the beginning paragraphs** can help you to understand the **attitude of the interviewee** (person who was interviewed) toward his subject before you read about all the details.

Scan the first two paragraphs of the reading and find the answer to the question. Write it on the lines.

What did Tolstoy think of movies?

_____

_____

Now read the rest of the article to find out what Tolstoy thought about cinema as business and art.

A Conversation with Leo Tolstoy on Film

By David Bernstein

This article is based on remarks made by Tolstoy on his 80th birthday when cameramen came to take pictures of the event. A news reporter asked Tolstoy about the movies.

1   "You will see that this little clicking **contraption** with the revolving handle [the movie camera] will make a revolution in our life — in the life of writers. It is a direct attack on the old methods of literary art. We shall have to adapt ourselves to the shadowy screen and to the cold machine. A new form of writing will be necessary. I have thought of that and I can feel what is coming.

2   But I rather like it. This **swift** change of scene, this **blending** of emotion and experience — it is much better than the heavy, **long-drawn-out** type of writing we are used to. It is closer to life. In life, too, changes and transitions flash by before our eyes, and emotions of the soul are like a hurricane. The films are wonderful! Drr! and a scene is ready! Drr! and we have another scene! The cinema has captured the mystery of motion and that is greatness."

3   Someone spoke of the **domination** of the films by businessmen interested only in profits. "Yes, I know, I've been told about that before," Tolstoy replied. "The films have fallen into the clutches of the businessmen and art is weeping! But the businessmen are everywhere." And he began to tell one of those little **parables** for which he is famous.

4   "A little while ago, I was standing on the banks of our pond. There on the shore by the reeds[1] I saw an insect with little lavender spots on its wings. It would **flutter** about, **obstinately**, and its circles became smaller and smaller. In among the reeds sat a green toad with staring eyes on each side of his flat head. The toad looked up, opened his mouth wide and — remarkable! — the butterfly flew in willingly! The toad snapped his jaws shut quickly, and the butterfly disappeared.

5   "Then I remembered that thus the insect reaches the stomach of the toad, leaves its seed there to develop and become a larva,[2] a caterpillar. The caterpillar becomes a chrysalis,[3] and out of the chrysalis springs a new butterfly. And then the creating of new life begins all over again.

6   "It is the same way with the cinema. In the reeds of film art sits the toad — the businessman. Above him **hovers** the insect — the artist. A glance, and the jaws of the businessman **devour** the artist. But that doesn't mean destruction. In the belly of the businessman is carried on the process of impregnation and the development of the seeds of the future. These seeds will come out on God's earth and will begin their beautiful, brilliant lives all over again."

---

[1] *reed:* a type of tall plant like grass that grows in wet places

[2] *larva:* the immature form of animals like insects, when they look completely different from the adult that they will become; the larva of the butterfly is the caterpillar

[3] *chrysalis:* an insect pupa that holds a butterfly before it's ready to come out

COMPREHENSION

A Main Ideas

Check (✓) the main ideas in the reading. Compare answers with a partner.

According to Tolstoy's remarks about the cinema:

☐ 1. The movie camera will have a great influence on writers' approach to writing.

☐ 2. Business and art have nothing in common.

☐ 3. Business and art are interdependent.

☐ 4. Business will destroy the hopes of all artists.

☐ 5. The toad is to the butterfly as the businessman is to the artist.

B Close Reading

Read the quotes from the reading. Circle the statement that best explains each quote. Share your answers with a partner.

1. "You will see that this little clicking contraption with the revolving handle [the movie camera] will make a revolution in our life — in the life of writers. It is a direct attack on the old methods of literary art." *(paragraph 1)*

   a. The camera will change the way writers write.

   b. The camera will be a threat to writers.

   c. The camera will make writing less realistic.

2. "The toad looked up, opened his mouth wide and — remarkable! — the butterfly flew in willingly! The toad snapped his jaws shut quickly, and the butterfly disappeared." *(paragraph 4)*

   a. The toad hunted the butterfly.

   b. The butterfly accepted the toad's invitation.

   c. The butterfly escaped the toad in the end.

3. "A glance, and the jaws of the businessman devour the artist. But that doesn't mean destruction. In the belly of the businessman is carried on the process of impregnation and the development of the seeds of the future." *(paragraph 6)*

   a. The artist understands that from destruction comes creation.

   b. The artist has no hope but to be eaten up and exploited by the businessman.

   c. The artist needs the businessman to realize his art.

A **Guessing from Context**

Read each quote from the reading. Try to guess the meaning of the words in bold from the context. Write your guess. Then consult a dictionary and write the definition.

1. "You will see that this little clicking **contraption** with the revolving handle [the movie camera] will make a revolution in our life — in the life of writers." (*paragraph 1*)

   contraption   Guess: _a machine that looks strange or funny_

   Dictionary: _a strange-looking piece of machinery_

2. "This **swift** change of scene, this **blending** of emotion and experience — it is much better than the heavy, **long-drawn-out** type of writing we are used to. It is closer to life. In life, too, changes and transitions flash by before our eyes, and emotions of the soul are like a hurricane. The films are wonderful! Drr! and a scene is ready! Drr! and we have another scene! The cinema has captured the mystery of motion and that is greatness." (*paragraph 2*)

   swift   Guess: _____

   Dictionary: _____

   blending   Guess: _____

   Dictionary: _____

   long-drawn-out   Guess: _____

   Dictionary: _____

3. "Someone spoke of the **domination** of the films by businessmen interested only in profits. 'Yes, I know, I've been told about that before,' Tolstoy replied. 'The films have fallen into the clutches of the businessmen and art is weeping! But the businessmen are everywhere.'" (*paragraph 3*)

   domination   Guess: _____

   Dictionary: _____

4. "A glance, and the jaws of the businessman **devour** the artist. But that doesn't mean destruction." (*paragraph 6*)

   devour   Guess: _____

   Dictionary: _____

B Synonyms

Complete the sentences with the words from the box. Use the synonym in parentheses to help you select the correct word. Compare answers with a partner.

blending	devoured	flutter	long-drawn-out	parables
contraption	domination	hovers	obstinately	swift

1. It is interesting to see how a _____ *contraption* _____ like the motion-picture
   (strange-looking machine)
   camera has revolutionized the world of art.

2. The movies we see today represent a _____ of two
   (mixture)
   seemingly "opposite" but interrelated forces: art and business.

3. Yet the spirit of Susan Sontag _____ over the debate even
   (floats)
   today: Have films degenerated because of the pressure of money?

4. Although many people believe that modern-day finances have _____
   (consumed)
   the world of art by destroying the creative spirit, such a perception is not

   necessarily accurate.

5. With a deadline, screenwriters know there is an end in sight to the

   _____ creative process, and they become more efficient
   (time-consuming)
   about getting their work done.

6. Without a deadline, artists might _____ continue to seek
   (stubbornly)
   perfection, and their work would never be produced.

7. The film industry has enjoyed its unrivaled _____ over
   (control)
   the public imagination because moving pictures can tell fabulous stories in

   amazing ways.

8. The _____ succession of images and visual stimulation
   (rapid)
   have given motion pictures a universal power of communication.

9. Animals can make tools, but as far as we know, human beings are the only

   storytelling animals. From the beginning of language, people have told

   _____ to teach the young people of the next generation.
   (simple stories with lessons)

10. Like butterflies that _____ around a flower, people seem
    (fly up and down)
    to dance around movie stars looking for some sign of the good life.

C Connotations

> A **connotation** is a feeling or an idea that a word makes you think of. This **feeling** can be **positive** or **negative**.

1 Look at each word. Decide if it generally has mainly *Positive*, *Negative*, or *Neutral* connotations. Check (✓) the appropriate box. Discuss your answers with a partner.

	POSITIVE	NEGATIVE	NEUTRAL
1. obstinate	☐	☐	☐
2. persistent	☐	☐	☐
3. stubborn	☐	☐	☐
4. devour	☐	☐	☐
5. eat	☐	☐	☐
6. contraption	☐	☐	☐
7. machine	☐	☐	☐
8. dominate	☐	☐	☐
9. control	☐	☐	☐

2 Complete the sentences with the appropriate words. Choose from the two words in parentheses. Compare answers with a partner.

1. The writing student's _____ *obstinate* _____ attitude made his teacher
   (persistent / obstinate)
   stop sending him what she considered to be constructive criticism.

2. Because of the actor's _____ efforts to learn the accent of
   (persistent / stubborn)
   his character, his speech coach was very pleased.

3. The director _____ lunch on the set just like all the crew
   (ate / devoured)
   members and the actors.

4. The angry businessman _____ every word of the artist's
   (ate / devoured)
   explanation, with eyes to kill.

5. An early computer called the ENIAC was a complicated and impractical

   _____ using vacuum tubes that looked like light bulbs.
   (contraption / machine)

6. A new special-effects _____ can make even imaginary
   (contraption / machine)
   people look real.

7. It is hard for small independent films to avoid the _____
   (domination / control)
   of the market by big Hollywood studios.

8. Creative _____ of the final cut should always stay with the
   (domination / control)
   director, not with the studios.

CRITICAL THINKING

Discuss the questions in a small group. Be prepared to share your answers with the class.

1. Do you think that Tolstoy is successful in getting his point across with the parable he tells? Why did he use such a story?

2. Do you prefer books or movies? When you read a book and then see the movie, which one do you like best? Can you think of some books that were better than the movies? Can you think of some movies that were better than the books? What does the book provide that the film does not provide? What does the film provide that the book does not provide?

3. Tolstoy was enthusiastic about the new technology of cinema even though he was a very old man at the time. Do most older people usually like technology? Why or why not? How do you think Tolstoy would feel about movies today?

LINKING READINGS ONE AND TWO

The author of Reading One, Susan Sontag, and the writer featured in Reading Two, Leo Tolstoy, both expressed their concerns about cinema. Which concerns do they share?

Work with a partner. Write _S/T_ next to the concerns that Sontag and Tolstoy had in common. Write _S_ next to concerns that were Sontag's only, and _T_ next to concerns that were Tolstoy's only.

_____S_____ 1. cinema's history

_____ 2. the joy of going to the movies

_____ 3. the current state of cinema

_____ 4. business and the arts

_____ 5. the love of cinema

_____ 6. technology and the writer's art

_____ 7. hope for cinema's future

A Warm-Up

1 Can you match the director with the correct movie?

_____	1. *The Lord of the Rings*	**a.**	James Cameron
_____	2. *The Godfather*	**b.**	Michael Hazanavicius
_____	3. *Jurassic Park*	**c.**	Steven Spielberg
_____	4. *Inception*	**d.**	Peter Jackson
_____	5. *Titanic*	**e.**	George Lucas
_____	6. *Gangs of New York*	**f.**	Francis Fort Coppola
_____	7. *The Artist*	**g.**	Christopher Nolan
_____	8. *Star Wars*	**h.**	Martin Scorsese

2 Where do you think directors get their ideas for their movies? Check (✓) your answers and discuss them with a partner.

☐ **a.** from books or stories

☐ **b.** from history

☐ **c.** from their imagination

☐ **d.** from the desire to use special effects

B Reading Strategy

Skimming an Interview

Before you read an interview, you can skim it to **get a quick general idea** of what will be discussed by **looking at the questions** asked by the interviewer.

Reading Three is an interview with James Cameron, the director of *Titanic* and *Avatar*. To get a general idea of what Cameron will discuss, skim the interview. Look at the questions asked by the interviewer and find a keyword for each question. Write the keywords on the line.

QUESTION 1: _____

QUESTION 2: _____

QUESTION 3: _____

Now read the whole interview to find out how James Cameron answered these three questions.

An Interview with James Cameron

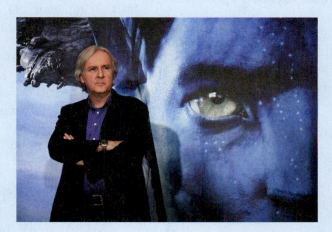

James Cameron is a film director, film producer, screenwriter, visual artist, and editor. Inspired by Star Wars, Cameron left his job as a truck driver and began working in special effects. His dream was to unite science and art. He began by making miniature models for films and worked his way up to art director, production designer, and finally director. His films include The Abyss, the Terminator films, Aliens, Titanic, and Avatar, as well as films about deep-sea exploration. In 2012, he dove 7 miles down to the bottom of the Pacific Ocean by himself in a 24-foot submarine. In the future, he hopes to mine asteroids of their valuable minerals in a commercially built rocket ship.

1 **INTERVIEWER:** When you make a movie, how involved are you in the **fiscal** aspect and the marketing?

2 **CAMERON:** I don't want to be overly involved because selling movies is what the studio does 24/7.[1] I want them to do their job and I want to do my job. My job is to make the movie and make it as excellent a film experience as you can have and let them figure out how to sell it based on what they know about selling movies.

3 **INTERVIEWER:** How did the concept of Avatar occur to you?

4 **CAMERON:** How you decide to make a film is different for each one. For Terminator, for example, I thought,

"OK, what kind of movie can I make as a first-time director? Should it involve effects? Because I know effects and I can sell that. But it's got to be shot in the streets of L.A. **on the cheap**, so that's my setting. So how do I get effects into that setting? Well, something comes from space or it comes from the future. Space has been done so let's do the future . . ." So I have these very **mercenary** things that drove me to a story, then I came up with a story that fit those **parameters**.

5 Avatar is very similar in that I was the CEO of Digital Domain, which overnight had sprung to being the second-best visual effects house in the world, and I didn't want to be

---

[1] **24/7:** every hour of the day and every day of the week

(continued on next page)

second-best. ILM (Industrial Light and Magic) had a big lead, having done the *Jurassic Park* films. And Stan Winston, with whom I founded the company, and I wanted to really **push** the art of CGI[2] character creation, creature creation, all of that. So I collected every bit of character creation that I'd done as an illustrator, just **doodling around** since I was in middle school, **hunkered down** behind the textbooks in class.

6   I had thousands and thousands of drawings, lots and lots of ideas, so I just worked it all up into one big story. But the **consensus** was that the idea of doing photo-realistic expressive characters in CGI was not possible, at that time. So I thought, "Alright guys, I'm giving you fair warning: I'm going to go make *Titanic*. When I come back let's talk again."

7   But of course, if you don't have a project driving the technology, it just lies dormant. Everything is done for a reason. I came back two years later and nothing had happened. And then I started thinking, "Well, I want to make my next feature in 3-D. *Avatar*'s probably not a good choice for that because it's just way too complicated, I've got to do something simpler first." And Stan said, "No, no, no. If you want to do *Avatar*, do *Avatar*." He said, "You do your biggest and your best idea in 3-D because that's what this deserves." He just had

***

[2] *CGI:* Computer Generated Imagery — a method of making animated movies using computers

this strong, **visceral** reaction to it, and you know Stan and I had been friends and partners for a long time, so I actually listened to that. I looked at *Avatar* and I thought, "Well hmm, maybe the time is right."

8   **INTERVIEWER:** Do you see political parallels in Avatar?

9   **CAMERON:** What I was doing with *Avatar* — by the way *Avatar* was written long before even the First Gulf War[3] — was more in response to a kind of human history at large and the way the history of the human race has been written in blood by technically or militarily superior people taking from those who are less capable. That's how Rome worked, that's how Greece worked, that's how China worked, you name it — name your empire. You couldn't get people to come to a movie theater and watch a film about the conquest of New Spain[4] and how the Aztecs were **slaughtered** by the Spaniards for their gold. But you can get them to come to a movie theater and see how the Pandoran Na'vi are being slaughtered for [the fictional element] unobtanium. It's the same story.

***

[3] *First Gulf War* (January–February 1991): A coalition force of 34 nations led by the United States invaded Iraq in response to the Iraqi invasion and annexation of Kuwait.

[4] *New Spain* (1521–1821): This name was given to the Spanish colonial empire in North America, which was ruled from Mexico City after the conquest of the Aztecs and their virtual enslavement. Silver and gold were the "unobtanium" that the colonial empires wanted.

COMPREHENSION

A Main Ideas

Read each statement. Decide if it is *True* or *False* according to the reading. Check (✓) the appropriate box. If it is false, change it to make it true. Discuss your answers with a partner.

	TRUE	FALSE
1. Cameron's original inspiration comes from literature.	☐	☐
2. Using cutting-edge technology is important to his vision of filmmaking.	☐	☐
3. He was inspired by current events to do the movies he directed.	☐	☐
4. Cameron is not competitive with other filmmakers.	☐	☐
5. Cameron writes as well as directs his films.	☐	☐

B Close Reading

> In a **paraphrase**, you express the meaning of the writer or speaker **in your own words**. Paraphrases are usually **shorter** than the original statement. Paraphrasing what you read helps to **ensure understanding** of the material.

Read the quotes from the reading. Write a paraphrase that best explains each quote. Share your answers with a partner.

1. "My job is to make the movie and make it as excellent a film experience as you can have and let them figure out how to sell it based on what they know about selling movies." *(paragraph 2)*

   Paraphrase: _Cameron worries about making the movie, not selling it._

2. "'OK, what kind of movie can I make as a first-time director? Should it involve effects? Because I know effects and I can sell that. But it's got to be shot in the streets of L.A. on the cheap, so that's my setting.' . . . So I have these very mercenary things that drove me to a story, then I came up with a story that fit those parameters." *(paragraph 4)*

   Paraphrase: _____

3. "But of course, if you don't have a project driving the technology, it just lies dormant." *(paragraph 7)*

   Paraphrase: _____

(continued on next page)

4. "What I was doing with *Avatar* . . . was more in response to . . . the way the history of the human race has been written in blood by technically or militarily superior people taking from those who are less capable." *(paragraph 9)*

Paraphrase: _____

5. "You couldn't get people to come to a movie theater and watch a film about the conquest of New Spain and how the Aztecs were slaughtered by the Spaniards for their gold. But you can get them to come to a movie theater and see how the Pandoran Na'vi are being slaughtered for [the fictional element] unobtanium. It's the same story." *(paragraph 9)*

Paraphrase: _____

VOCABULARY

Ⓐ Synonyms

Read the sentences about James Cameron. Match each word or phrase in bold with its synonym in the box below. Compare answers with a partner.

_h_ **1.** Because he began his career in special effects, Cameron was always interested in making movies that **push** technology forward.

____ **2.** He never accepted the conventional **parameters** that dictate what could and could not be done on film.

____ **3.** Computer-Generated Imagery (CGI) is difficult to use in movies because you need a very successful movie to make the expense worthwhile. CGI can't be made **on the cheap**.

____ **4.** Even though most specialists thought that expressive human faces were impossible to do in CGI, Cameron wanted to disprove the **consensus** in the profession and do it successfully.

____ **5.** Cameron was always a very visual person; even as a child he was always **doodling around** in class, **hunkering down** behind his book to hide from the teacher.

____ **6.** **Fiscal** considerations are very important in his career.

____ **7.** Cameron is very honest about the limits of his inspiration: He has very **mercenary** reasons to choose certain stories, but then he weaves emotion into the film.

____ **8.** He wants the viewer to have a very **visceral** reaction to his movies.

____ **9.** *Avatar* was a fictional story, but it reminded us of the **slaughter** of native peoples in the Americas.

a. unity of opinion	**f.** at bargain prices
b. sketching	**g.** limitations
c. financial	**h.** propel
d. crouching	**i.** massacre
e. money-oriented	**j.** emotional and instinctive

B Using the Dictionary

Read the dictionary entry for the verb *push*.

> **push** *v.*
> **1** MOVE to make someone or something move by pressing with your hands, arms, shoulders, etc.: *Help me push the car into the garage.*
> **2** TRY TO GET PAST SB to use your hands, arms, shoulders, etc. to make someone move, especially so that you can get past them: *Stop pushing and wait your turn.*
> **3** ENCOURAGE/PERSUADE to encourage or try to persuade someone to accept or do something: *My boss is pushing me to work more overtime.*
> **4** INCREASE/DECREASE to increase an amount, number, or value: *Inflation has pushed up prices by 35%.*
> **5** ADVERTISE to try to sell more of a product by advertising it a lot: *We need new ways to push our products.*

Now read each sentence. Decide which meaning of *push* is being used. Write the number of the appropriate definition.

__4__ **a.** James Cameron **pushed** the capacities of CGI in *Avatar*.

_____ **b.** In her essay, Susan Sontag tried to **push** young people into learning more about the history of cinema.

_____ **c.** The studio is **pushing** this film as science fiction, but it's really a horror movie.

_____ **d.** *Star Wars* was the highest grossing movie until *Titanic* **pushed** ahead of the competition.

_____ **e.** Tolstoy felt that films would **push** writers to write in a more modern and exciting way.

_____ **f.** In the second film, the Terminator **pushed** the evil cyborg into a vat of acid.

NOTE-TAKING: Organizing Notes to Write a Summary

1 Go back to the reading and read it again. Take notes by underlining the keywords and writing a few comments in the margin. Then use the chart to organize your notes.

	QUESTION TOPIC	CAMERON'S ANSWER
1.	Involvement with finances	*Not involved. Not my job. Studio's job.*
2.	Finding ideas for movies	
3.	Political aspects of *Avatar*	

2 Using your notes in the organizer, complete this short summary of the interview with James Cameron.

James Cameron starts his interview by saying that selling movies is not his responsibility. It's the studio's job to sell the movies; his job is to create films that moviegoers will enjoy...

CRITICAL THINKING

Discuss the questions in a small group. Be prepared to share your opinions with the class.

1. First-time filmmakers have to be successful; otherwise, they won't get to make another major film. How did Cameron make sure his *Terminator* movie was a success?

2. Tolstoy tries to get his point across to the reader by using a parable. How does Cameron use a parable in *Avatar*?

3. Why is technology so important in films today? Did Cameron succeed in blending science and art?

4. Is Cameron a money-maker or an artist? Has he succeeded in blending business and art?

5. Cameron was an illustrator before he was a director. How do you think that helped him in his career?

BRINGING IT ALL TOGETHER

Work in groups of four. Role-play a discussion about cinema between a journalist, Susan Sontag, Leo Tolstoy, and James Cameron. The journalist will ask questions of the others. Sontag, Tolstoy, and Cameron will express their opinions. Use some of the vocabulary you studied in the chapter (for a complete list, go to page 82).

TOPIC: Movies: Art or Business?

ROLES:
- Journalist
- Leo Tolstoy
- Susan Sontag
- James Cameron

QUESTIONS:
- What do you think of movie-making: Is it an art or business?
- What do you think of modern movies with Computer Generated Imagery?
- Movies are now a billion-dollar entertainment. Is this a good thing?
- Should young people know more about the history of cinema?
- Should we continue seeing movies in theaters?

WRITING ACTIVITY

Write a three-paragraph essay about your favorite movie. Use more than five of the words and idioms you studied in the chapter.
- **Introduction:** Give the name of the movie, and tell what it is about.
- **Body Paragraph:** Give three reasons why you think it is a good movie. Refer to specific scenes as support for your opinion.
- **Conclusion:** Explain how the movie illustrates any of the ideas of Sontag, Tolstoy, or Cameron.

DISCUSSION AND WRITING TOPICS

Discuss these topics in a small group. Choose one of them and write a paragraph or two about it. Use the vocabulary from the chapter.

1. Movie stars and film celebrities are constantly in the news. Why do people like to read about them? Are they role models for young people? Should they be?

2. Do you like to see movies like *Avatar* on cell phones or tablets? Why or why not?

3. Do you read the reviews of movie critics in newspapers? Online? Do you follow their recommendations? What should be the role of a movie critic?

4. Do you like to see movies from many countries? Or just Hollywood movies? Just movies from your country? Do you think it's fair that Hollywood movies dominate world entertainment?

VOCABULARY

Nouns	Verbs	Adjectives	Adverbs
blending	devour	dazzling	astonishingly
consensus	flutter	fervent	obstinately
contraption	herald	fiscal	
domination*	hover	grounded	**Phrases and Idioms**
era	overwhelm	irreversible	doodle around
masterpiece	push	long-drawn-out	on the cheap
parable	resurrect	mercenary	
parameters*	slaughter	soaring	
tip	wane	swift	
trend*		visceral	
	Phrasal Verb		
	hunker down		

* = AWL (Academic Word List) item

SELF-ASSESSMENT

In this chapter you learned to:

O Find the thesis statement in an essay

O Skim an interview for the general idea, and scan for the interviewee's attitude towards his subject

O Guess the meaning of words from the context

O Use dictionary entries to learn the meanings of words

O Understand and use synonyms, idioms, connotations, and increase/decrease verbs

O Recognize and use parallel structure for emphasis and contrast

O Take notes to identify the main ideas of a text and the supporting details

O Take margin notes, organize the notes, and write a summary of the text

What can you do well? ✓

What do you need to practice more? ✓

MEDIA STUDIES: The Internet and Social Media

MEDIA STUDIES: an academic discipline that deals with the contents, history, and effects of various mass media of communication

OBJECTIVES

To read academic texts, you need to master certain skills.

In this chapter, you will:

- Predict the content of a text from the title

- Skim the first paragraph of a text to preview the most important idea

- Understand scholarly references

- Guess the meaning of words from the context

- Use dictionary entries to learn the meanings of words

- Understand and use synonyms, collocations, different word forms, and the prefix *anti-*

- Identify imperatives used as illustrative devices and the reasons for their use

- Take notes to identify the details that support the main ideas of a text, and complete an outline

Consider These Questions

Discuss the questions with a partner.

1. Do you have a Facebook page? Why do people use Facebook? Should they worry about putting so much personal information on the Internet?

2. Do you use Twitter? Why do you think people like it?

3. Do you use Internet services on a computer or a telephone or a tablet? Which do you prefer?

4. Do you check your email many times a day? What are the positive and negative consequences of always being available for contact through email?

5. How do you think social media have changed society?

READING ONE: Mind Control and the Internet

A Warm-Up

Discuss the questions in a small group.

1. How does the Internet affect your life?

2. Do you see any dangers in the Internet?

B Reading Strategy

Predicting Content from Title

Predicting or getting some idea of a text before you start reading it will help you improve your reading speed and comprehension. The **title** of a text can often help you predict or **guess the author's most important idea** and guide you through the reading with the proper focus.

Look at the title of the reading. Do you think the author will focus on the positive or the negative aspects of the Internet? Check (✓) your answer.

☐ the positive aspects of the Internet

☐ the negative aspects of the Internet

What do you expect to learn in this article? Write your answer on the lines.

_____

_____

Now read the article to find out if your guess was correct.

Mind Control and the Internet

By Sue Halpern

1   In its **inaugural** days, the Web was a strange, **eclectic** collection of personal homepages, a kind of digital wall art that did not rely on **mainstream** media companies or corporate cash, and was not driven by commercial interests. But then commerce moved in, almost by accident, when Larry Page and Sergey Brin, the duo who started Google, reluctantly paired small ads with their masterful search engine as a way to fund it. It was not their intent, at first, to create the largest global advertising platform in the history of the world. But that is what happened. Write the word "blender" in an email and the next set of ads you're likely to see will be for Waring and Oster.[1] Search for information on bipolar disease, and drug ads will pop up when you are reading baseball scores.

2   Targeted ads may seem harmless enough — after all, if there is going to be advertising, isn't it better if it is for products and services that might be useful? But to pull you into a transaction, companies believe they need to know not only your current interests, but what you have liked before, how old you are, your gender, where you live, how much education you have, and on and on. There are something like five hundred companies that are able to track every move you make on the Internet, **mining** the raw material of the Web and selling it to marketers. That you are overweight, have missed a car payment or two, read historical novels, support Republicans, and spend a lot of time on airplanes is not only known to people other than yourself, it is of great monetary value to them as well. So, too, where you are and where you've been, as we recently learned when it was revealed that both Apple and Google have been tracking mobile phone and tablet users and storing that information as well. Even reading devices like Amazon's Kindle pay attention to what users are doing: highlight a passage in a Kindle book and the passage is sent back to Amazon. Clearly the potential for privacy and other civil liberty[2] abuses here is vast. And if marketing companies can do this, why not political candidates, the government, or companies that want to **sway** public opinion?

3   Facebook users who click on the "like" button for a product may trigger the appearance of an ad for that product on the pages of their "friends." Companies like Twitanalyzer and Klout analyze data from Twitter, Facebook, and LinkedIn to determine

(continued on next page)

[1] **Waring and Oster:** two famous kitchen appliance companies

[2] *civil liberties:* our freedoms, our First Amendment rights — to say and write what we believe, to think what we want, etc.

who has the most influence online and sell that information to businesses that entice the influencers to pitch[3] their products.

4   The **paradox** of personalization and the self-expression promoted by the Internet through Twitter, Facebook, and even Chatroulette is that it **simultaneously** diminishes the value of personhood and individuality. Read the comments that **accompany** many blog posts and articles, and it is overwhelmingly evident that violating dignity — someone else's and therefore, one's own — is a cheap and widely circulated currency. This is not only true for subjects that might ordinarily **incite** partisanship and passion, like sports or politics, but for pretty much anything.

_____

[3] *pitch:* to sell

5   The point of *ad hominem* attacks[4] is to take a swipe at[5] someone else's character, to **undermine** their integrity. The "hive mind" created through our electronic connections necessarily obviates[6] the individual — indeed, that's what makes it a collective consciousness. Anonymity, which **flourishes** when there is no individual accountability, is one of its key features, and behind it, meanness, **antipathy**, and cruelty have a tendency to rush right in.

_____

[4] *ad hominem attacks:* arguments based on the personal facts or failings of the opponent rather than on the merits of the case; personal attacks

[5] *take a swipe at:* to criticize someone publicly

[6] *obviate:* to remove; to prevent or dispose of effectively

COMPREHENSION

A   **Main Ideas**

Complete the sentences according to your understanding of the reading. Discuss your answers with a partner.

1. The Internet began as an informal group of homepages without any connection to business, but today _____.

2. A great deal of data collection occurs on the Web, such as _____

_____.

3. This data collection seems harmless, but _____.

4. People's activities are tracked on computers and other devices. The author worries about these records because _____.

5. Although the Internet seems to encourage individualism, it _____

_____.

Read the quotes from the reading. Circle the statement that best explains each quote. Share your answers with a partner.

1. "But then commerce moved in, almost by accident, when Larry Page and Sergey Brin, the duo who started Google, reluctantly paired small ads with their masterful search engine as a way to fund it." *(paragraph 1)*

   a. Google founders Larry Page and Sergey Brin were not really happy about having to finance Google with small ads.

   b. The Internet was a business proposition right from the beginning.

   c. It was a coincidence that business started to flood the Internet at the same time that Google founders Larry Page and Sergey Brin decided to finance Google with small ads.

2. "Targeted ads may seem harmless enough — after all, if there is going to be advertising, isn't it better if it is for products and services that might be useful? But to pull you into a transaction, companies believe they need to know not only your current interests, but what you have liked before, how old you are, your gender, where you live, how much education you have, and on and on." *(paragraph 2)*

   a. Targeted ads are harmless.

   b. Companies shouldn't be allowed to know anything about us.

   c. Companies know too much about us.

3. "Companies like Twitanalyzer and Klout analyze data from Twitter, Facebook, and LinkedIn to determine who has the most influence online and sell that information to businesses that entice the influencers to pitch their products." *(paragraph 3)*

   a. Based on information that they receive from companies like Twitanalyzer and Klout, businesses get in touch with social networks.

   b. Based on the data that they receive from companies like Twitanalyzer and Klout, businesses offer deals to individuals who will agree to recommend the business products to their friends and contacts online.

   c. Based on information that they receive from sites like Twitter and Facebook, businesses decide what products to market.

4. "The 'hive mind' created through our electronic connections necessarily obviates the individual — indeed, that's what makes it a collective consciousness." *(paragraph 5)*

   a. The "hive mind" created by electronic media reflects an individual consciousness rather than a collective one.

   b. The "hive mind" created by electronic media gives the individual a critical role in collective consciousness-raising.

   c. The "hive mind" created by electronic media reflects a collective consciousness, not an individual one.

VOCABULARY

Guessing from Context

Read each quote from the reading. Try to guess the meaning of the words in bold from the context. Write your guess. Then consult a dictionary and write the definition.

1. "In its **inaugural** days, the Web was a strange, eclectic collection of personal homepages, a kind of digital wall art that did not rely on **mainstream** media companies or corporate cash, and was not driven by commercial interests. But then commerce moved in." *(paragraph 1)*

   inaugural   Guess: _first_

                       Dictionary: _the first in a series_

   mainstream   Guess: _regular_

                       Dictionary: _the most usual or normal in a society_

2. "Clearly the potential for privacy and other civil liberty abuses here is vast. And if marketing companies can do this, why not political candidates, the government, or companies that want to **sway** public opinion?" *(paragraph 2)*

   sway   Guess: _____

                       Dictionary: _____

3. "The **paradox** of personalization and the self-expression promoted by the Internet through Twitter, Facebook, and even Chatroulette is that it **simultaneously** diminishes the value of personhood and individuality." *(paragraph 4)*

   paradox   Guess: _____

                       Dictionary: _____

   simultaneously Guess: _____

                       Dictionary: _____

4. "Read the comments that **accompany** many blog posts and articles, and it is overwhelmingly evident that violating dignity — someone else's and therefore, one's own — is a cheap and widely circulated currency." *(paragraph 4)*

   accompany   Guess: _____

                       Dictionary: _____

5. "This is not only true for subjects that might ordinarily **incite** partisanship and passion, like sports or politics, but for pretty much anything." *(paragraph 4)*

   incite   Guess: _____

                       Dictionary: _____

B Synonyms

Read each paragraph. Match each word in bold with its synonym in the box below. Compare answers with a partner.

In these days of advanced technology, the Internet is __flourishing__ all over
1.
the world. With all the powerful tools at our disposal, we can order products from
faraway countries and speak to people all over the globe. However, we have to be
careful that the new online world does not __undermine__ our personal freedoms.
2.
When we purchase an item on the Web, we are __simultaneously__ being monitored
3.
and spied on by businesses that keep a record of what we are doing. Knowing our
personal information is only one item in an __eclectic__ list of things businesses
4.
can know: they can find out what schools we went to, what newspapers and books
we read, even what we like when we highlight a passage in an e-book. Some people
say this spying can __accompany__ our every move on the Internet. We'd like to
5.
take a swipe at these companies, but we don't usually even know who or what they
are. Our aim is not to __incite__ paranoia and fear but to increase people's
6.
awareness of what is going on in the online community.

____ **a.** follow	____ **c.** at the same time	_1_ **e.** doing well
____ **b.** diverse	____ **d.** provoke	____ **f.** weaken

In this era of mass media, we face a scary __paradox__. It's very easy
1.
to communicate with many people on blogs, for example, but in order to
__sway__ opinions, many Internet users resort to insults. Somehow,
2.
the innocence of the __inaugural__ days of the Web has been lost. Even on
3.
__mainstream__ sites like YouTube, people are often insulting each other in cruel
4.
comments that express __antipathy__ rather than understanding. Cyberbullying
5.
is another problem. Young people gang up on some of their peers and insult them
without mercy. Undoubtedly, we need to encourage less heartless behavior.

____ **a.** beginning	____ **c.** dislike	____ **e.** influence
____ **b.** contradiction	____ **d.** well-established	

C Word Forms: Dictionary Work

1 Some words can be used either as a noun or as a verb. Read the different meanings for the noun and verb forms of *mine*.

	NOUN	VERB
mine	**1** a deep hole or series of holes in the ground from which coal, gold, etc. is dug	**1** to dig into the ground in order to get gold, coal, etc.
	2 A type of bomb that is hidden below the surface of the ground or in the water, which explodes when touched	**2** (often passive: *to be mined*) to hide bombs in the ocean or under the ground
	3 someone or something that can give you a lot of information about a particular subject	**3** to get information, ideas etc. from something

2 Read each sentence. Decide which word form is being used (noun or verb) and what its specific meaning is. Write the name of the word form and the number of the appropriate definition.

_____*verb (2)*_____ **a.** The Internet is **mined** with all kinds of temptations to get consumers to go on buying sprees.

_____ **b.** Finding the reasons for the students' cruel behavior was like digging deep in a **mine** without finding anything to show for the hard work done.

_____ **c.** Rather than go to the library, the students often **mine** the Internet first in order to get the information they need.

_____ **d.** The mother of five children was a **mine** of information about child rearing.

D Prefix: *anti-*

Anti- is a prefix meaning **against** or **opposite**.

EXAMPLE:
antipathy   a strong feeling of dislike (***pathos*** is a Greek root meaning "feeling," as in "sympathy")

Based on an understanding of the root of the word and the prefix, what do you think these words mean?

1. antibacterial *(adj.)* _____   **3.** antiseptic *(n.)* _____

2. antisocial *(adj.)* _____   **4.** antifreeze *(n.)* _____

Now look the words up in the dictionary.

GRAMMAR FOR READING: Using an Imperative to Illustrate a Point

There are many ways of **illustrating what would happen in certain conditions:**

EXAMPLES:

      condition   result

- **Use** a mobile phone, **and** Apple will know where you are at all times.
- **If you use** a mobile phone, Apple will know where you are at all times.
- **When you use** a mobile phone, Apple knows where you are at all times.

Q: Do these three sentences say the same thing?
A: Yes. All three express the same condition and result.

Q: Which sentence is the most direct and the most economical in language?
A: The first one, which starts with an imperative.

When you want to illustrate in the **most direct and precise way** what would happen in certain conditions, use an **imperative**. It creates a strong link between the writer and the reader. Note that the imperative clause (condition) is linked to the other clause (result) with **and**.

1 Work with a partner. Go back to the reading and find the three paragraphs where imperatives are used. Identify each paragraph here, and write the sentences with imperatives on the lines.

PARAGRAPH: _____

_____

_____

_____

PARAGRAPH: _____

_____

_____

PARAGRAPH: _____

_____

_____

_____

2 Discuss the questions.

1. Why does the writer use this construction?

2. Does the sentence pattern serve the same purpose in all three paragraphs?

NOTE-TAKING: Completing an Outline

Go back to the reading and read it again. Working with a partner, complete the outline showing the main ideas and supporting details.

A. The Internet has become a huge commercial enterprise.

    1. It began as an alternative to big media.

    2. Then Brin and Page started _taking ads to finance Google_____.

    3. _____ by money interests.

B. Targeted ads are dangerous to privacy.

    1. Companies collect _____.

    2. Apple, Google, Kindle _____.

    3. There is the danger that _____.

C. Facebook _____.

    1. What you click on will lead to ads popping up.

    2. People with many friends _____.

D. Anonymity seems like freedom, but it's not.

    1. The paradox is that there's a lot of self-expression on the web . . .

    2. But _____.

E. _____.

    1. The "hive-mentality" destroys individual responsibility.

    2. It also encourages meanness.

CRITICAL THINKING

Discuss the questions in a small group. Be prepared to share your points of view with the class.

1. Do you think the Web would have developed as much as it has today if it had remained in its original state, without the influence of commerce? Why or why not?

2. Why is the title of the reading perfect for the content? What danger to individual liberties does "mind control" pose? How does this control operate in a commercial environment? Why is it dangerous in a government context?

3. Cyberbullying has become a problem on the Web, especially for children and teenagers. How does this problem reflect the power of the "hive mind" and the potential loss of respect for the individual that it causes? What other problems make us more aware of our "meanness, antipathy, and cruelty" as human beings?

(A) Warm-Up

Discuss the question in a small group.

Some people think that the Internet keeps us locked up in our rooms, interacting only with machines.

Do you agree? Does the Internet isolate us from society, or does it make us more a part of society?

(B) Reading Strategy

Understanding Scholarly References

In-Text Citations:
References to the work of scholars and researchers are a vital part of academic texts. Citations are essential in order to give credit to other professionals and to assure readers that your study or article is following best professional practices.

- Modern media practices have evolved significantly from their traditional forms, with the key concepts of the new media being participation and interactivity (O'Reilly, 2005, p. 1 and Anderson, 2007).
  This means that the new media concepts can be found on page 1 of a study written in 2005 by a researcher named O'Reilly and also in a study written in 2007 by a researcher named Anderson. The concepts are **paraphrases** *in the writer's own words of what she read in the two researchers' works. Even though the report writer does not use the exact words of the academic studies, the ideas are used and have to be cited.*

- As Boyd and Ellison (2007) reveal, "While the key technological features are fairly consistent, the cultures that emerge around [social networking sites] are varied."
  The use of **quotation marks** *means that the writer is using the* **exact words** *of researchers Boyd and Ellison, from their study written in 2007.*

Bibliography or References:
To find the exact names of the studies referred to and the names of the publications in which they appeared, you must look at the bibliography or references at the end of each chapter or in the back of the book. In that way, you can identify the sources of the facts and look up the publications to get further information.

Work with a partner. Find three different citations in the reading. Write them on the lines. Then explain each one.

_____

_____

_____

Examine the bibliography at the end of the reading. Where did the writer do most of her research?

_____

Now read the text to find out more about the positive effects of social networking sites according to different scholars and researchers.

THE POSITIVE EFFECTS OF SOCIAL NETWORKING SITES

By Ebony Wheeldon, Curtin University of Technology, Australia

1   Modern media practices have evolved significantly from their traditional forms, with the key concepts of the new media being participation and interactivity (O'Reilly, 2005, p. 1 and Anderson, 2007). This paper aims to look at the positive effect that interaction through social networking sites has on today's society.

2   A social networking site is described as "a website where individuals can set up an online profile, describing his/her interests" (Hawkins, n.d.[1]). However, as Boyd and Ellison (2007) reveal, "While the key technological features are fairly **consistent**, the cultures that **emerge** around [social networking sites] are varied. Most sites support the maintenance of pre-existing social networks, but others help strangers connect based on shared interests, political views, or activities."

3   The significance placed on interaction and participation within these social networking sites is evident in the numerous ways in which communication is encouraged. For example, some social networking sites such as MySpace and Facebook offer users the ability to create sub-groups (or message boards) of people based on similar interests. These can vary from support groups, to fan groups, to community organizations or school groups, **analogous** to clubs in the offline world. Apart from using these groups to interact, people have the ability (depending on privacy settings) to comment and respond to "status updates" and statements or comments that others have posted, thereby **initiating** communication. On sites such as YouTube, people may even give a video response. By allowing such feedback, there is the **prospect** of conversation, of debate, of sharing information or perceiving new ideas.

4   By forming groups of people with similar interests (particularly if the interest or hobby is not mainstream), the **proliferation** of social networking sites can create a sense of unity and belonging in people who might previously have felt **alienated** in society. Particularly in areas with smaller populations, the chance of discovering others with similar interests is infrequent, but by removing these location barriers through online communication, the chance of meeting people with the same interests is greatly increased. Social networking sites give the impression that it is a much *smaller world*.

---

[1] *n.d.* = "no date" known for the reference

5   Social networking sites also offer the chance of communication in cases where mobility is often a **hindrance** to social interaction. Elderly people and those with physical disabilities who are unable to leave their house are able to stay in touch with existing relations and friends, as well as get in touch with people who have similar issues (Lecky-Thompson, 2009). The ability to incorporate blogging in social networking can also be **therapeutic**. "Blogging is a form of journal therapy and," according to renowned therapist Kathleen Adams, "studies indicate that the release offered by writing has a direct impact on the body's capacity to **withstand** stress and fight off infection and disease" (Market Wire, 2008). People find it easier to reach out online because it can be anonymous and it allows people more control over what information they disclose.

6   For all the benefits of social networking sites in today's society, it is evident that any impact they have is due not merely to the sites themselves but "the communication layer **embedded** within them" (Young, 2006). According to Siegler (2009), they are "simply an extension of social networking in the real world." At different points in time, Siegler (2009) asserts, "It has been said that [social networking] would be both the downfall of mankind, and the thing that would bring the planet together [but] the truth is that social networking, while great in many respects, does not fulfill a fundamental human desire: To be in the actual presence of other people."

Bibliography

Anderson, T. (2007). "Web 2.0 and New Media Definitions." Retrieved April 22, 2010, from http://www.newcommbiz.com/web-20-and-new-media-definitions/

Boyd, D. & Ellison, N. (2007). "Social Network Sites: Definition, History, and Scholarship." *Journal of Computer-Mediated Communication*, 13(1), article 11. Retrieved March 10, 2010, from http://jcmc.indiana.edu/vol 13/issue1/boyd.ellison.html

Hawkins, K. (n.d.). "What Is a Social Networking Site?" Retrieved April 21, 2010, from http://www.wisegeek.com/what-is-a-social-networking-site.htm

Lecky-Thompson, G. (2009). "Facebook: Good or Bad for Communication." Retrieved March 10, 2010, from http://social-networking-tagging.suite101.com/article.cfm/facebook_good_or_bad_for_communication

Market Wire. (Ed.). (2008). "Can Social Networking Benefit Your Mental Health?" Retrieved April 1, 2010, from http://findarticles.com/p/articles/mi_pwwi/is_200804/ai_n25368225/

O'Reilly, T. (2005). "Design Patterns and Business Models for the Next Generation of Software." Retrieved April 2, 2010, from http://oreilly.com/web2/archive/what-is-web-20.html

Siegler, M. (2009). "Location Is the Missing Link between Social Networks and the Real World." Retrieved March 10, 2010, from http://techcrunch.com/2009/11/18/location-is-the-missing-link-between-social-networks-and-the-real-world/

Young, R. (2006). "The Future of Social Networks — Communication." Retrieved March 10, 2010, from http://gigaom.com/2006/10/09/the-future-of-social-networks-communication/

COMPREHENSION

A Main Ideas

Check (✓) the statements that best express the main ideas in the reading. Discuss your answers with a partner.

☐ **1.** Interaction and participation are the main features of social networking sites.

☐ **2.** Real communication between individuals is not possible on social networking sites.

☐ **3.** The negative effects of social networking sites are many and varied.

☐ **4.** Social networking sites can lessen the alienation felt by some people.

☐ **5.** Participating in social networking sites yields therapeutic benefits.

☐ **6.** Social networking satisfies a basic human need, to be in the company of others.

B Close Reading

Read the quotes from the reading. Circle the statement that best explains each quote. Share your answers with a partner.

1. "By forming groups of people with similar interests (particularly if the interest or hobby is not mainstream), the proliferation of social networking sites can create a sense of unity and belonging in people who might previously have felt alienated in society." *(paragraph 4)*

   a. Getting people of common interests together on social networking sites makes them feel more mainstream.

   b. Social networking sites can bring together people with minority interests and make them feel more mainstream.

   c. The spread of social networking sites has helped to reduce the number of outsiders.

2. "Social networking sites give the impression that it is a much *smaller world*." *(paragraph 4)*

   a. The world seems smaller because people from all over can communicate with each other.

   b. The world seems smaller because the traditional customs have been overcome.

   c. The world seems smaller because the larger world is no longer as impressive as it once was.

3. " 'Blogging is a form of journal therapy and,' according to renowned therapist Kathleen Adams, 'studies indicate that the release offered by writing has a direct impact on the body's capacity to withstand stress and fight off infection and disease.' " *(paragraph 5)*

   a. Therapist Kathleen Adams believes that we should blog when we are ill.

   b. Therapist Kathleen Adams believes that self-expression can reduce stress.

   c. Therapist Kathleen Adams believes that writing can provide release.

VOCABULARY

A Word Forms

1 Fill in the chart with the correct word forms. Some categories can have more than one form. Use a dictionary if necessary. An **X** indicates there is no form in that category.

	NOUN	VERB	ADJECTIVE	ADVERB
1.	alienation		alienated	X
2.		X	analogous	X
3.		X	consistent	
4.	X		emerging / emergent	X
5.	hindrance		X	X
6.	proliferation			X
7.	therapy /	X	therapeutic	

2 Complete the sentences with the correct form of the words. Choose from the two forms in parentheses. Compare answers with a partner.

1. Society often _____ alienates _____ people who are very different from
   (alienation / alienates)
   the average person.

2. In every culture, this unfortunate habit of isolating others has been
   _____ evident across the globe for centuries.
   (consistent / consistently)

3. Being cut off from others can be _____ to being dead.
   (analogy / analogous)

4. When people are marginalized, they are _____ from
   (hindrance / hindered)
   participating fully in society.

5. What can also _____ from such a situation is a society that
   (emerge / emerging)
   is prone to discrimination and injustice.

6. The _____ of social networking has lessened the
   (proliferation / proliferate)
   alienation felt by some.

7. It has provided a _____ link to others with common
   (therapeutic / therapeutically)
   interests that will hopefully benefit society as a whole.

B Synonyms

Complete the essay with the words from the box. Use the synonym in parentheses to help you select the correct word. Compare answers with a partner.

alienation	embedded	initiate	therapeutic
analogous	emerges	proliferation	withstand
consistently	hindrance	prospect	

Blogs and Healing

Research findings throughout the world about the _____therapeutic_____
1. (healing)
effects of blogging have _____ shown that the process of
2. (always)
writing a personal diary provides a release from emotional distress. This is especially

true for teens who write blogs. What _____ constantly in
3. (comes out)
the literature is the fact that writing public blogs (even more than writing private

diaries) helps teens find ways to cope with their lives. Problems with self-esteem,

social anxiety, and emotional distress have become _____
4. (implanted)
in our current world. For some young people, these problems can become a[n]

_____ to living a happy life. In many ways, blogging helps
5. (obstacle)
teens to overcome their social _____.
6. (estrangement)

In her study "The Therapeutic Value of Adolescent Blogging about Social-

Emotional Difficulties," Dr. Meyran Boniel-Nissim of the University of Haifa

reports that those teens who wrote blogs in which they talked about the difficulties

that they could no longer _____ ended up seeing positive
7. (endure)
changes in their behavior. Many of these changes came as a result of the supportive

comments they received from strangers on their blogs, once they had the courage to

_____ contact and reach out to others. On the other hand,
8. (begin)
teens who wrote private diaries that were not open to comments saw no progress.

Dr. Alice Flaherty, a neuroscientist at Harvard University and Massachusetts

General Hospital, also notes that blogging might trigger dopamine release, which

is _____ to the kinds of stimulants that people who listen to
9. (similar)
music, run, and look at works of art enjoy.

With the _____ of blogging all over the

10. (spread)

world, such information bodes well for our future. Knowing that the

_____ of making people feel better about themselves is

11. (hope)

inherent in the sharing of expressive writing with others is something that we

cannot ignore.

C Using the Dictionary

Read the dictionary entries for the word *prospect*.

> **prospect** *n.* **1** something that is possible or likely to happen in the future: *The idea of traveling in Europe was an exciting prospect.* **2** a person, job, plan that has a good chance of success in the future: *Wilder is considered a good prospect for the next election.* **3** [usually plural] chances of future success: *You can't marry a man with no job and no prospects!* **4** [usually singular] a view of a wide area of land, especially from a high place: *a fine prospect of the valley below*
>
> **prospect** *v.* **1** to examine an area of land or water in order to find gold, silver, oil, etc.: *prospecting for gold* **2** to look for something, especially business opportunities: *The charity is prospecting for new donors.*

Read each sentence. Decide which word form is being used and what its specific meaning is. Write the name of the word form and the number of the appropriate definition.

_____noun (3)_____ **a.** You can't get involved with a company that has no **prospects**.

_____ **b.** The **prospect** is that when the company goes public, all the people who own shares in it will make a lot of money.

_____ **c.** In 1848, many people came to California to **prospect** for gold.

_____ **d.** Today they come to Silicon Valley to get a job with Internet start-ups that have a **prospect** of future success.

_____ **e.** From the Santa Cruz Mountains, you can look down at the beautiful **prospect** of the Santa Clara Valley, now called Silicon Valley, with its more than 6,000 high technology companies.

_____ **f.** The beautiful setting is all the more impressive because finding a job in this location is a more likely **prospect**.

_____ **g.** It is not unusual for recent college graduates to **prospect** for career opportunities there.

_____ **h.** Few areas in the country offer as many **prospects** in the computer industry as Silicon Valley does.

NOTE-TAKING: Identifying Details That Support Main Ideas

Go back to the reading and read it again. Then for each main idea, write down in your own words the details that support it. Share your answers with a partner.

	MAIN IDEA	SUPPORTING DETAILS
1.	Interaction and participation are the main features of social networking sites.	• Communication encouraged through subgroups, message boards, people who share interests . . . •
2.	Social networking sites can lessen the alienation felt by some people.	• •
3.	Participating in social networking sites yields therapeutic benefits.	• • •

CRITICAL THINKING

Discuss the questions in a small group. Be prepared to share your points of view with the class.

1. The author's purpose is to write about the positive effects of social networking communication. However, she ends her paper with a quote from another researcher that says: "[But] the truth is that social networking, while great in many respects, does not fulfill a fundamental human desire: To be in the actual presence of other people." Has the author weakened or strengthened her argument with this ending?

2. Why did this paper need a scholarly bibliography? What did the references bring to the paper?

3. Does social networking provide the answer to all human ills? For instance, if shy people spend all their time online without ever putting themselves in real contact with people, has this "interactivity" been worth it? Why or why not?

4. Bloggers usually talk about their problems anonymously, and to anonymous strangers. Why is it easier for us to discuss our problems with people we do not know? Would you recommend this as the first step to take in resolving the problems that often emerge in our relationships with the people we do know? Why or why not?

5. How is using social media different from calling someone on the telephone?

6. The writer says that through social media the world has become smaller. Do you agree? Why or why not?

LINKING READINGS ONE AND TWO

Work with a partner. Look at the three themes. What would Sue Halpern and Ebony Wheeldon, the authors of the two readings, say about each one? Read their possible answers for the first theme. Then try to imagine their answers for the other two themes, and write them in the chart.

	THEME	SUE HALPERN (READING ONE)	EBONY WHEELDON (READING TWO)
1.	The Power of the Internet	The Internet has taken over our lives. Businesses dominate, and all kinds of privacy and civil liberties issues are now becoming a concern. (negative)	The Internet has taken over our lives. It has given people the potential to participate and interact with each other online. (positive)
2.	Anonymity		
3.	Individuality		

READING THREE: The Use of Social Media in the Arab Spring

 Warm-Up

Read a brief explanation of the term "Arab Spring" and then answer the question that follows.

The term "Arab Spring" is used to describe the protest movements that began in Tunisia in 2011 and spread to many countries in the Middle East and North Africa. The aim of these movements was to overthrow dictators or authoritarian monarchies. The "spring" was in contrast to the "winter" of oppression that people in many of these countries had experienced in the past.

What role do you think social media played in such movements?

Skimming First Paragraph for Most Important Idea

Skimming (reading quickly) the first paragraph of a news article can give you a **preview of the most important idea** explored in the text.

Skim the first paragraph of the reading and answer the questions. Check (✓) the appropriate box.

1. What is the most important idea of the article?

   ☐ **a.** International discussions in social media contributed to the protests.

   ☐ **b.** The Arab Spring contributed to increased interest in social media.

2. What is the support for this idea?

   ☐ **a.** Analysis of televised stories

   ☐ **b.** Analysis of 3 million tweets, YouTube videos, and blogs

Now read the rest of the article. Were your guesses correct?

The Use of Social Media in the Arab Spring

By Catherine O'Donnell, *UW News and Information*

1 In the 21st century, the revolution may not be televised — but it likely will be tweeted, blogged, texted and organized on Facebook, recent experience suggests. After analyzing more than 3 million tweets, gigabytes of YouTube content and thousands of blog posts, a new study finds that social media played a central role in shaping political debates in the Arab Spring. Conversations about revolution often preceded major events, and social media has carried inspiring stories of protest across international borders.

Young woman tweeting during an Arab Spring demonstration

2 "Our evidence suggests that social media carried a **cascade** of messages about freedom and democracy across North Africa and the Middle East, and helped **raise expectations** for the success of political uprising," said Philip Howard,

the project lead and an associate professor in communication at the University of Washington. "People who shared interest in democracy built extensive social networks and organized political action. Social media became a **critical** part of the toolkit for greater freedom." During the week before Egyptian president Hosni Mubarak's resignation, for example, the total rate of tweets from Egypt — and around the world — about political change in that country **ballooned** from 2,300 a day to 230,000 a day. Videos featuring protest and political commentary **went viral** — the top 23 videos received nearly 5.5 million views. The amount of content produced online by opposition groups, in Facebook and political blogs, increased **dramatically**.

3 "Twitter offers us the clearest evidence of where individuals engaging in democratic conversations were located during the revolutions," Howard said. "Twitter provides a window into the broader world of digital conversations, many of which probably involved cell phones to send text, pictures or voice messages," he said. In Tunisia, for example, less than 20 percent of the population uses social media, but almost everyone has access to a mobile phone.

4 Political discussion in blogs **presaged** the turn of popular opinion in both Tunisia and Egypt. In Tunisia, conversations about liberty, democracy and revolution on blogs and on Twitter often immediately preceded mass protests. Twenty percent of blogs were evaluating Ben Ali's leadership the day he resigned from office (Jan. 14), up from just 5 percent the month before. Subsequently, the primary topic for Tunisian blogs was "revolution" until a public rally of at least 100,000 people eventually forced the old regime's remaining leaders to **relinquish** power.

5 In the case of both Tunisia's and Egypt's revolutions, discussion **spanned** borders. In the two weeks after Mubarak's resignation, there was an average of 2,400 tweets a day from people in neighboring countries about the political situation in Egypt. In Tunisia after Ben Ali's resignation, there were about 2,200 tweets a day.

6 "In other words," Howard said, "people throughout the region were drawn into an extended conversation about social uprising. The success of demands for political change in Egypt and Tunisia led individuals in other countries to pick up the conversation. It helped create discussion across the region." Howard said that although social media did not cause the **upheaval** in North Africa, they altered the capacity of citizens to affect domestic politics. Online activists created a virtual ecology of civil society, debating **contentious** issues that could not be discussed in public. Ironically, government efforts to crack down on social media may have incited more public activism, especially in Egypt. "People who were isolated by efforts to shut down the Internet, mostly middle-class Egyptians, may have gone to the streets when they could no longer follow the unrest through social media," Howard said.

7 "Recent events show us that the public sense of shared **grievance** and potential for change can develop rapidly," he said. "These dictators for a long time had many political enemies, but they were **fragmented**. So opponents used social media to identify goals, build **solidarity** and organize demonstrations."

COMPREHENSION

A Main Ideas

Read each statement. Decide if it is *True* or *False* according to the reading. Check (✓) the appropriate box. If it is false, change it to make it true. Discuss your answers with a partner.

	TRUE	FALSE
1. Social media were responsible for the Arab Spring.	☐	☐
2. Social media brought together people with an interest in democracy.	☐	☐
3. Social media restricted people's views to one country.	☐	☐
4. When governments shut down the social media, the political movement died.	☐	☐
5. According to the article, an increase in activity in social media came after all the large demonstrations.	☐	☐
6. Social media defeated censorship for a certain time.	☐	☐
7. Most people in the Middle East have a computer to access social media.	☐	☐

B Close Reading

Read the quotes from the reading. Circle the statement that best explains each quote. Share your answers with a partner.

1. "After analyzing more than 3 million tweets, gigabytes of YouTube content and thousands of blog posts, a new study finds that social media played a central role in shaping political debates in the Arab Spring." *(paragraph 1)*

   a. Social media gathered crowds for demonstrations.

   b. Social media contributed to clarifying ideas.

2. "Ironically, government efforts to crack down on social media may have incited more public activism, especially in Egypt." *(paragraph 6)*

   a. Governments weren't able to block social media.

   b. Blocking social media may have backfired on governments.

3. "These dictators for a long time had many political enemies, but they were fragmented." *(paragraph 7)*

   a. "They" refers to the enemies.

   b. "They" refers to the dictators.

VOCABULARY

A **Guessing from Context**

Read each quote from the reading. Try to guess the meaning of the words in bold from the context. Write the clues that helped you guess and your guess. Then consult a dictionary and write the definition.

1. "Political discussion in blogs **presaged** the turn of popular opinion in both Tunisia and Egypt. In Tunisia, conversations about liberty, democracy and revolution on blogs and on Twitter often immediately preceded mass protests." (*paragraph 4*)

   presage Clues: _preceded (came before)_

   Guess: _announce_

   Dictionary: _to be a warning that something is going to happen_

2. "Twenty percent of blogs were evaluating Ben Ali's leadership the day he resigned from office (Jan. 14), up from just 5 percent the month before. Subsequently, the primary topic for Tunisian blogs was "revolution" until a public rally of at least 10,000 people eventually forced the old regime's remaining leaders to **relinquish** power." (*paragraph 4*)

   relinquish Clues: _____

   Guess: _____

   Dictionary: _____

3. "Online activists created a virtual ecology of civil society, debating **contentious** issues that could not be discussed in public." (*paragraph 6*)

   contentious Clues: _____

   Guess: _____

   Dictionary: _____

4. "These dictators for a long time had many political enemies, but they were **fragmented**. So opponents used social media to identify goals, build solidarity and organize demonstrations." (*paragraph 7*)

   fragmented Clues: _____

   Guess: _____

   Dictionary: _____

B Synonyms

Complete each sentence with a word or phrase from the box. Use the synonym in parentheses to help you select the correct word. Compare answers with a partner.

ballooned	critical	fragmented	presaged	spans
cascade	dramatically	go viral	relinquish	upheavals
contentious	expectations	grievances	solidarity	

1. Censorship of the Internet is a very _____ *contentious* _____ issue in some
   (controversial)
   countries; blogs often criticize politicians online, but some people think such
   criticism is too dangerous.

2. People have _____ against corruption or other issues and
   (complaints)
   have nowhere else to go to protest.

3. The opposition was _____ into small groups.
   (split)

4. Communicating with others through social media raises _____
   (hopes)
   that by joining together, change can happen.

5. Social media like YouTube, Facebook, and Twitter also develop feelings of
   _____ for the victims of oppression all over the world.
   (empathy)

6. YouTube videos of government repression can _____ in a
   (become extremely popular)
   matter of minutes.

7. Governments are afraid of _____ if opponents gather too
   (rebellions)
   many allies online.

8. In some countries, controlling the Internet is a _____
   (very important)
   function of the secret services of the police.

9. Censorship of the Internet _____ borders when countries
   (spreads across)
   pressure Google, Yahoo, and Facebook to refuse content that the government
   doesn't like.

10. In their defense, governments say that the Internet has to obey the laws of their
    country and, if those laws forbid criticism of politicians, the Internet companies
    must _____ power to governments.
    (give up)

11. Businesses also monitor our logins: Information from our Internet activities has increased _____ in recent years.
    (greatly)

12. At first, the Internet had no profit motive, but the early ads on Google _____ a change.
    (warned about)

13. Advertisements on the Web have _____ in the past few years to the point that ads are everywhere.
    (expanded)

14. There has been a _____ of programs that show businesses where and when we have logged in, what sites and browsers we use, what news we are interested in, and what products we buy.
    (series)

C **Collocations**

Check (✓) the words that are often paired together. Discuss your answers with a partner and the meaning of the collocations.

☐ 1. raise expectations

☐ 2. increase expectations

☐ 3. lower expectations

☐ 4. contentious issues

☐ 5. contentious details

☐ 6. contentious expectations

☐ 7. relinquish power

☐ 8. relinquish energy

☐ 9. relinquish control

CRITICAL THINKING

Discuss the questions in a small group. Be prepared to share your ideas with the rest of the class.

1. Why are universities interested in an academic study of social media?

2. Some people say that without social media the Arab Spring wouldn't have happened. What do you think?

3. Should governments have control of the Internet? Or should the Internet be entirely free? What about dangerous content?

4. Huge media giants have been created by the Internet: Google, Amazon, iTunes. Is this a good thing or something to be worried about?

BRINGING IT ALL TOGETHER

Work in groups of four. Organize a debate about the Internet and social media. Follow the instructions.

Topic: Should the Internet and social media be free of government control?

Instructions:
- Each group decides which two students will defend the idea of government control of the Internet and social media and which two students will argue against government control of the Internet and social media. (Social media would be Facebook, YouTube, Twitter, and blogs.)
- Before you begin, each team of two people should brainstorm the ideas they will need to express, and make a list (FOR government control or AGAINST government control). Use information from all three readings in this chapter.

During the debate, use some of the vocabulary you studied in the chapter (for a complete list, go to page 109).

WRITING ACTIVITY

Write a three-paragraph essay on the Internet service or type of social media that is the most interesting or worrisome to you. Use more than five of the words and idioms you studied in the chapter.
- **Introduction:** Explain what services the Internet company or social media site provides for the public.
- **Body Paragraph:** Give three reasons for your opinion (for or against) maintaining these services.
- **Conclusion:** Explain how life will change in the future if most people adopt the opinion you have expressed in the essay.

DISCUSSION AND WRITING TOPICS

Discuss these topics in a small group. Choose one of them and write a paragraph or two about it. Use the vocabulary from the chapter.

1. Some governments wanted to block Internet content from controversial sites, such as WikiLeaks, which leaked information about corruption, the treatment of prisoners, and the conduct of the Afghan war on the part of several governments, including the United States. Should some content on the Internet be blocked or not? Is it really possible to block the Internet completely?

2. Some employers are requiring job seekers to give them their Facebook password. Why are they doing this? Would you give your password? Should employers be allowed to ask for it?

3. Do you think it's a good idea for universities to use students' Facebook pages to introduce people to each other? Why or why not?

VOCABULARY

Nouns	Verbs	Adjectives	Adverbs
antipathy	accompany *	alienated	dramatically *
cascade	balloon	analogous *	simultaneously
grievance	emerge *	consistent *	
hindrance	flourish	contentious	**Phrases and Idioms**
paradox	incite	critical	go viral
proliferation	initiate *	eclectic	raise
prospect *	mine	embedded	expectations
solidarity	presage	fragmented	
upheaval	relinquish	inaugural	
	span	mainstream	
	sway	therapeutic	
	undermine		
	withstand		

* = AWL (Academic Word List) item

SELF-ASSESSMENT

In this chapter you learned to:

○ Predict the content of a text from the title

○ Skim the first paragraph of a text to preview the most important idea

○ Understand scholarly references

○ Guess the meaning of words from the context

○ Use dictionary entries to learn the meanings of words

○ Understand and use synonyms, collocations, different word forms, and the prefix **anti-**

○ Identify imperatives used as illustrative devices and the reasons for their use

○ Take notes to identify the details that support the main ideas of a text, and complete an outline

What can you do well? ✔

What do you need to practice more? ✔

CHAPTER 5

NEUROSCIENCE:
The Brain and Memory

NEUROSCIENCE: the scientific study of the nervous system and the brain

OBJECTIVES

To read academic texts, you need to master certain skills.

In this chapter, you will:

- Visualize the content of a text to understand it better

- Scan a chart to find specific information

- Skim the first two paragraphs of a text to get an idea of what it will discuss

- Guess the meaning of words from the context

- Use dictionary entries to learn the meanings of words

- Understand and use synonyms, collocations, different word forms, and words of Greek or Latin origin

- Recognize and use figurative language and rhetorical questions

- Take notes by making lists and using keywords as study tools

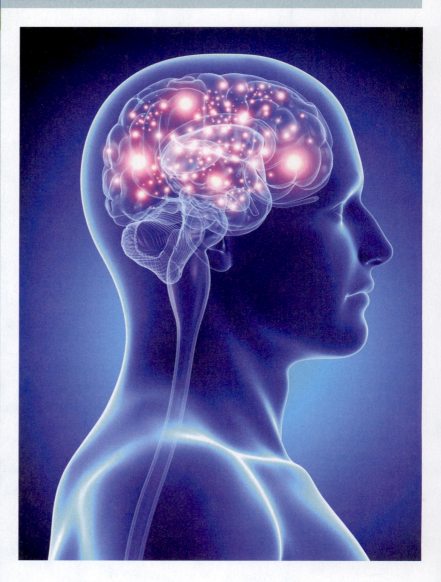

Consider These Questions

Discuss the questions with a partner.

1. What are the best memories of your childhood? Are these memories important to you? What people do you remember best?

2. How can we avoid remembering painful and hurtful things?

3. What do you do to help yourself remember? How do you memorize material for school?

READING ONE: In Search of Memory

 A **Warm-Up**

Consider the question. Check (✓) the reasons that are relevant to you. Discuss your answers with a partner.

Why are memories so important to people?

☐ **a.** to relive a lost love

☐ **b.** to recall a wonderful vacation

☐ **c.** to remember those who have died

☐ **d.** to remember time spent with family

☐ **e.** to remember one's roots

☐ **f.** to define one's identity

B **Reading Strategy**

Visualizing Content

Visualizing the pictures the author creates with words can help you understand the **emotional meaning** of a text.

Read the first paragraph of "In Search of Memory". Discuss the questions with a partner.

1. What pictures come to mind as you read?

2. Why do you think these images have stayed in the author's mind?

3. Why is he telling these stories to the reader?

Now read the text to see how the author's childhood memories are linked to his further interest in memory in his professional life.

In Search of Memory

By Eric Kandel

Eric Kandel is a Nobel Prize winner and University Professor of Neuroscience and co-director of the Center for Brain Science at Columbia University. He began his career with psychoanalysis, studying Freud's insights. Later, he decided to study neurology to understand more about how the mind works. In addition to major textbooks in the field, his recent publications include In Search of Memory: The Emergence of a New Science of Mind *and* The Age of Insight: The Quest to Understand the Unconscious Mind in Art, Mind, and Brain.

1   Memory has always fascinated me. Mental time travel allows me to leave the writing of this sentence in my study at home overlooking the Hudson River and project myself backward sixty-seven years and eastward across the Atlantic Ocean to Vienna, Austria, where I was born and where my parents owned a small toy store. The memories of those days — hearing the bangs on the door, being ordered by the Nazi policemen to go to a stranger's apartment, finding ourselves robbed of our belongings, the disappearance and reappearance of my father — are the most powerful memories of my early life. **In retrospect**, my family was fortunate. After one **humiliating** and frightening year, Ludwig, then fourteen, and I were able to leave Vienna for the United States to live with our grandparents in New York. Our parents joined us six months later. The **bewilderment**, poverty, humiliation, and fear I experienced that last year in Vienna made it a defining period[1] in my life. I cannot help but link my later interest in mind — in how people behave, the unpredictability of motivation, and the persistence of memory — to my last year in Vienna.

2   The insights provided by the new science of mind are most evident in our understanding of the molecular mechanisms the brain uses to store memories. Memory — the ability to acquire and store information as simple as the routine details of daily life and as complex as **abstract** knowledge of geography or algebra — is one of the most remarkable

---

[1] *defining period:* a time in your life that determined the direction of your future

aspects of human behavior. Memory enables us to solve the problems we confront in everyday life by gathering several facts at once, an ability that is vital to problem solving. In a larger sense, memory provides our lives with continuity. It gives us a **coherent** picture of the past that puts current experience in perspective. The picture may not be rational or accurate, but it **persists**. Without the **binding** force of memory, experience would be broken into as many fragments as there are moments in life. Without the mental time travel provided by memory, we would have no awareness of our personal history, no way of remembering the joys that serve as the **luminous** milestones of our life. We are who we are because of what we learn and remember.

3 Our memory processes serve us best when we can easily recall the joyful events of our lives and diminish the painful impact of **traumatic** events and disappointments. But sometimes, horrific memories persist and damage people's lives, as happens in post-traumatic stress disorder,[2] a condition suffered by some people who have experienced first-hand the terrible events of genocide, war, rape, or natural disasters.

4 Memory is essential not only for the continuity of individual identity, but also for the **transmission** of culture and for the evolution and continuity of societies over centuries. Although the size and structure of the human brain have not changed since *Homo sapiens* first appeared in East Africa some 150,000 years ago, the learning capabilities of individual human beings and their historical memory have grown over the centuries through shared learning — that is, through the transmission of culture.

5 Much as shared memory enriches our lives as individuals, loss of memory destroys our sense of self. It **severs** the connection with the past and with other people, and it can **afflict** the developing infant as well as the mature adult. Down's syndrome,[3] Alzheimer's disease,[4] and age-related memory loss are familiar examples of the many diseases that affect memory.

6 The new science of mind holds out the hope that greater understanding of the science of memory will lead to better treatments for both memory loss and persistent painful memories. Yet it goes beyond a search for solutions to devastating illnesses. The new science of mind attempts to penetrate the mystery of consciousness, including the **ultimate** mystery: how each person's brain creates the consciousness of a unique self and the sense of free will.

---

[2] *post-traumatic stress disorder (P.T.S.D.):* a mental illness that can develop after a very bad experience, such as fighting in a war

[3] *Down's syndrome:* a condition that some people are born with, that stops them from developing in a normal way, both mentally and physically

[4] *Alzheimer's disease:* an illness that attacks and gradually destroys parts of the brain, especially in older people, so that they forget things and lose their ability to take care of themselves

COMPREHENSION

A Main Ideas

Complete the sentences based on the main ideas of the reading. Use your own words.

1. The events in Austria affected the author's mind because _____

   _____

   _____

2. Storing memories is essential to human life because _____

   _____

   _____

3. Knowing more about the way the brain functions can help us _____

   _____

   _____

B Close Reading

Read the quotes from the reading. Circle the statement that best explains each quote. Share your answers with a partner.

1. "In retrospect, my family was fortunate." *(paragraph 1)*

   a. It didn't seem that way at the time.

   b. Other families didn't suffer as much.

   c. His family suffered a lot.

2. "The bewilderment, poverty, humiliation, and fear I experienced that last year in Vienna made it a defining period in my life. I cannot help but link my later interest in mind — in how people behave, the unpredictability of motivation, and the persistence of memory — to my last year in Vienna." *(paragraph 1)*

   a. I can't help the unpredictability of art and the persistence of memory.

   b. I can't help how people behave or the facts of my last year in Austria.

   c. What happened to me as a child determined my scientific career.

3. "Without the binding force of memory, experience would be broken into as many fragments as there are moments in life." *(paragraph 2)*

   a. If we didn't have memory, every experience would be an isolated event.

   b. With the help of memory, every moment in life is experienced separately.

   c. Without memory, there would be no experiences.

4. "Although the size and structure of the human brain have not changed since *Homo sapiens* first appeared in East Africa some 150,000 years ago, the learning capabilities of individual human beings and their historical memory have grown over the centuries through shared learning — that is, through the transmission of culture." (*paragraph 4*)

   a. Culture has increased the size and structure of the human brain.

   b. The human brain hasn't changed over the years.

   c. Shared learning has increased our knowledge and historical memory.

5. "The new science of mind holds out the hope that greater understanding of the science of memory will lead to better treatments for both memory loss and persistent painful memories. Yet **it** goes beyond a search for solutions to devastating illnesses." (*paragraph 6*)

   a. "It" refers to "the hope."

   b. "It" refers to "the new science of mind."

   c. "It" refers to "greater understanding."

6. "Yet it goes beyond a search for solutions to devastating illnesses. The new science of mind attempts to penetrate the mystery of consciousness, including the ultimate mystery: how each person's brain creates the consciousness of a unique self and the sense of free will." (*paragraph 6*)

   a. The insights of brain science relate only to the secrets of devastating illnesses.

   b. The insights of brain science can unlock the mysteries of a unique person.

   c. The insights of brain science relate to philosophical questions as well as medical issues.

VOCABULARY

Ⓐ Guessing from Context

Read each quote from the reading. Try to guess the meaning of the words in bold from the context. Write the clues that helped you guess and your guess. Then consult a dictionary and write the definition.

1. "Memory — the ability to acquire and store information as simple as the routine details of daily life and as complex as **abstract** knowledge of geography or algebra — is one of the most remarkable aspects of human behavior." (*paragraph 2*)

   abstract   Clues: _complex / algebra_

   Guess: _theoretical_

   Dictionary: _existing only as an idea rather than something you_

   can see or touch

   (continued on next page)

2. "In a larger sense, memory provides our lives with continuity. It gives us a **coherent** picture of the past that puts current experience in perspective." *(paragraph 2)*

coherent   Clues: _____

                   Guess: _____

                   Dictionary: _____

3. "Without the **binding** force of memory, experience would be broken into as many fragments as there are moments in life." *(paragraph 2)*

binding   Clues: _____

                   Guess: _____

                   Dictionary: _____

4. "Without the mental time travel provided by memory, we would have no awareness of our personal history, no way of remembering the joys that serve as the **luminous** milestones of our life. We are who we are because of what we learn and remember." *(paragraph 2)*

luminous   Clues: _____

                   Guess: _____

                   Dictionary: _____

5. "Our memory processes serve us best when we can easily recall the joyful events of our lives and diminish the painful impact of **traumatic** events and disappointments. But sometimes, horrific memories persist and damage people's lives." *(paragraph 3)*

traumatic   Clues: _____

                   Guess: _____

                   Dictionary: _____

6. "Much as shared memory enriches our lives as individuals, loss of memory destroys our sense of self. It **severs** the connection with the past and with other people, and it can afflict the developing infant as well as the mature adult." *(paragraph 5)*

sever   Clues: _____

                 Guess: _____

                 Dictionary: _____

B Word Forms

1 Fill in the chart with the correct word forms. Some categories can have more than one form. Use a dictionary if necessary. An *X* indicates there is no form in that category.

	NOUN	VERB	ADJECTIVE	ADVERB
1.	*affliction*		afflicted / *afflicting*	X
2.			bewildered /	bewilderingly
3.	humiliation		humiliated /	
4.		persist		
5.			traumatic	

2 Complete the sentences with the correct form of the words from the chart. The first letter of each word has been given to you as a clue. Compare answers with a partner.

1. As a child, Kandel was b ewildered _____ by the political changes in his native Vienna, Austria.

2. The h _____ of having all his things taken away is difficult for a child to endure.

3. Kandel was t _____ by his experiences, but fortunately he and his family were able to escape to America.

4. Sometimes the t _____ is so painful that people can never forget.

5. The p _____ of his memories led him not to bitterness but to a career in biology.

6. As a researcher, he worked p _____ with the neural system of a simple animal called Aplysia, a snail with very large nerve cells.

7. His work will teach us more about the way the brain works and will help people who suffer from the many a _____ of the brain.

8. The b _____ changes brought about by advanced age may one day find a solution.

C Synonyms

Complete the essay with the words or phrases from the box. Use the synonym in parentheses to help you select the correct word. Compare answers with a partner.

abstract	binding	in retrospect	sever	ultimate
afflicted	coherent	luminous	transmitted	
bewildering	humiliating	persists	traumatic	

Freud's theory of mind was a _____ luminous _____ milestone
1. (brilliant)

in the history of science because it provided a way to understand the

_____ hidden processes of the brain. Despite their faults,
2. (confusing)

Freud's theories offered a humane way to treat people _____
3. (tormented)

by mental problems or suffering from _____ memories.
4. (painful)

Freud felt that by appealing to the rational mind, unconscious fears and

_____ obsessions would diminish in intensity. If people could
5. (demeaning)

be brave and _____ their emotional ties to painful memories
6. (cut)

of the past, they could form a _____ and realistic picture of
7. (understandable)

their future.

_____, many of Freud's insights aimed at linking
8. (Looking backward)

psychology to physiology — _____ the workings
9. (connecting)

of the mind to the workings of the brain — have proven fruitful. Only an

interdisciplinary approach linking psychology to biology can answer the

_____ questions about the meaning of consciousness.
10. (theoretical)

In the 1980s, cognitive neuroscience made enormous progress with the invention

of brain imaging, a technology that allows scientists to realize their dream of looking

into the human brain. The activity of different parts of the brain is measured and

_____ to a computer screen. As people perceive a visual
11. (communicated)

image, think about a spatial route, or start a voluntary action, scientists can see the

activity that _____ in various parts of the brain. Eventually,
12. (continues)

scientists hope to address the _____ questions of how we
13. (final)

think, feel, learn, and remember.

D Collocations

Check (✓) the collocations (words that are often paired together). Discuss your answers with a partner.

☐ 1. confront a problem

☐ 2. confront an issue

☐ 3. confront the inevitable

☐ 4. sever ties

☐ 5. sever contact

☐ 6. sever discussion

☐ 7. binding ties

☐ 8. binding contracts

☐ 9. binding events

NOTE-TAKING: Making Lists

Go back to the reading. As you read it again, make a list of all the reasons given for the importance of memory. Make another list of the ways we can benefit from future discoveries in the science of mind.

WHY MEMORY IS IMPORTANT	HOW BRAIN SCIENCE CAN HELP US
1. is essential for problem solving and reasoning	1. helps us understand how the brain functions
2.	2.
3.	3.
4.	4.

CRITICAL THINKING

Discuss the questions in a small group. Be prepared to share your answers with the class.

1. Sometimes forgetting is a blessing, and remembering is a curse. Explain why this could be true. Has this ever happened to you?

2. Why are childhood memories so important?

3. Why is it so hard to study the way the brain functions?

4. How would you feel if a close relative lost his or her memory? How would you feel if you realized that you were losing your memory?

A **Warm-Up**

Discuss the question in a small group. Share your answers with the class.

Which of these are easier to remember? Why?

☐ how to ride a bike

☐ how to do algebra

☐ how to play an instrument

☐ how to dance

☐ how to remember vocabulary words

B **Reading Strategy**

Scanning a Chart

Many textbooks use a **chart to summarize the important information** presented in each chapter. The chart is therefore a valuable reading and study tool. Knowing how to read a chart — by **first scanning (examining) its general layout** (structure) and then studying its contents — is a skill that all students need to master.

Scan the layout of the chart in the reading. Then answer the questions. Write your answers on the lines.

1. To which column of the chart (1, 2, or 3) would you go to read about how the amygdala functions?

_____

2. Identify five different kinds of memory referred to in the chart. Where did you find this information?

_____

3. Which region of the brain is responsible for processing spatial memory?

_____

4. What kind of memory is processed by the amygdala?

_____

Now, as you read the text, you will be able to learn more about how the brain helps humans remember things.

THE BRAIN AND HUMAN MEMORY

The human brain has about 100 billion cells. Most of these cells are neurons or nerve cells. A neuron is either in a resting state or shooting an electrical impulse down an axon. A neuron has a cell body and a long little thread or fiber called an axon; at the very end it shoots out a chemical called a transmitter. This chemical goes across a gap (synapse) where it triggers another neuron to send a message. This is the biological basis of the functioning of the brain in all its activities, including memory.

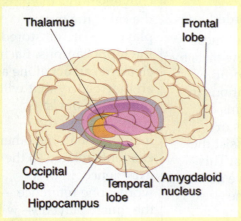

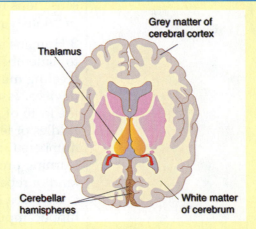

The brain is responsible for human memory. This **phenomenon** of remembering is a complex one that calls upon the work of several regions of the brain.

REGIONS OF THE BRAIN	MAJOR OPERATING FUNCTIONS	KINDS OF MEMORY PROCESSED
The **pre-frontal lobe:** It is located at the very front of the brain.	**1** It allows humans to **hold on to** a piece of information temporarily while they complete a task. **2** Its intense activity in matters related to thinking and decision-making explains why human foreheads are so much higher than those of their primate relatives, the apes, whose pre-frontal lobes are much less developed.	SHORT-TERM MEMORY (WORKING MEMORY) — related to what a person is currently aware of or thinking about — is made possible by the pre-frontal lobe.

(continued on next page)

REGIONS OF THE BRAIN	MAJOR OPERATING FUNCTIONS	KINDS OF MEMORY PROCESSED
The **hippocampus:** It is located in the inner fold of the temporal lobe and has been given its name because it **resembles** the curved tail of a seahorse (*hippokampos* in Greek).	**1** It helps humans transfer information from their short-term memory to their long-term memory (memory put into storage). **2** Because data communicated in the various sensory areas of the cortex[1] **converge** in the hippocampus, it can be thought of as a **sorting** center that compares new sensations with previously recorded ones. **3** Humans sometimes try to remember new facts by creating **mnemonic devices**, associations in the form of poems or riddles or letters or numbers that assist the learning process. This kind of repetitive activity takes place in the hippocampus. **4** The hippocampus creates associations of objects' various properties.[2] When such associations have finally been recorded in the hippocampus, the cortex is able to **reconstitute** the associations into what we call memory.	DECLARATIVE MEMORY — the memory of facts and events — is made possible by the hippocampus, the cortical structures surrounding it, and the neural pathways connected to the cortex. For instance, all the elements of an "episode" such as a friend's birthday party — the people's faces, the conversations, the gifts, the cake, the music played — are all stored in the hippocampus. Each element can act alone as an index entry that will **retrieve** to one's consciousness the memory of all the other elements related to the experience. In other words, one reference — the music played — will automatically "cross-refer" and trigger a memory of the other elements of the episode.
The **right hippocampus**	Its "place cells" help create space maps in the mind.	SPATIAL MEMORY — the memory that records information about one's environment — is **restricted** to the right hippocampus alone.

[1] *cortex:* the outer layer of the brain

[2] *properties:* qualities or powers that belong naturally to something

REGIONS OF THE BRAIN	MAJOR OPERATING FUNCTIONS	KINDS OF MEMORY PROCESSED
The **amygdala:** It is part of the limbic system.[3]	**1** It **brings** emotional memory **into play**. **2** It also helps humans manage fear.	EMOTIONAL MEMORY — the memory of events evoking particularly strong emotions — is made possible by the amygdala.
The **cerebellum, basal ganglia,** and **motor cortex:** The cerebellum is located in the back of the brain stem and is attached to the midbrain; the basal ganglia is located in the forebrain; the motor cortex is located in the back region of the frontal lobe.	These regions are all involved with motor control.	PROCEDURAL MEMORY — motor memory of skills that require practice such as knowing how to ride a bicycle — is established in these regions. (Amnesia caused by lesions[4] to the hippocampus does not affect a person's procedural memory.)

[3] *limbic system:* includes brain structures concerned with emotion, behavior, motivation, and memory, including the hippocampus, amygdala, anterior thalamic nuclei, septum, limbic cortex, and fornix

[4] *lesion:* an abnormal change or scar in a part of someone's body such as their lungs or brain, caused by injury or illness

COMPREHENSION

Ⓐ   Main Ideas

Match the different types of memory with their functions and the parts of the brain directly involved. Compare answers with a partner.

TYPE OF MEMORY	FUNCTION	PART OF THE BRAIN
1. short-term memory	**a.** encoding information to remember at a later time	**i.** amygdala and limbic system
_____ **2.** long-term memory	**b.** a mental map	**ii.** right hippocampus
_____ **3.** declarative memory	**c.** remembering motor skills	**iii.** hippocampus
_____ **4.** spatial memory	**d.** intense personal experiences	**iv.** cerebellum
_____ **5.** emotional memory	**e.** remembering episodes	**v.** pre-frontal lobe
_____ **6.** procedural memory	**f.** holding information temporarily	

B Close Reading

Read the quotes from the reading. Circle the statement that best explains each quote. Share your answers with a partner.

1. "[The pre-frontal lobe's] intense activity in matters related to thinking and decision-making explains why human foreheads are so much higher than those of their primate relatives, the apes, whose pre-frontal lobes are much less developed." *(Major Operating Functions, pre-frontal lobe, 2)*

   a. The physical development of the pre-frontal lobe in both humans and apes is directly related to higher-level thinking abilities.

   b. The physical development of the pre-frontal lobe is more advanced in apes than in humans.

   c. The physical development of the pre-frontal lobe is the same in humans and apes.

2. "Declarative memory — the memory of facts and events — is made possible by the hippocampus, the cortical structures surrounding it, and the neural pathways connected to the cortex." *(Kinds of Memory Processed, hippocampus)*

   a. For declarative memory to be activated, the hippocampus works all by itself.

   b. For declarative memory to be activated, the hippocampus receives help from the surrounding cortex and nerves.

   c. For declarative memory to be activated, the cortex plays a more prominent role than the hippocampus.

3. "Amnesia caused by lesions to the hippocampus does not affect a person's procedural memory." *(Kinds of Memory Processed, the cerebellum, basal ganglia, and motor cortex)*

   a. Damage to one part of memory implies damage to all other parts of memory.

   b. Damage to one part of the brain doesn't mean all types of memory are impossible.

   c. Damage to motor skills implies damage to higher-level thinking skills.

VOCABULARY

A Synonyms

Read the sentences about brain science. Match each word or phrase in bold with its synonym in the box below. Compare answers with a partner.

 1. Functional magnetic resonance imaging (fMRI) is a relatively new procedure that **brings into play** the magnetic properties of blood flow in the brain.

_____ 2. With the fMRI, scientists can **reconstitute** on a computer the brain processes related to perception and motor activity.

_____ 3. The use of this machine is not **restricted** to research; it is also used to diagnose the effects of strokes and Alzheimer's disease.

_____ 4. To improve long-term memory, **mnemonic devices** are used to make memorization easier.

_____ 5. Memory aids can be poems or easy-to-remember visual or auditory clues that allow people to **retrieve** the information they need.

_____ 6. An example of a mnemonic device can be found in musical notation: the lines in the treble clef represent the notes EGBDF — Every Good Boy Deserves Fun — which **resembles** a little poem.

_____ 7. These memory aids work over long periods of time because it is easier to **hold on to** meaningful information as opposed to arbitrary sequences.

_____ 8. The brain **sorts** information and stores it in different places.

_____ 9. Many memory functions **converge** in the hippocampus.

_____ 10. The **phenomenon** of neuroplasticity means that the brain can adapt and change even into old age.

a. makes use of	**f.** reassemble
b. come together	**g.** is similar to
c. retain	**h.** limited
d. memory aids	**i.** recall
e. existence	**j.** classifies

B **Singular and Plural of Words of Greek or Latin Origin**

WORDS OF GREEK OR LATIN ORIGIN	SINGULAR	PLURAL
Human memory is a complex **phenomenon**.	phenomen**on**	phenomen**a**
This part of the brain has a single **stratum** of cells.	strat**um**	strat**a**
Each of these elements alone could act as an **index** entry.	ind**ex**	ind**ices**
This is the biological **basis** of the functioning of the brain.	bas**is**	bas**es**

Look at the list of words of Greek or Latin origin. What are their plural forms? Write them on the lines.

SINGULAR	PLURAL		SINGULAR	PLURAL
1. criterion	_criteria_		6. parenthesis	_____
2. datum	_____		7. synthesis	_____
3. analysis	_____		8. medium	_____
4. bacterium	_____		9. appendix	_____
5. matrix	_____		10. addendum	_____

CRITICAL THINKING

Discuss the questions with a partner.

1. What would happen if someone's amygdala were injured in an accident?

2. What would happen to someone if that person's hippocampus were injured?

3. What would happen if someone's cerebellum were injured?

LINKING READINGS ONE AND TWO

Fill in the chart linking what Kandel discussed in Reading One with the different types of memory and parts of the brain presented in Reading Two. Compare answers with a partner.

	KANDEL DISCUSSED	TYPE OF MEMORY AND PART OF BRAIN INVOLVED
1.	Being chased from his home	*Emotional memory / amygdala*
2.	Post-traumatic stress disorder	
3.	Acquiring/storing abstract knowledge	
4.	Continuity	
5.	Luminous joys	
6.	Alzheimer's disease	

A Warm-Up

Discuss the questions in a small group. Share your answers with the class.

Based on the information communicated in Reading Two:

1. Where do you think the ability to play music is stored in the brain?

2. Does it involve one or more than one part of the brain?

B Reading Strategy

Skimming First Two Paragraphs

Skimming the first two paragraphs of a text and circling **keywords** help you to have a clearer **idea of what the text will discuss**.

Skim the first two paragraphs of the reading and circle one or two keywords you find in each paragraph. Then write them on the lines.

PARAGRAPH 1: _____

PARAGRAPH 2: _____

Now read the text. Did you circle the most appropriate keywords?

Music and the Brain

By Oliver Sacks

Oliver Sacks is a world-renowned neurologist and professor of neurology and psychiatry at Columbia University. His work was depicted in the film Awakenings. *He has written many best-selling books, including* The Man Who Mistook His Wife for a Hat, An Anthropologist on Mars, Musicophilia, *and the autobiographical study* Uncle Tungston.

In the following excerpt from his book Musicophilia, *Oliver Sacks describes what happened to a well-known British musician and musicologist, Clive Wearing.*

(continued on next page)

Clive Wearing suffered an infection (herpes encephalitis) in 1985, which affected parts of his brain concerned with memory. He was left with a memory span of only seconds, which Oliver Sacks calls "the most devastating case of amnesia ever recorded." Here, Sacks examines how Clive and his wife struggle to cope with his condition.

1   Clive Wearing's life as an **eminent** musician and musicologist was over. To imagine the future was no more possible than to remember the past — both were **engulfed in** amnesia. Yet somehow he always recognized Deborah as his wife every time she visited. How, when he recognized no one else with any **consistency**, did Clive recognize Deborah?

2   There are clearly many sorts of memory and emotional memory is one of the deepest and least understood. His passionate relationship with Deborah, a relationship that began before the encephalitis infection and one that centers, in part, on their shared love for music, has engraved itself in him so deeply in areas of his brain unaffected by the disease that the worst amnesia ever recorded cannot **eradicate** it.

3   The other miracle was the discovery Deborah made early on that his musical powers were totally intact. Clive could sit down at the organ and play with both hands on the keyboard, as if this were easier than riding a bicycle. He **retained** his remarkable knowledge of music, his ability to sight-read,[1] to play the piano and organ, sing, conduct a choir, in the masterful way he did before he became ill.

4   It's very clear that two different sorts of memory can exist: a conscious memory of events (episodic memory) and an unconscious memory for procedures, and that such procedural memory is **unimpaired** in amnesia.

5   This is dramatically clear with Clive, too, for he can shave, shower, look after his toilet, and dress elegantly with taste and style, he moves confidently and is fond of dancing. He talks fluently and abundantly, using a large vocabulary; he can read and write in several languages. He is good at calculation. If he is asked how to do these things, he cannot say, but he does them. Whatever involves a sequence or pattern of action, he does fluently, unhesitatingly.

6   But can Clive's beautiful playing and singing, his masterly conducting, his powers of improvisation be adequately characterized as simple "skills" or "procedure"? His playing is filled with intelligence and feeling. Can any artistic or creative performance **of this caliber** be explained by "procedural memory"?

---

[1] *sight-read:* to play or sing written music when you look at it for the first time, without practicing it first

7   Each time Clive sings or plays the piano or conducts a choir, automatism comes to his aid. But what comes out in an artistic or creative performance, though it depends on automatisms, is anything but automatic. The actual performance reanimates him, engages him as a creative person; it becomes fresh and alive, perhaps contains new improvisations or **innovations**. Clive's performance self seems, to those who know him, just as **vivid** and complete as it was before his illness.

8   The rope that is let down from heaven for Clive comes not with recalling the past but with performance — and it holds only as long as the performance lasts. Without performance, the thread is broken and he is thrown back once again into the **abyss**. It is not the remembrance of things past,[2] the "once" that Clive **yearns for**, but can never achieve. It is the filling of the present, the now, and this is only possible when he is totally **immersed in** the successive moments of an act. It is the "now" that bridges the abyss.

_____

[2] *remembrance of things past:* an allusion to French author Marcel Proust's novel *À la recherche du temps perdu (Remembrance of Things Past/In Search of Lost Time)*

COMPREHENSION

 Main Ideas

Read each statement. Decide if it is *True* or *False* according to the reading. Check (✓) the appropriate box. If it is false, change it to make it true. Discuss your answers with a partner.

	TRUE	FALSE
1. Despite his amnesia, Clive's musical genius has not disappeared.	☐	☐
2. Episodic memory explains how the unconscious is working these days in Clive's life.	☐	☐
3. Clive hesitates to do anything that has a pattern to it.	☐	☐
4. When Clive plays music, he goes beyond automatic recall and becomes creative.	☐	☐
5. Clive has to keep performing in order to find his connection to the past.	☐	☐

B Close Reading

Read the quotes from the reading. Circle the statement that best explains each quote. Share your answers with a partner.

1. "His passionate relationship with Deborah, a relationship that began before the encephalitis infection and one that centers, in part, on their shared love for music, has engraved itself in him so deeply in areas of his brain unaffected by the disease that the worst amnesia ever recorded cannot eradicate it." *(paragraph 2)*

   "It" at the end of the sentence refers to . . .

   a. the disease.

   b. his passionate relationship with Deborah.

   c. the worst amnesia.

2. "Whatever involves a sequence or pattern of action, he does fluently, unhesitatingly." *(paragraph 5)*

   a. He can do anything that involves a series of logical steps, without any difficulty.

   b. He can do anything that involves fluency and confidence, without any difficulty.

   c. He can do anything that involves a pattern with fluency and hesitation.

3. "Can any artistic or creative performance of this caliber be explained by 'procedural memory'?" *(paragraph 6)*

   With this question, the author is wondering . . .

   a. if procedural memory can explain such great creativity.

   b. if procedural memory will allow other creative performances.

   c. if procedural memory has such a caliber.

4. "The rope that is let down from heaven for Clive comes not with recalling the past but with performance — and it holds only as long as the performance lasts." *(paragraph 8)*

   a. Performing saves Clive from the feeling of being lost.

   b. Performing leaves Clive hanging by a thread in space and time.

   c. Performing well depends on the strength of the rope Clive holds on to.

5. "It is the 'now' that bridges the abyss." *(paragraph 8)*

   a. The present causes the emptiness.

   b. It is through the present that he finds the past.

   c. The present is lost in the abyss of the past.

VOCABULARY

A Synonyms

Read the sentences. Match each word or phrase in bold with its synonym in the box below. Compare answers with a partner.

__f__ 1. Brain diseases can plunge patients into an **abyss** that isolates them from friends and family.

_____ 2. For example, a patient with Alzheimer's, an incurable brain disease, will not even recognize members of the family with any **consistency**.

_____ 3. As the patient becomes more and more **engulfed in** the devastating effects of the illness, participation in normal social interactions becomes impossible.

_____ 4. The caregivers themselves, usually family members, become **immersed in** the treatment of their loved ones and forget that there is a "normal" life beyond the sickroom.

_____ 5. Fronto-temporal dementia is different from Alzheimer's disease because patients usually **retain** their memory at first, but fall into long periods of silence, showing indifference and odd personality changes.

_____ 6. A **vivid** picture of the disease at work could be the following scenario.

_____ 7. A distinguished gentleman, once an **eminent** cook, burns every pot in the house, and sits withdrawn and silent, no longer speaking to his wife at dinner.

_____ 8. Although he seems **unimpaired** when you look at him, his inability to communicate has affected all his work relationships to such an extent that he has lost his job.

_____ 9. In one respect, knowing the unfortunate diagnosis of fronto-temporal dementia at least explains to the confused wife how a man **of this caliber** — her intelligent, kind, and hard-working husband — has become responsible for such troubling behavior.

_____ 10. Nevertheless, she **yearns for** a cure, but with very little hope.

_____ 11. Yet, there may eventually be a way to **eradicate** this disease.

_____ 12. Recently, thanks to **innovations** in science and technology, researchers have identified drugs that may treat the accumulation of abnormal proteins in the brain, which is a biochemical and genetic defect that causes some forms of the disease. Tests on human subjects are expected to start soon.

a.	eliminate	**g.**	undamaged
b.	of this quality	**h.**	keep
c.	new methods	**i.**	desperately desires
d.	swallowed up by	**j.**	regularity
e.	completely involved in	**k.**	well-known
f.	deep emptiness	**l.**	dramatic

B Using the Dictionary

Read the dictionary entries for *eminent*, *immanent*, and *imminent*.

> **eminent** *adj.* famous and admired by many people: *an eminent anthropologist*
>
> **immanent** *adj.* **1** a quality that is immanent seems to be naturally present: *Hope seems immanent in human nature.* **2** God or another spiritual power that is immanent is present everywhere.
>
> **imminent** *adj.* an event that is imminent is an event that will happen very soon: *A new trade agreement is imminent.*

Now complete each sentence with the appropriate word.

1. _____ throughout the medical profession is the hope to find cures for certain diseases.

2. When researchers say that the discovery of a cure for any disease is _____, people become very optimistic.

3. Ironically, the _____ brain surgeon was now suffering from the disease that he had studied all his life.

4. Even if danger was _____, the doctor made light of it so as not to get his patients into a panic.

5. Everyone hoped that this _____ statesman would receive the best medical treatment possible.

C Collocations

Check (✓) the collocations (words that are often paired together). Discuss your answers with a partner.

□ **1.** yearn to be free

□ **2.** yearn to see her

□ **3.** yearn to have dinner

□ **4.** a vivid color

□ **5.** a vivid vocabulary

□ **6.** a vivid personality

□ **7.** eradicate a disease

□ **8.** eradicate a person

□ **9.** eradicate an issue

With **figurative language**, writers are able to get their point across **more dramatically** and effectively by means of the **pictures that they draw with words**.

EXAMPLE:
- Night's candles are burned out. (Shakespeare, *Romeo and Juliet*)

INTERPRETATION:
Here Shakespeare uses figurative language. His "night's candles" refer to the stars. The "candles" are "burned out" because the day is beginning and the stars are disappearing from the sky.

In paragraph 8 of the reading, the author uses figurative language. Reread the paragraph. Pay attention to the underlined words and discuss their meaning with a partner.

The rope that is let down from heaven for Clive comes not with recalling the past but with performance — and it holds only as long as the performance lasts. Without performance, the thread is broken and he is thrown back once again into the abyss. It is not the remembrance of things past, the "once" that Clive yearns for, but can never achieve. It is the filling of the present, the now, and this is only possible when he is totally immersed in the successive moments of an act. It is the "now" that bridges the abyss.

	FIGURATIVE LANGUAGE	INTERPRETATION
1.	a rope let down from heaven	*a heavenly gift; a chance to climb up from deep emptiness*
2.	the broken thread	
3.	thrown back into the abyss	
4.	yearning for the past	
5.	bridging the abyss	

GRAMMAR FOR READING: Rhetorical Questions

> A **rhetorical question** may look like a question, but it is a **way of making a statement** or introducing a new idea **without expecting a reply**. Unlike questions of fact, rhetorical questions often have no answer or no universally accepted answer. Rhetorical questions often serve as a **way to prepare the reader for the author's opinions**.
>
> **EXAMPLE:**
> **Question of Fact:** When was the new law passed?
> **Rhetorical Question:** What could that law possibly mean?

1 Identifying Rhetorical Questions

Work with a partner, Read the questions and decide if they are *rhetorical questions (R)* or *questions of fact (F)*. Discuss the reasons for your answers.

___F___ 1. What caused Clive's amnesia?

_____ 2. Is procedural memory an unconscious memory?

_____ 3. Isn't music a universal language?

_____ 4. Has Clive been able to sight-read since his amnesia set in?

_____ 5. Can there be anything worse than not having a way to remember the past and look into the future?

_____ 6. Does love conquer all?

_____ 7. Does Clive still have a large vocabulary?

_____ 8. Are Clive's piano performances merely a sign of rote learning?

2 Considering the Author's Point of View

Go back to the reading. Underline the three rhetorical questions asked by the author. Then write each one on the lines and answer the questions that follow.

1. _____

   Q: What answer does the author give to this question? Is his opinion clearly stated?

   A: _____

2. _____

   Q: What answer does the author give to this question? Is his opinion clearly stated?

   A: _____

3. _____

   Q: What answer does the author give to this question? Is his opinion clearly stated?

   A: _____

NOTE-TAKING: Using Keywords as a Study Tool

Go back to the reading and read it again. For each paragraph, write down the keywords and a few notes next to each one. You should try to predict the questions the teacher will ask. For each paragraph, write a possible question.

1. Keywords: *Clive Wearing's life / amnesia*

   Notes: *recognized Deborah, no one else*

   Question: *As a patient with amnesia, how many people did Clive recognize?*

2. Keywords: _____

   Notes: _____

   Question: _____

3. Keywords: _____

   Notes: _____

   Question: _____

4. Keywords: _____

   Notes: _____

   Question: _____

5. Keywords: _____

   Notes: _____

   Question: _____

6. Keywords: _____

   Notes: _____

   Question: _____

7. Keywords: _____

   Notes: _____

   Question: _____

8. Keywords: _____

   Notes: _____

   Question: _____

Now ask a partner your questions. Writing questions and answering them is a good way to prepare for an exam.

CRITICAL THINKING

1 Discuss the questions in a small group. Be prepared to share your answers with the class.

   1. Which parts of Wearing's brain were affected by memory loss? Which parts were not?

   2. Some people say that love conquers all. Do you think the story of Clive Wearing supports this idea?

   3. Who do you believe suffers more from Clive's amnesia, Clive or Deborah?

   4. Dr. Oliver Sacks writes with great sympathy and humanity about people affected by brain disorders. In paragraph 3, he calls Wearing's ability to still play music "a miracle" because Dr. Sacks understands how important music was to this man. Look at the word choices in paragraphs 7 and 8. How does the author's choice of words show his compassion and feeling for Clive Wearing?

2 Read this list of events and decide whether they are directed by the conscious *episodic memory (E)* or the unconscious *procedural memory (P)*.

_____ 1. A young man remembers the first time he had a piano lesson.

_____ 2. A woman always combs her hair after using the dryer.

_____ 3. After many years, a man goes into the ocean and remembers how to swim.

_____ 4. A woman returns to a restaurant she went to on her honeymoon and remembers what she ordered.

_____ 5. A man remembers how to make an omelet.

_____ 6. A woman remembers her first kiss.

AFTER YOU READ

BRINGING IT ALL TOGETHER

Work in groups of three. Role-play an interview with Eric Kandel and Oliver Sacks about memory and memory loss. The journalist will ask questions of the others. Kandel and Sacks will express their opinions. Use some of the vocabulary you studied in the chapter (for a complete list, go to page 138).

TOPIC: The different types of memory and memory loss

ROLES:
- Journalist
- Eric Kandel
- Oliver Sacks

Questions:

- Professor Kandel: How was your life affected by events in your childhood?
- Professor Sacks: What does the case of Clive Wearing tell us about the functioning of the brain?
- Professor Kandel: What is your opinion about this case?
- Professor Sacks: How does what Professor Kandel say about memory make us appreciate all the more the tragic condition in which Clive Wearing finds himself?

Add your own questions:

- _____

- _____

WRITING ACTIVITY

Write a three-paragraph essay about your most important memory — a memory that was a "defining moment" for you. How did your attitude toward love, studies, a career, or life values change as result of this experience? Use more than five of the words or idioms you studied in the chapter.

- **Introduction:** Explain the moment to the reader.

- **Body Paragraph:** Tell the reader how this event or situation affected your life and the choices you have made.

- **Conclusion:** Discuss the future.

DISCUSSION AND WRITING TOPICS

Discuss these topics in a small group. Choose one of them and write a paragraph or two about it. Use the vocabulary from the chapter.

1. What do you do to help yourself remember? How do you memorize material for school? For professional purposes?

2. Oliver Sacks's books deal with very extreme cases of neurological difficulties. Why do people find it very interesting to learn about cases like that of Clive Wearing? What do such cases teach us? Do you find these studies interesting? Useful?

3. Eric Kandel calls memory "mental time travel." Why does he say this? Do you agree or disagree? Can you give examples from your life?

4. Kandel calls understanding individual consciousness and free will the "ultimate mystery." How does his thinking seem to be close to philosophy or religion? Do you think that science can or should deal with these problems?

VOCABULARY

Nouns	Verbs	Adjectives	Phrases and Idioms
abyss	afflict	abstract *	bring sth into play
bewilderment	converge	binding	engulfed in
consistency *	eradicate	coherent *	hold on to
innovation *	persist *	eminent	immersed in
phenomenon *	reconstitute	humiliating	in retrospect
transmission *	resemble	luminous	mnemonic device
	retain *	restricted *	of this caliber
	retrieve	sorting	yearn for
	sever	traumatic	
		ultimate	
		unimpaired	
		vivid	

* = AWL (Academic Word List) item

SELF-ASSESSMENT

In this chapter you learned to:

○ Visualize the content of a text to understand it better

○ Scan a chart to find specific information

○ Skim the first two paragraphs of a text to get an idea of what it will discuss

○ Guess the meaning of words from the context

○ Use dictionary entries to learn the meanings of words

○ Understand and use synonyms, collocations, different word forms, and words of Greek or Latin origin

○ Recognize and use figurative language and rhetorical questions

○ Take notes by making lists and using keywords as study tools

What can you do well? ☑

What do you need to practice more? ☑

CHAPTER 6

ZOOLOGY:
Animals and Language

ZOOLOGY: the scientific study of animals and their behavior

OBJECTIVES

To read academic texts, you need to master certain skills.

In this chapter, you will:

- Scan a text for specific information

- Find the link between the title of a text and the first paragraph

- Predict the author's point of view from the first paragraph of a text

- Guess the meaning of words from the context

- Understand and use synonyms, collocations, phrasal verbs, and different word forms

- Recognize and use hedging language

- Take notes to identify the arguments for or against the author's thesis

- Complete an outline with the necessary details

Consider These Questions

Discuss the questions with a partner.

1. What kinds of animal sounds are you used to hearing? Do you understand some of them?

2. Whale songs from the ocean and elephant sounds from the jungle are available on the Web. Have you ever heard them? How do scientists obtain these sounds?

3. Why do you think scientists want to study animal sounds?

4. Can some animals understand human language?

5. Can some animals imitate human language and communicate with humans?

READING ONE: Bridges to Human Language

(A) Warm-Up

Discuss the question in a small group.

Both animals and humans communicate with sounds. What is the difference between animal sounds and human language?

(B) Reading Strategy

Scanning for Specific Information

Scanning a text means reading it **quickly and superficially** to find **specific information** like names, dates, places, definitions, etc.

Scan the reading to find out (1) the name of the animal it focuses on, and (2) the kind of information this animal needs to communicate. Write the name and information on the lines.

1. _____

2. _____

Now read the text to learn more about this animal and its "language."

Bridges to Human Language

By Jared Diamond

Jared Diamond, currently professor of geography at the University of California, Los Angeles, is an American scientist and the author of The Third Chimpanzee: The Evolution and Future of the Human Animal, Collapse: Why Societies Choose to Fail or Succeed, *and* Guns, Germs, and Steel. *This text is an excerpt from* The Third Chimpanzee.

1   Human language origins constitute the most important mystery in understanding how we became uniquely human. Between human language and the vocalizations of any animal lies a seemingly unbridgeable **gulf**. Unfortunately, the origins of language prove harder to **trace** than the origins of the human pelvis,[1] skull,[2] tools, and art. All those latter things may survive, and can be recovered and dated, but the spoken word vanishes in an instant.

2   Many wild animals communicate with each other by sounds, of which bird songs and the barking of dogs are especially familiar to us. Despite this long history of intimate association, our understanding of these **ubiquitous** familiar sounds has suddenly exploded because of the application of new techniques: the use of modern tape recorders to record animal calls, electronic analysis of the calls to detect **subtle** variations **imperceptible** to the unaided human ear, broadcasting recorded calls back to animals to observe how they react, and observing their reactions to electronically reshuffled calls. These methods are revealing animal communication to be much more language-like than anyone would have guessed thirty years ago.

3   The most sophisticated "animal language" studied to date is that of a common cat-sized African monkey known as the vervet. Equally at home in trees and on the ground of savanna and rain forest, vervets are among the monkey species that visitors to East African game parks are most likely to see.

4   About three quarters of wild vervet deaths are caused by **predators**. If you're a vervet, it's essential to know the differences between a martial eagle, one of the leading killers of vervets, and a white-backed vulture, an equally large soaring bird that eats carrion[3] and is no danger to live monkeys. It's essential to act appropriately when the eagle appears, and to tell your relatives. Besides these problems posed by predators, vervets have complex social relationships with each other. For all these reasons, vervets would profit from efficient ways of communicating about and representing their world.

(continued on next page)

---

[1] *pelvis:* the set of large, wide curved bones at the base of the spine, to which the legs are joined

[2] *skull:* the bones of a person's or animal's head

[3] *carrion:* dead flesh that is decaying

5   When they see a large broad-winged soaring hawk, vervets usually respond with the eagle call if the hawk is a martial eagle or crowned eagle, their two most dangerous avian predators. They usually do not respond if the hawk is a black-chested snake eagle or white-backed vulture, which do not prey on vervets. Seen from below, black-chested snake eagles look rather similar to martial eagles in their shared pale underparts, banded tail, and black head and throat. Vervets rate as good bird-watchers, because their lives depend on it! These examples demonstrate that vervet alarm calls are not involuntary expressions of either fear or intent. They have an external referent[4] that may be quite exact.

6   **Skeptics** go on to dispute proposed analogies between animal sounds and human speech on the further grounds that[5] human speech is learned, but that many animals are born with the instinctive ability to **utter** the sounds characteristic of their species. However, young vervets appear to learn how to utter and respond to sounds appropriately, just as do human infants. The grunts of an infant vervet sound different from those of an adult. "Pronunciation" gradually improves with age. Infant vervets don't learn reliably to give the correct response to an adult's call until the age of six or seven months. Not until the age of two years does the infant consistently **emit** each alarm call in the correct context.

7   Unfortunately, vocal communication by wild chimps and other apes has never been studied by the methods applied to vervets, because of logistical problems.[6] Several groups of scientists have nevertheless spent years training captive gorillas, common chimps, and pygmy chimps to understand and use **artificial** languages based on plastic chips of different sizes and colors, or on hand signs similar to those used by deaf people, or on consoles like typewriters with each key bearing a different symbol. At a minimum, these studies of trained apes reveal that they possess the intellectual capabilities for mastering large vocabularies, begging the obvious question[7] whether they have evolved such vocabularies in the wild.

---

[4] *referent:* reference

[5] *on the grounds that:* because

[6] *logistical problem:* practical problem

[7] *beg the question:* If something begs the question, it avoids dealing with the question discussed.

8   Humans don't just have vocabularies of thousands of words with different meanings. We also combine those words and vary their forms in ways **prescribed** by grammatical rules (such as rules of word order) that determine the meaning of the word combinations. Grammar thereby lets us construct a potentially infinite number of sentences from a finite number of words. Most linguists would not dignify an animal's system of vocal communication with the name of language, no matter how large its vocabulary, unless it also involved grammatical rules.

9   No hint of syntax has been discovered in the studies of vervets to date. Most of their grunts and alarm calls are single utterances. In short, while the gulf between animal and human vocal communication is surely large, scientists are rapidly gaining understanding of how that gulf has been partly bridged from the animal side.

COMPREHENSION

A Main Ideas

Read each statement. Decide if it is *True* or *False* according to the reading. Check (✓) the appropriate box. If it is false, change it to make it true. Discuss your answers with a partner.

	TRUE	FALSE
1. The use of modern tape recorders in the wild has confirmed the ideas researchers had about animal language 30 years ago.	☐	☐
2. Vervets vocalize special calls that alert each other to specific dangers.	☐	☐
3. Evidence seems to point to the fact that vervets' sound patterns are instinctive rather than learned.	☐	☐
4. Although chimps and wild apes in captivity seem capable of learning human language, we know that they do not develop large vocabularies on their own in the wild.	☐	☐
5. For the majority of linguists a system of communication cannot be considered a language unless it depends on grammatical rules.	☐	☐
6. Animals communicate with each other by using sounds that are more "language-like" than we thought.	☐	☐
7. It is not hard to trace human language origins.	☐	☐

Read the quotes from the reading. Circle the answer that best explains each quote. Share your answers with a partner.

1. "If you're a vervet, it's essential to know the differences between a martial eagle, one of the leading killers of vervets, and a white-backed vulture, an equally large soaring bird that eats carrion and is no danger to live monkeys. It's essential to act appropriately when the eagle appears, and to tell your relatives." *(paragraph 4)*

   Acting appropriately means . . .

   a. ignoring the eagle and telling others what to do.

   b. realizing it is an eagle and telling others what to do.

2. "Seen from below, black-chested snake eagles look rather similar to martial eagles in their shared pale underparts, banded tail, and black head and throat." *(paragraph 5)*

   The author's purpose in writing this statement is . . .

   a. to tell you about the characteristics of eagles.

   b. to make you see how carefully vervets must look at eagles.

3. "These examples demonstrate that vervet alarm calls are not involuntary expressions of either fear or intent. They have an external referent that may be quite exact." *(paragraph 5)*

   The author's purpose in writing this statement is . . .

   a. to clarify that vervet sounds are very specific and not just the result of emotion or chance.

   b. to clarify that the argument about how vervets have the beginnings of real language is false.

4. "Not until the age of two years does the infant consistently emit each alarm call in the correct context." *(paragraph 6)*

   The author's purpose in writing this statement is . . .

   a. to show that vervet sounds are inborn and instinctive.

   b. to show that vervet sounds are learned like language.

5. "Most linguists would not dignify an animal's system of vocal communication with the name of language, no matter how large its vocabulary, unless it also involved grammatical rules." *(paragraph 8)*

   This statement emphasizes that . . .

   a. the essence of human language is the ability to understand and use grammar.

   b. the essence of human language is the ability to understand and use vocabulary.

VOCABULARY

A **Guessing from Context**

Read each quote from the reading. Try to guess the meaning of the words in bold from the context. Write the clues that helped you guess and your guess. Then consult a dictionary and write the definition.

1. "Unfortunately, the origins of language prove harder to **trace** than the origins of the human pelvis, skull, tools, and art. All those latter things may survive, and can be recovered and dated. . ." *(paragraph 1)*

   trace   Clues: _origins / recovered and dated_

                  Guess: _discover_

                  Dictionary: _to study the history, or progress, of something_

2. "Many wild animals communicate with each other by sounds, of which bird songs and the barking of dogs are especially familiar to us. Despite this long history of intimate association, our understanding of these **ubiquitous** familiar sounds has suddenly exploded." *(paragraph 2)*

   ubiquitous Clues: _____

                  Guess: _____

                  Dictionary: _____

3. "**Skeptics** go on to dispute proposed analogies between animal sounds and human speech on the further grounds that human speech is learned, but that many animals are born with the instinctive ability to **utter** the sounds characteristic of their species." *(paragraph 6)*

   skeptic   Clues: _____

                  Guess: _____

                  Dictionary: _____

   utter   Clues: _____

                  Guess: _____

                  Dictionary: _____

4. "Humans don't just have vocabularies of thousands of words with different meanings. We also combine those words and vary their forms in ways **prescribed** by grammatical rules (such as rules of word order) that determine the meaning of the word combinations." *(paragraph 8)*

   prescribe   Clues: _____

                  Guess: _____

                  Dictionary: _____

B Synonyms

Complete each sentence with a word from the box. Use the synonym in parentheses to help you select the correct word. Compare answers with a partner.

artificial	imperceptible	skeptics	ubiquitous
emit	predators	subtle	utter
gulf	prescribe	trace	

The Secret Language of Elephants

For 20 years Andrea Turkalo has studied a group of wild elephants in the Congo basin rain forest, collecting an archive of elephant behavior and sounds.

1. In the Dzanga Clearing, elephants are _____ubiquitous_____; the clearing
   (everywhere)
   is a watering hole, a spa, and a sanctuary of peace for all of them.

2. In this area, the elephants can be studied in their natural habitat, not in an

   _____ setting like a zoo.
   (unnatural)

3. Humans are the only _____[1] for forest elephants, but in
   (natural enemies)
   this rain forest, the elephants are safe.

4. Elephants _____ complicated, sophisticated sounds that
   (make)
   scientists are trying to record along with videos of the specific behavior that

   accompanies the sound.

5. Researchers use cutting-edge acoustic devices to record _____
   (slight)
   changes in pitch in elephant sounds.

6. Once or twice a year, Andrea Turkalo takes her recordings to Cornell University,

   where researchers are collecting the early stages of a dictionary on elephant

   vocalizations. To facilitate this process, the researchers are following rules that

   _____ proper sound classification techniques.
   (set down)

7. Researchers find it difficult to _____ elephant
   (follow)
   vocalizations by ear because most elephant sounds are at very low frequencies,

   below what humans can hear.

_____

[1] Old elephants or weak baby elephants can be killed by lions or tigers.

8. Although the sounds elephants _____ are almost
   (give voice to)
   _____ to the human ear, these vocalizations carry far to
   (inaudible)
   other elephants in the dense forest.

9. _____ may refuse to call elephant vocalizations a
   (doubters)
   language, but the sounds have a meaning in the social life of elephants.

10. Many countries want to protect elephants but don't have enough money for

    guards to protect the sanctuaries. There is a _____
                                                      (gap)
    between theory and practice, between the law and the manpower to enforce it.

C Word Usage: *prescribe* vs. *proscribe*

> Use the verb **prescribe**:
> 1. to officially say what medicine or treatment a sick person should have
>   • Doctors **prescribe** medication to help their patients get better.
>
> 2. to state officially what should be done in a particular situation
>   • Federal law **prescribes** a jail sentence of four years for this type of crime.
>
> Use the verb **proscribe**:
>   to officially say that something is not allowed to exist or be done
>   • Their religion **proscribes** gambling.

Complete each sentence with the correct word form. Choose from the two forms in parentheses. Compare answers with a partner.

1. The guidelines _____ insulting people because of their
                    (prescribe / proscribe)
   origins, religious affiliation, or sexual orientation.

2. The law _____ animal abuse.
            (prescribes / proscribes)

3. The law _____ fair treatment for animals and punishes
            (prescribes / proscribes)
   animal abuse with fines or jail time.

4. Some medicines that are allowed in one state in the United States may be

   _____ in another.
   (prescribed / proscribed)

5. Bed rest is often _____ for a sprained ankle.
                      (prescribed / proscribed)

NOTE-TAKING: Identifying Arguments for or against the Author's Thesis

Go back to the reading and read it again, taking notes on the implied arguments. Then fill in the chart with information from each side.

AUTHOR'S THESIS: Animal communication is much more language-like than anyone would have guessed.

	FOR	AGAINST
1.	Vervets communicate about eagles.	No, it's just involuntary sounds of fear.
2.		
3.		
4.		

CRITICAL THINKING

Discuss the questions in a small group. Be prepared to share your points of view with the class.

1. Why would vervets have evolved such sophisticated communication? Do you think the author proved his point that animals are capable of developing a vocabulary in the wild?

2. Why is this reading called "Bridges to Human Language"?

3. Many people want us to treat animals more kindly than we do. Why would discussing animal language help this movement?

4. If you know the vocabulary of a language, is it enough? Why do linguists think that grammar is more important?

Warm-Up

Discuss the question with a partner.

How would you set up an experiment to see if chimps or apes could learn human language? Remember, they are not physically able to reproduce all the sounds of any human language.

B **Reading Strategy**

Finding the Link between Title and First Paragraph

There is often a **direct link** between the **title** of a text and the contents of its **introductory paragraph**. Understanding this **link helps the reader focus** with more confidence on the rest of the text.

Look at the title of the reading. Then read the first paragraph and the first word of the second paragraph. Discuss the questions with a partner.

1. What does the title imply? Who are the "relatives," and whose relatives are they?

2. How does the first paragraph clarify the subject of the text? What do linguists sharing Chomsky's point of view think?

3. The second paragraph begins with "But." What do you think it will discuss?

Now read the whole text to find out if your predictions were correct.

Speaking to the Relatives
From the Why Files

1   Where did our capacity for language originate? Many linguists, **echoing** the influential Noam Chomsky,[1] argue that it's a **uniquely** human gift. According to this school, chimpanzees and other close relatives could not use language because they lack the human brain structures that create language.

2   But other researchers disagree, pointing out that a few apes can use, at least to some extent, symbolic communications systems — languages — like American Sign Language. E. Sue Savage-Rumbaugh,[2] a Georgia State University biology professor, says the accepted wisdom reflects a long-standing **bias** and that modern studies are **refuting** it.

(continued on next page)

---

[1] *Noam Chomsky:* linguist, philosopher, cognitive scientist, and political activist; has taught at MIT for 50 years and has been described as the father of modern linguistics

[2] *Dr. Sue Savage-Rumbaugh:* originally based at Georgia State University's Language Research Center in Atlanta, and now serves as executive director and head scientist at Great Ape Trust in Des Moines, Iowa

3   Savage-Rumbaugh studies bonobos — a relative of ours that, like chimpanzees, shares 98 to 99 percent of human genes. When you spend all day with bonobos, she says, "the differences don't **loom** very large. . . . They look like us, care like us, smell like us, think like us. They are like us." Speaking at the recent American Association for the Advancement of Science meeting in Philadelphia, Savage-Rumbaugh observed that since apes don't have a vocal tract, they can't make the sounds of human language. Previous researchers have tried to overcome that liability by teaching apes sign language. Savage-Rumbaugh, however, uses a "keyboard"[3] consisting of 400 symbols, and what she finds is controversial. "If you talk to apes and point to little symbols, they learn to understand language just as I'm talking to you."

4   Instead of using behaviorism — rewarding the apes with food each time they use a word correctly — she allows the animals to **pick up** words in "normal" conversation. This seems to work. "Watching Kanzi [an experimental bonobo] in casual 'conversation,' one is struck by the intense give-and-take," wrote journalist Stephen Hart, author of *The Language of Animals*. Furthermore, the researchers found Kanzi's understanding of new sentences to be about equal to that of a two-and-a-half-year-old child, Hart found.

5   Savage-Rumbaugh suspects that bonobos are using language in the wild, but since they **congregate** in trees in groups of about 100, "it's almost impossible to study them." And on the ground, they are silent to avoid predators. Savage-Rumbaugh **contends** that wild bonobos — only an estimated 4,000 to 40,000 survive in Congo, formerly Zaire — have a second communication system. This one resembles road signs built of smashed plants rather than steel.

6   The finding grew from the observation that troops of bonobos hang out in various locations during the day. When bonobos go **foraging** on the ground, the small groups must maintain "radio silence" to **evade** predators. Savage-Rumbaugh began wondering how one group manages to follow another to the next hangout.

7   In 1995, Savage-Rumbaugh spent two months studying bonobos at a research station operated by Takayoshi Kano, a Japanese primate researcher in the Congo forest. During two days of following troops with local bonobo trackers, she observed that their trails were clearly marked by smashed plants and branches planted at an angle to the direction of travel.

8   Although skeptics could **counter** that she was just seeing trampled plants, she contends they actually were road signs since they occurred only at trail intersections. "These clues are not left at arbitrary points in the vegetation but rather at locations where trails split and where an individual following might be confused as to the correct direction to take." While the finding has not been replicated in other primates, Savage-Rumbaugh suspects that it might represent the kind of symbolic communication system humans rely on.

---

[3] *keyboard:* also referred to as a "lexigram" in the literature on this topic

COMPREHENSION

A Main Ideas

Read each statement. Decide if it is *True* or *False* according to the reading. Check (✓) the appropriate box. If it is false, change it to make it true. Discuss your answers with a partner.

	TRUE	FALSE
1. Bonobos can speak human languages.	☐	☐
2. Some bonobos can use sign language or communication symbols to some extent.	☐	☐
3. Kanzi can listen and respond in conversation.	☐	☐
4. All scientists believe that bonobos use communication symbols in the wild.	☐	☐
5. Savage-Rumbaugh is a famous scientist working with bonobos and sign language.	☐	☐

B Close Reading

Read the quotes from the reading. Circle the statement that best explains each quote. Share your answers with a partner.

1. "Many linguists, echoing the influential Noam Chomsky, argue that [the capacity for language] is a uniquely human gift. According to this school, chimpanzees and other close relatives could not use language because they lack the human brain structures that create language." (*paragraph 1*)

   a. According to Chomsky, chimps and bonobos cannot use language.

   b. Chomsky is the only one who believes that chimps and bonobos cannot use language.

2. "'Watching Kanzi [an experimental bonobo] in casual "conversation," one is struck by the intense give-and-take,' wrote journalist Stephen Hart, author of *The Language of Animals*." (*paragraph 4*)

   The "give-and-take" Stephen Hart refers to is . . .

   a. the turn-taking that humans share in their conversations with one another.

   b. the mutual sharing and bonding that seems to be occurring in the conversations between bonobos and humans.

3. "Although skeptics could counter that [Savage-Rumbaugh] was just seeing trampled plants, she contends they actually were road signs since they occurred only at trail intersections." (*paragraph 8*)

   a. Savage-Rumbaugh thinks the animals are signaling to each other.

   b. Skeptics don't believe the road signs occurred only at trail intersections.

(continued on next page)

4. "Savage-Rumbaugh suspects that bonobos are using language in the wild, but since they congregate in trees in groups of about 100, 'it's almost impossible to study them.' And on the ground, they are silent to avoid predators." *(paragraph 5)*

    a. Savage-Rumbaugh can prove that bonobos communicate with each other in the wild, not just with humans in the laboratory.

    b. Savage-Rumbaugh thinks bonobos communicate with each other in the wild, not just with humans in the laboratory.

VOCABULARY

Ⓐ Word Forms

1 Fill in the chart with the correct word forms. Use a dictionary if necessary. An *X* indicates there is no form in that category.

	NOUN	VERB	ADJECTIVE	ADVERB
1.	congregation	congregate	X	X
2.		contend	X	X
3.		echo		X
4.		evade		
5.		refute		X

2 Complete the sentences with the correct form of the words from the chart. The first letter of each word has been given to you as a clue. Compare answers with a partner.

1. Although bonobos congregate_____ in trees, they often walk on

   two legs on the ground. Their closeness to the human genome and their peaceful

   social life are what attracts researchers to their habitat in the Congo.

2. Savage-Rumbaugh's work is a r_____ of the idea that

   bonobos cannot use human language to some degree.

3. Although the animals cannot speak, Savage-Rumbaugh's c_____

   is that they can understand words and use them to communicate.

4. Her critics, on the other hand, c_____ that knowing words

   is not enough; they e_____ Chomsky in saying that

   animals cannot have language because they don't know grammar and syntax.

5. We may try to e_____ the issue and say that grammar and syntax are not everything in language; linguists, however, maintain that without grammar, language does not exist.

6. Still, it is hard to r_____ the fact that specially trained bonobos can have conversations with humans using the keyboard.

B Synonyms

Complete each paragraph with the words or phrases from the box. Use the synonym in parentheses to help you select the correct word or phrase. Compare answers with a partner.

congregate	contend	evade	forage

Bonobos and the natural habitat where they _____congregate_____
1. (gather)
are endangered. Bonobos have been all but destroyed by hunters. Many of the
villagers living in the area _____ the rules about entering
2. (get around)
the sanctuary park because they want to _____ for food.
3. (search for)
Researchers _____ that greater education is needed in the
4. (claim)
remote villages along with better signs indicating the park boundaries.

bias	counter	echoing	loom	pick up	refute	uniquely

Kanzi is a _____ talented male bonobo who lives at the Great
5. (very especially)
Ape Trust of Iowa. He has demonstrated a great ability to _____
6. (learn)
language. Skeptics of bonobo research _____ the validity of
7. (argue against)
some of the research team's conclusions. They _____ that
8. (answer)
Kanzi's sentence structure is very simple, _____ Chomsky's
9. (repeating)
concerns about grammar. Most of the work done with Kanzi concerns comprehension
rather than production of language. Savage-Rumbaugh claims that there is a

_____ against realizing that animals can use language. No one
10. (prejudice)
knows what research findings _____ on the horizon that will
11. (are likely to appear)
confirm either point of view.

C Phrasal Verbs with *pick*

> A **phrasal verb** is a combination of a **verb** and a **particle** (or two). The combination has a special meaning, different from the meaning of the verb.
>
> **Pick up** is a phrasal verb with many different meanings, including the meaning used in the reading: "to learn."
> - She allows the animals to **pick up** words in "normal" conversation.
>
> **Pick** is also used with other particles, like **at**, **out**, **up on**, etc. The resulting phrasal verbs have many different meanings.

Read the dictionary entries for the phrasal verbs *pick at*, *pick out*, *pick up*, and *pick up on*. The entries give some of these verbs' many meanings.

> **pick at** *phr. v.* **1** to eat something by taking small bites but without much interest **2** to touch something repeatedly with your fingers, often pulling it slightly
>
> **pick out** *phr. v.* **1** to choose someone or something carefully **2** to recognize someone or something in a group of people or things
>
> **pick up** *phr. v.* **1** to lift someone or something up from a surface **2** to improve **3** to learn something without much effort or without being taught in a class **4** to begin something (a conversation, a meeting, a life) again, starting from the point where it stopped earlier **5** to find someone and take him/her to the police station for questioning
>
> **pick up on** *phr. v.* **1** to notice something, especially when it is difficult **2** to return to a point or an idea that has been mentioned and discuss it more

Now read each sentence. Decide which meaning of the verb is being used. Write the number of the appropriate meaning.

__1__ **a.** The dog just **picked at** his tray of dog food. It didn't seem hungry.

_____ **b.** The dog's owner **picked at** a scar on her arm because it itched badly.

_____ **c.** Following his master's orders, the dog **picked out** a doll from the pile of toys in the other room.

_____ **d.** It was hard to **pick out** the one dog in the animal shelter that they would take home with them because all the dogs were adorable.

_____ **e.** Many people believe that an animal's understanding of words **picks up** as it hears the words over and over again.

_____ **f.** Might it be easier for dogs to **pick up** their master's language than for their masters to **pick up** their dogs' language?

_____ **g.** The young girl **picked** the puppy **up** from the ground and held him in her arms when he refused to walk any more.

_____ **h.** A dog's learning speed will **pick up** with a trainer who knows how to gradually increase the difficulty of challenges.

_____ **i.** A dog can **pick up on** his master's anxiety and will show compassion by rubbing his head against the master's leg.

_____ **j.** People discussed the newspaper article again and **picked up on** the part about the dog understanding so many commands in English.

GRAMMAR FOR READING: Hedging Language

When we **hedge**, we **avoid giving an absolute answer** or using strong language. We do not use words like "is," "declare," "maintain," and "insist on." We use:

MODALS: **may, might, could, must**
- The research **may** help us understand the origins of language.

VERBS: **appear to, seem to, tend to; suspect that, contend that, suggest that, propose that, argue that, claim that**
- The results **appear to** support the scientists' hypothesis.

ADVERBS: **probably, seemingly, generally, perhaps**
- **Perhaps** linguists will revise their theories.

By using **hedging language**, researchers leave room for further interpretations and findings. Although their statements are based on evidence, they realize that the evidence they present is not always absolute; it **suggests possibilities** but not 100% certitude.

1 Check (✓) the sentences that use hedging language.

☐ **1.** The languages that animals speak do not seem to follow grammatical rules.

☐ **2.** Jared Diamond's discussion may give us insights into the origin of language.

☐ **3.** The vervets are among the monkey species that visitors to East African game parks usually see.

☐ **4.** The Great Ape Trust, where Kanzi and his sister, mother, nephew, and four other bonobos now reside, is North America's largest great ape sanctuary.

☐ **5.** Psychologist Sue Savage-Rumbaugh suggests that the uniqueness of human language may now come under question as we learn more and more about other species' language ability.

2 Find three sentences in Reading One using *seemingly*, *may*, and *appear*. Write them on the lines.

1. _____

2. _____

3. _____

3 Find three sentences in Reading Two using *argue that*, *seem to*, and *suspect that*. Write them on the lines.

1. _____

2. _____

3. _____

NOTE-TAKING: Completing an Outline with the Necessary Details

Go back to the reading and read it again. Using the cues given here, fill in the necessary details of the outline with notes in your own words.

I. Argument about Bonobos' Language Ability

    A. Chomsky and some linguists

        1. humans: *language is spoken only by humans*

        2. chimps/other relatives: *do not have the brain structure to create language*

    B. Rumbaugh-Savage and other researchers

        1. few apes: _____

        2. modern research and bias: _____

II. Research with Apes and Language

    A. Lab experiments

        1. sign language: _____

        2. keyboard: _____

        3. Kanzi: _____

    B. Experiments with apes in the wild

        1. difficulties for researchers: _____

        2. predators/marking of trails: _____

    C. Skeptics

        1. Skeptics' argument: _____

        2. Rumbaugh's response: _____

CRITICAL THINKING

Discuss the questions in a small group. Be prepared to share your answers with the class.

1. Why do you think universities in many countries give money to programs about animal life? What can we learn from them?

2. In the experiments at the Great Ape Trust, Savage-Rumbaugh's bonobos are learning to respond to human language. Are Savage-Rumbaugh's findings important for what we would like to know about bonobos in the wild? Does her research give us an idea of how they communicate in their natural setting? Why or why not?

3. Is the fact that Kanzi can learn words in the give-and-take of "normal" conversation important for Savage-Rumbaugh's experiment? Why or why not?

4. Does the information we learned about vervets strengthen or weaken what Savage-Rumbaugh claims about bonobos communicating among themselves in the wild? Why?

LINKING READINGS ONE AND TWO

Go back to Readings One and Two and read them again. Compare vervets and bonobos regarding their ability to use language.

1 Put a check (✓) under *Vervets* or *Bonobos* if the corresponding reading provides significant information about the topic. Put an *X* in the box if no significant information is given about the topic.

	TOPIC	VERVETS (READING ONE)	BONOBOS (READING TWO)
1.	Life in the wild	✓	✓
2.	Life in captivity		
3.	Social relationships		
4.	Language as a voluntary tool (i.e., wanting to communicate something)		
5.	Artificial language		
6.	Natural language		

2 Complete this short summary of what Readings One and Two teach us about animals and language.

> The information about vervets in Jared Diamond's text shows that animals in the wild have natural vocal communication. Their calls can make fine distinctions as they warn each other about the appearance of predators. Although this does not constitute a complete language, it shows that . . .

READING THREE: Language and Morality

Ⓐ Warm-Up

Discuss the questions with a partner.

Can animals understand right and wrong? Fair and unfair?

Ⓑ Reading Strategy

Predicting Author's Point of View from First Paragraph

The first paragraph of a text often helps us to **predict** the **author's point of view** or **opinion** about the topic he or she is writing about.

Read the first paragraph of the reading. Then answer the questions. Discuss your answers with a partner.

1. Do the authors think animals have moral behavior?

_____

2. Is it the same moral behavior as in humans?

_____

Now read the rest of the text to find out if your predictions were correct.

Language and Morality

By Marc Bekoff and Jessica Pierce

Mark Bekoff is professor emeritus of ecology and evolutionary biology at the University of Colorado, Boulder. He is an ethologist, a scientist who studies animal behavior, and believes that we can understand the origin of goodness by studying the ethical behavior of animals. Jessica Pierce is a writer and bioethicist who is concerned about the ethical treatment of animals.

Examples of Moral Behavior?

- An older female elephant sees that a younger female elephant with an injured leg has been knocked over by a young male elephant. She chases the male away and goes back to the younger female and touches the hurt leg with her trunk.

- A rat in a cage refuses to push a lever for food when it sees another rat receive an electric shock as a result.

- In a group of chimpanzees, individuals punish others who are late for dinner because no one eats until everyone is present.

Do these examples show that animals display moral behavior: that they can be kind, **altruistic**, and fair?

---

1 We've argued that humans share with other social mammals the same basic group of moral behaviors, namely fairness, cooperation, and **empathy**. We've also suggested that morality may exist along a **continuum**, from simpler to more complex patterns of behavior. But humans appear to have evolved an unusually high level of moral complexity.

2 The human prefrontal cortex, the area of the brain responsible for judgment and rational thought, is more highly developed in humans than in other animals. With judgment and rational thought (what is often called *reason*), we gain self-consciousness about the grounds of our actions and gain a corresponding capacity for **self-governance** and conscious control. It is because animals lack this capacity for reflective self-control that we don't hold

them responsible. We don't hold them morally **culpable** for following their strongest impulses.

3 Humans use language to **articulate** and enforce moral norms, another potential difference in kind. As Robin Dunbar's work on gossip and reputation suggests, language and morality are

(continued on next page)

inextricably bound. Dunbar, who works at the Institute of **Cognitive** and Evolutionary Anthropology at the University of Oxford in the United Kingdom, argues that language has been evaluative from its origins; it has been used to communicate socially important information about each other, such as who is trustworthy and who will **reciprocate**. Our words express anger, **contempt**, and approval in our public utterances. But does language separate humans from other animals? Anthropologist Terrence Deacon thinks it does. In his book *The Symbolic Species*, Deacon argues that although there is undoubtedly an unbroken continuity between human and nonhuman minds, there is also a singular **discontinuity**: humans use language to communicate.

The use of words has changed our brain over time. Deacon notes, "[T]he first use of symbolic reference by some distant ancestors changed how natural selection processes have affected hominid[1] brain evolution ever since."

4   If our brains are significantly different, and morality is essentially a product of the brain, then wouldn't we possibly be unique in this respect? Animals communicate about morality, but not with language. This would be an important subject for comparative work.

---

[1] *hominid:* member of a group of animals that includes humans

COMPREHENSION

 Main Ideas

Complete the paragraph based on the main ideas of the reading. Use your own words.

   Bekoff and Pierce believe that we can understand the origin of goodness by

studying the ethical behavior of animals. Human morality is much more complex

because _____

_____1._____.

Human beings use language to strengthen morality. Robin Dunbar argues that

language has always been about _____

_____2.

Terrence Deacon thinks that although human minds and animal minds exist along a

continuum, _____

_____3.

_____.

Close Reading

Read the quotes from the reading. Circle the answer that best explains each quote. Share your answers with a partner.

1. "We've also suggested that morality may exist along a continuum, from simpler to more complex patterns of behavior. But humans appear to have evolved an unusually high level of moral complexity." *(paragraph 1)*

   a. The authors think that animals and humans have the same morality.

   b. The authors think that human morality is superior because animals and humans have a completely different sense of morality.

   c. The authors think that animals and humans share some aspects of morality, but human morality is more complicated.

2. "It is because animals lack this capacity for reflective self-control that we don't hold them responsible." *(paragraph 2)*

   a. If animals had more self-control, they could be held responsible for what they do.

   b. Animals are too self-centered.

   c. Animals have no sense of responsibility.

3. "[Language] has been used to communicate socially important information about each other, such as who is trustworthy and who will reciprocate." *(paragraph 3)*

   a. Language is not a social activity.

   b. Language gives us information about others.

   c. Language is not reliable communication.

VOCABULARY

 Synonyms

Cross out the word that is NOT a synonym for the word in bold. Compare answers with a partner.

1. **altruistic**	~~selfish~~	generous	self-sacrificing
2. **articulate**	express	communicate	silence
3. **cognitive**	learning	instinctive	understanding
4. **contempt**	cowardice	disrespect	scorn
5. **continuum**	range	spectrum	continuation
6. **culpable**	capable	guilty	blameworthy
7. **discontinuity**	break	connection	gap
8. **empathy**	apathy	understanding	compassion
9. **inextricably**	completely	incapably	totally
10. **reciprocate**	keep	exchange	give back
11. **self-governance**	voting	self-control	independence

Check (✓) the collocations (words that are often paired together). Discuss your answers with a partner.

- ☐ 1. inextricably bound
- ☐ 2. inextricably chained
- ☐ 3. inextricably linked
- ☐ 4. cognitive psychology
- ☐ 5. cognitive neuroscience
- ☐ 6. cognitive emotion
- ☐ 7. culpable homicide
- ☐ 8. culpable story
- ☐ 9. culpable neglect
- ☐ 10. culpable behavior

CRITICAL THINKING

Discuss the questions in a small group. Be prepared to share your ideas with the class.

1. Do you think that language is on a continuum — that animals and humans engage in language behavior but in different ways — or do you think language is uniquely human? What evidence can you point to for your opinion?

2. It is said that everyone has bad thoughts and impulses, but self-governance is having the control not to act on them. Where do humans get this capacity for self-control? Do animals have it?

3. Can animals feel empathy? Bekoff and Pierce gave some examples. Are they convincing? What moral behavior have you noticed in animals?

AFTER YOU READ

BRINGING IT ALL TOGETHER

Work in groups of five. Role-play a discussion between a skeptic and the four authors or researchers you've encountered in the chapter. The skeptic will question the others about the work they have done. Use some of the vocabulary you studied in the chapter (for a complete list, go to page 164).

ROLES:

- Skeptic
- Jared Diamond
- Sue Savage-Rumbaugh
- Marc Bekoff
- Jessica Pierce

QUESTIONS:

- Professor Diamond: You write that vervets communicate about eagles and that their language is learned. How can you call that language if they are only reacting to their fear of predators?

- Dr. Savage-Rumbaugh: Your research shows how bonobos can respond to human language in the laboratory by using a keyboard. But you have not been able to study bonobos' communications with one another in the wild. How, then, can you justify your belief that bonobos use "language"?

- Professor Bekoff: You have observed rats in experiments protecting other rats from receiving an electric shock. Why do you think this gives us proof of animal morality?

- Ms. Pierce: You have written about elephants *seeming* to give one another love and empathy. Is it possible that you are being fooled by these "appearances"?

Add your own questions:

- _____

- _____

WRITING ACTIVITY

This chapter is about language and animals. Write a short essay about how you have experienced learning a second language. Answer the questions. Use more than five of the words or idioms you studied in the chapter.

- What was more difficult for you: grammar or vocabulary? What other difficulties did you have?

- How did you solve the problem of learning a new language?

- What were the enjoyable aspects (if any)?

DISCUSSION AND WRITING TOPICS

Discuss these topics in a small group. Choose one of them and write a paragraph or two about it. Use the vocabulary from the chapter.

1. What can we learn about language from studying how animals communicate?

2. Why does language make human beings unique? What else is unique about humans?

3. What might be the danger in considering human beings to be completely unique? How can such thinking affect the way in which we treat animals?

4. Do you think animals have rights that humans should respect? What are some animal rights?

5. Why do people want to prove that animals have some capacity for moral behavior?

VOCABULARY

Nouns	Verbs	Adjectives	Adverbs
bias *	articulate	altruistic	inextricably
contempt	congregate	artificial	uniquely *
continuum	contend	cognitive	
discontinuity	counter	culpable	
empathy	echo	imperceptible	
gulf	emit	subtle	
predator	evade	ubiquitous	
skeptic	forage		
self-governance	loom		
	prescribe		
	reciprocate		
	refute		
	trace *		
	utter		

Phrasal Verb

pick up

* = AWL (Academic Word List) item

SELF-ASSESSMENT

In this chapter you learned to:

○ Scan a text for specific information

○ Find the link between the title of a text and the first paragraph

○ Predict the author's point of view from the first paragraph of a text

○ Guess the meaning of words from the context

○ Understand and use synonyms, collocations, phrasal verbs, and different word forms

○ Recognize and use hedging language

○ Take notes to identify the arguments for or against the author's thesis

○ Complete an outline with the necessary details

What can you do well? ✓

What do you need to practice more? ✓

POLITICAL SCIENCE:
The Rulers and the Ruled

POLITICAL SCIENCE: a social science that studies the principles of government and political institutions

OBJECTIVES

To read academic texts, you need to master certain skills.

In this chapter, you will:

- Skim a text to identify the author's point of view

- Highlight the important information in a text

- Think about the title of a text and predict its content

- Guess the meaning of words from the context

- Use dictionary entries to learn the meanings of words

- Understand and use synonyms, different word forms, figurative language, and expressions of similarity and contrast

- Use a dash or dashes to isolate and emphasize a point

- Take notes to compare and contrast the ideas of two thinkers

*The Statue of Liberty
(Liberty Enlightening the World)*

A Consider These Statements

Read the statements and decide whether you *Agree* or *Disagree*. Check (✓) your choice. Discuss your answers and your reasons for them with a partner.

	AGREE	DISAGREE
1. Governments exist to ensure the happiness of their people.	☐	☐
2. Politicians are mostly liars.	☐	☐
3. Kings and princes make good leaders.	☐	☐
4. Voting is a good way to choose a leader.	☐	☐

B Types of Governments

Many different kinds of governments have existed in human history. Working with a partner, match the types of governments with their defining characteristics.

TYPES OF GOVERNMENTS	DEFINING CHARACTERISTICS
_____ **1.** democracy	**a.** an individual without hereditary claims to power rules; either absolute rule by one person or by a group unrestricted by law
_____ **2.** dictatorship	**b.** power belongs to a small elite part of society, usually wealthy, privileged, and powerful families
_____ **3.** monarchy	
_____ **4.** oligarchy	**c.** a ruler, usually from a hereditary dynasty (family), holds power for his or her lifetime
_____ **5.** theocracy	**d.** the leaders of the state are the same as the religious leaders; government leaders take orders from religious leaders
	e. citizens choose their own leaders and their rights are protected by law

ANSWERS: 1. e   2. a   3. c   4. b   5. d

Warm-Up

Look at the timeline. Read the information about the Italian Renaissance (1400–1550), the Scientific Revolution (1550–1700), and the Enlightenment (1700s).

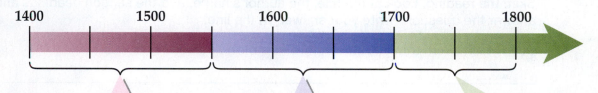

| 1400 | 1500 | 1600 | 1700 | 1800 |

1400–1550
The Italian Renaissance

- a rediscovery or "rebirth" of interest in Greek and Roman philosophy, art, and science
- a new respect for learning
- a change from religious subjects to the human and natural world
- the growing importance of the artist; Leonardo da Vinci and Michelangelo
- changes that affected mainly the elites

1550–1700
The Scientific Revolution

- development of the scientific method using observation, experimentation, and reason → laws of nature understood better
- inspired by Copernicus (the sun is the center of the solar system, not the earth) and Galen (the circulation of blood in the body), Galileo (astronomy and physics), and Newton (the laws of gravity, optics, and mathematics)
- positive effect on business, education, careers in science

1700s
The Enlightenment

- applied reason to all life decisions
- supported reason rather than religion
- valued political freedom, religious tolerance, and humanism
- included Diderot (the *Encyclopedia*), Montesquieu (separation of powers to avoid dictatorship), Rousseau (the "social contract" underlying government), Voltaire (religious tolerance, liberty), and Adam Smith (free trade and capitalism)

Now discuss the questions with a partner.

1. What changed during the Renaissance?

2. Niccolò Machiavelli wrote a book of advice for political leaders during the Renaissance. What form of government did he probably have to deal with at that time?

3. How did the Scientific Revolution change people's views on human nature?

4. What kind of government would probably be favored by the philosophers of the Enlightenment?

Skimming for the Author's Point of View

Being able to **identify the author's point of view** by skimming a reading selection can **help you read the text** with more confidence and purpose.

Skim the reading. Look at the title, the author's name, and the section headings and answer the question. Write your answer on the line.

Does Machiavelli think a ruler should be a moral person?

_____

Now, as you read the text, you will be able to compare your ideas with the author's. In what ways do you agree? In what ways do you disagree?

The Morals of the Prince

By Niccolò Machiavelli

Niccolò Machiavelli

Niccolò Machiavelli (1469–1527), the son of a lawyer, lived in Florence during the Italian Renaissance. It was a very chaotic time, when many foreign governments were trying to take over the city-states of Italy. Machiavelli was an official of the Florentine Republic. He was also a philosopher, diplomat, writer, playwright, and politician, and is considered one of the founders of modern political science. He was a true "Renaissance man" because he excelled in so many areas. In 1513, he wrote The Prince, *which was intended to be advice to the Medici rulers of Florence.*

1   Anyone who tries to follow a perfect standard of goodness must inevitably be ruined among the many who are not good. **Hence**, it is essential for a prince who wants to maintain his position to learn how not to be good.

Whether It Is Better to Be Loved or Feared

2   The question is whether it is better to be loved than feared, or feared rather than loved. We might wish to be both but since love and fear cannot exist together, if we must choose, it is far safer to be feared than

Lorenzo di Medici, Duke of Urbino (1492–1519)

loved. Men are generally thankless and **fickle**, liars and **deceivers**, wanting to avoid danger, and greedy of gain. Men are less careful how they offend a man who makes himself loved than a man who makes himself feared. Since men are a sorry breed and love is a tie of obligation, they will break this tie every time they see it to be in their own interest. But fear is bound by the **dread** of punishment, which never relaxes its grasp.

3   Nevertheless, a prince should inspire fear in such a way that if he does not win love he may escape hate. For a man may very well be feared and yet not hated, and this will be the case so long as he does not meddle[1] with the property or with the women of his subjects. If forced to put anyone to death, he should do so only when there is manifest cause[2] or reasonable justification. But, above all, he must abstain from **confiscating** the property of others. For men will sooner forget the death of their father than the loss of their **patrimony**.

The Way Princes Should Keep Their Word

4   We see from what has taken place in our own days that princes who have set little store by[3] their word, but have known how to **manipulate** men, have accomplished great things, and in the end, got the better of[4] those who trusted to honest dealing.

5   Since a prince should know how to use the nature of beasts wisely, he ought to imitate both the lion and the fox. The lion cannot guard himself from traps and the fox cannot protect himself from wolves. The prince must therefore be a fox to recognize traps and a lion to drive off wolves. A **prudent** prince neither can nor should keep his word when to keep it is not to his advantage. If all men were good, this would not be good advice, but since they are dishonest and do not keep faith with you, you in return need not keep faith with them. No prince was ever at a loss to find ways to hide his bad faith and deceitfulness.

6   The man who plays the fox has the best chance of success. To play this part, it is necessary to be a good liar and a **hypocrite**. Men are so simple, and governed so absolutely by their immediate needs, that the man who wishes to deceive will always find people willing to believe him. A new prince is often forced, in order to preserve the state, to act in opposition to good faith, **charity**, humanity, and religion. He must therefore keep his mind ready to shift as the winds of Fortune turn. As I have already said, he should not quit the good way if he can help it, but should know how to follow evil ways if he must.

7   A prince should appear to be the embodiment of **compassion**, good faith, **integrity**, humanity, and religion. There is no virtue more necessary for him to seem to possess than this last. Everyone sees what you *seem*, but few know what you are, and these few dare not oppose themselves to the power of the state. In the actions of all men, and most of all princes, we look to the end result. If a prince succeeds in maintaining his authority over the state, the means he uses will always be judged honorable and be approved by everyone because the masses are always taken in by appearances.

---

[1] *meddle [in/with]:* to intrude in other people's affairs

[2] *manifest cause:* an obvious cause or reason

[3] *set little store by [their word]:* not to care about breaking a promise

[4] *get the better of:* to defeat someone or deal successfully with a problem

COMPREHENSION

A **Main Ideas**

What does Machiavelli recommend a prince should do (or not do) and why? Fill in the chart. Use your own words.

	WHAT A PRINCE SHOULD DO	WHY
1.	A prince should make himself feared.	Only the fear of punishment will make men obey. Otherwise, they are changeable and "a sad lot."
2.		
3.		

	WHAT A PRINCE SHOULD NOT DO	WHY
4.	A prince shouldn't confiscate a family's property.	He will never be forgiven.
5.		
6.		

B **Close Reading**

Read the quotes from the reading. Circle the statement that best explains each quote. Share your answers with a partner.

1. "If forced to put anyone to death, he should do so only when there is manifest cause or reasonable justification." (*paragraph 3*)

   a. Violence is good.

   b. Violence must be avoided.

   c. Violence needs an excuse.

2. "For men will sooner forget the death of their father than the loss of their patrimony." (*paragraph 3*)

   a. People love property more than people.

   b. People love their family more than money.

   c. People can forget their losses quickly.

3. "A prudent prince neither can nor should keep his word when to keep it is not to his advantage." (*paragraph 5*)

    a. A prince should keep his word because it will serve his interests.

    b. A prince should not keep his word.

    c. A prince should think only of his own interests.

4. "In the actions of all men, and most of all princes, we look to the end result." (*paragraph 7*)

    a. The ends justify the means.

    b. The means justify the ends.

    c. The ends are their own reward.

5. "If a prince succeeds in maintaining his authority over the state, the means he uses will always be judged honorable." (*paragraph 7*)

    a. The primary aim of the prince is to insure the welfare of his people; as long as he is successful, no matter how he does it, people won't criticize him.

    b. The primary aim of the prince is to make sure he stays in power; as long as he is successful, no matter how he does it, people won't criticize him.

    c. The primary aim of the prince is to insure material prosperity; as long as he is successful, no matter how he does it, people won't criticize him.

VOCABULARY

 Synonyms

Cross out the word that is NOT a synonym for the word in bold. Compare answers with a partner.

1. **charity**	generosity	~~intolerance~~	love
2. **compassion**	empathy	kindness	modesty
3. **confiscate**	appropriate	seize	contribute
4. **deceiver**	debater	manipulator	liar
5. **dread**	refusal	horror	fear
6. **fickle**	disloyal	fun-loving	changeable
7. **hence**	thus	because	so
8. **hypocritical**	frank	lying	insincere
9. **integrity**	honesty	morality	sympathy
10. **manipulate**	mislead	mishandle	fool
11. **patrimony**	estate	economy	money
12. **prudent**	devious	careful	cautious

B Word Forms

1 Fill in the chart with the correct word forms. Some categories can have more than one form. Use a dictionary if necessary. An *X* indicates there is no form in that category.

	NOUN	VERB	ADJECTIVE	ADVERB
1.	charity	X	*charitable*	
2.	compassion	X		
3.	deception / *deceiver*	deceive		
4.	hypocrite /	X		
5.	manipulator /	manipulate		

2 Complete the sentences with the correct form of the words from the chart. Each item follows the order in which the words appear in the chart.

1. People who live in loving communities treat each other with

   _____*charity*_____ and respect. Such _____*charitable*_____

   behavior cultivates feelings of loyalty and trust in the society.

2. Sometimes it is dangerous to show too much _____

   toward others. _____ people do not always understand

   that their kind actions may make the people they are helping forget that they

   must learn how to help themselves. Treating people _____

   may therefore have unexpected negative consequences.

3. _____ may be useful for a while, but sooner or later

   the _____ is revealed for who he or she is. We can only

   _____ people for so long before we get caught.

4. A _____ is someone who pretends to do one thing

   and does the other. This _____ attitude is often seen in

   politicians, who are often criticized for their _____.

5. Some people _____ others in order to get what

   they want. Their _____ behavior may hide their

   selfishness for a while, but eventually those who are the victims of their

   _____ learn to see them for who they are.

C Figurative Language: Metaphors, Similes, and Analogies

> **Figurative language** uses **images and unusual comparisons** to make things **clearer** and more **interesting**.
>
> **EXAMPLES:**
> - The prince must therefore be **a fox** to recognize traps and **a lion** to drive off wolves.
> - The man who plays **the fox** has the best chance of success. To play this part, it is necessary to be a good liar and a hypocrite.
>
> By making these references to the "character of beasts," Machiavelli **paints a picture with figurative language**. For Machiavelli, human nature was not very far removed from the animal world.
>
> Here are **three ways to use figurative language**:
>
> **METAPHOR:** Stephen King **is a literary lion**. *(a famous writer)*
>
> **SIMILE:** **Like** a lion, the soldier is strong and brave. / He is **as brave as** a lion.
>
> **ANALOGY:** **Just like** a lion who has no fear or remorse, the prince destroyed his former friends without mercy.

Work with a partner. Identify what kind of figurative language is used in the sentences: **M** (metaphor), **S** (simile), or **A** (analogy). Then explain what the sentence means.

__M__ 1. As I was reading *The Prince*, the light dawned on me, and I thought of a plan to succeed.

"Light" = understanding "The light dawned on me" means "I understood."

_____ 2. Just as the sunrise brings the hope of a new day, so the crowning of a new king or queen brings the hope of better times.

_____

_____ 3. Like a father to his children, a king brings protection and guidance to his people.

_____

_____ 4. The prince was as stubborn as a mule.

_____

_____ 5. The revolution burned as bright as the sun, dazzling everyone with its radiance. But it burned those who came too close.

_____

_____ 6. The strongest noble got the lion's share of the good farmland in the region.

_____

CRITICAL THINKING

1 Agree or Disagree

Read each statement. Decide if you *Agree* or *Disagree*. Check (✓) the appropriate box. Discuss your answers with a partner.

	AGREE	DISAGREE
1. Machiavelli is immoral.	☐	☐
2. When Machiavelli says a ruler should be a "fox," he means the ruler should be an intellectual.	☐	☐
3. Machiavelli is an optimist.	☐	☐
4. According to Machiavelli, men are born to be subjects of a ruler, not citizens of a republic.	☐	☐

2 What Would Machiavelli Say?

Machiavelli has been assigned reading in some U.S. business schools. Books such as Antony Jay's *Management and Machiavelli* and Stanley Bing's *What Would Machiavelli Do?* apply Machiavelli's writings to a business context.

Here is a list of business decisions. Work with a small group. Decide whether Machiavelli would "probably agree" (*Yes*) or "probably disagree" (*No*) with these decisions. If there is not enough information to decide, write *Can't tell*. Explain your answers by referring to the reading.

_____ 1. The head of a company decides to put a new business plan to a vote among employees.

_____ 2. The directors of an insurance company saved from bankruptcy by taxpayers' bailout dollars decide to give millions of dollars in bonuses to their managers.

_____ 3. Businesses use advertising to encourage people to buy their products regardless of the usefulness of these products.

_____ 4. The head of the company involves all workers in discussion sessions to solve a company problem.

_____ 5. The company director decides to increase production.

_____ 6. A company decides to recall consumer products that have proven to be unsafe even though it costs them a lot of money.

_____ 7. Companies contribute a small percentage of their profits to support a charity for poor children and use this fact in their publicity.

A Warm-Up

You are about to read the Declaration of Independence, the document written by Thomas Jefferson that officially announced the separation of the thirteen American colonies from Britain. Discuss the questions with a partner.

1. We all seek "independence" in our lives. What does the word "independence" mean to you?

2. At what stage in life does a person seek independence? What must he or she do to prepare for this independence?

3. What potential risks or dangers exist when an individual or country seeks independence?

B Reading Strategy

Highlighting

Highlighting important information in a text is a very useful reading strategy that helps you **remember the important points**.

As you read the Declaration of Independence, highlight the rights all people are entitled to and what they should do if these rights are not respected.

The Declaration of Independence

The Declaration of Independence officially announced the separation of the thirteen American colonies from Britain. The Continental Congress, made up of elected representatives from each of the colonies, approved the Declaration on July 4, 1776. The Declaration was mainly written by **Thomas Jefferson**, *who was inspired by the political philosophers of the European Enlightenment. He was one of the Founding Fathers and later became the third president of the United States. This selection from the Declaration deals with the theoretical justification of independence. The rest of the Declaration provides examples of the abuses of the English king. The colonies fought for their freedom for seven years before the Revolutionary War ended with independence.*

(continued on next page)

Jefferson presenting the draft of the Declaration of Independence to Congress

1 When in the Course of human events it becomes necessary for one people to **dissolve** the political bands which have connected them with another, and to assume among the powers of the earth, the separate and equal station to which the Laws of Nature and of Nature's God entitle them, a decent respect to the opinions of mankind requires that they should declare the causes which **impel** them to the separation.

2 We hold these truths to be self-evident, that all men are created **equal**, that they are **endowed** by their Creator **with** certain unalienable[1] Rights, that among these are Life, Liberty and the pursuit of Happiness. That to **secure** these rights, Governments are instituted among Men, **deriving** their just powers from the **consent** of the governed. That whenever any Form of Government becomes destructive of these ends, it is the Right of the People to **alter** or to **abolish** it, and to institute new Government, laying its foundation on such principles and organizing its powers in such form, as to them shall seem most likely to effect[2] their Safety and Happiness. Prudence, indeed, will dictate that Governments long established should not be changed for light and **transient** causes; and accordingly all experience hath shewn[3] that mankind are more disposed to suffer, while evils are sufferable than to right themselves by abolishing the forms to which they are accustomed. But when a long train of abuses and usurpations,[4] pursuing **invariably** the same Object evinces a design[5] to reduce them under absolute Despotism,[6] it is their right, it is their duty, to throw off such Government, and to provide new Guards for their future security. — Such has been the patient sufferance[7] of these Colonies; and such is now the necessity which **constrains** them to alter their former Systems of Government.[8]

---

[1] *unalienable* [in modern English "inalienable"]: cannot be taken away

[2] *effect:* to produce, cause to happen

[3] *hath shewn:* has shown [in modern English]

[4] *abuses and usurpations:* injustices and illegal actions

[5] *design:* a plan, an intention

[6] *despotism:* absolute rule (sometimes involving cruel and harsh punishment) by a despot or tyrant; tyranny

[7] *sufferance:* suffering [in modern English]

[8] It is important to note here that **Thomas Jefferson** included a condemnation of slavery in the original version of the Declaration. But the representatives of the southern states, where slavery was customary, refused to sign the Declaration of Independence unless that part was taken out.

COMPREHENSION

A **Main Ideas**

1 Using the information in the Declaration of Independence, complete the sentences by matching their beginnings with their endings given in the box below. Compare answers with a partner.

_c_ 1. A nation that has been united with another nation for a period of time should explain why it wants to break up this union if . . .

____ 2. All people should have the right to . . .

____ 3. To protect these rights, governments should be established . . .

____ 4. When the government that has been created is no longer successful in protecting these rights, . . .

____ 5. A government that does not guarantee the people's . . .

____ 6. Although people get used to all kinds of abuses, it is time for them to demand a new form of government when they live under total . . .

> **a.** tyranny.
> **b.** life, liberty, and the pursuit of happiness.
> **c.** it is no longer desired.
> **d.** safety and happiness cannot possibly be a good government.
> **e.** it must be changed.
> **f.** with the agreement of the population.

2 In your own words summarize the main ideas of the Declaration as if you were explaining its meaning to a 10-year-old child. Work with a partner.

_____

_____

_____

_____

_____

_____

_____

_____

_____

Read the quotes from the reading. Circle the statement that best explains each quote. Share your answers with a partner.

1. "When in the Course of human events it becomes necessary for one people to dissolve the political bands which have connected them with another . . ., a decent respect to the opinions of mankind requires that they should declare the causes which impel them to the separation." *(paragraph 1)*

   a. Important political changes must be explained to the world.

   b. Important national decisions don't concern the international community.

   c. People must make their decisions to please others.

2. "All men are created equal." *(paragraph 2)*

   a. All men are the same.

   b. All men have the same rights.

   c. All men are brothers.

3. "That to secure these rights, Governments are instituted among Men . . ." *(paragraph 2)*

   a. The role of government is to assure the stability of the state.

   b. The role of government is to guarantee material prosperity.

   c. The role of government is to guarantee people's rights.

4. "[Governments derive] their just powers from the consent of the governed." *(paragraph 2)*

   a. Only an elected government is legitimate.

   b. A legitimate government has to be powerful.

   c. People must obey the government.

5. "That whenever any Form of Government becomes destructive of these ends, it is the Right of the People to alter or to abolish it." *(paragraph 2)*

   a. The people have a right to revolution.

   b. The people need to change leaders very often.

   c. The people may have to eliminate all governments.

6. "[All] experience hath shewn that mankind are more disposed to suffer, while evils are sufferable than to right themselves by abolishing the forms to which they are accustomed." *(paragraph 2)*

   a. People like change and will change governments easily.

   b. Change is difficult and revolutions happen only when people can't tolerate their situation anymore.

   c. People want to suffer and that's why they don't change their government.

VOCABULARY

A **Guessing from Context**

Read each quote from the reading. Try to guess the meaning of the words in bold from the context. Write your guess. Then consult a dictionary and write the definition.

1. "When in the Course of human events it becomes necessary for one people to **dissolve** the political bands which have connected them with another, and to assume among the powers of the earth, the separate and equal station to which the Laws of Nature and of Nature's God entitle them, . . ." *(paragraph 1)*

   dissolve   Guess: *undo (the connection)*

                   Dictionary: *to formally end, to make weaker, to make disappear*

2. "To **secure** these rights [i.e., Life, Liberty and the pursuit of Happiness], Governments are instituted among Men, **deriving** their just powers from the **consent** of the governed." *(paragraph 2)*

   secure   Guess: _____

                   Dictionary: _____

   derive   Guess: _____

                   Dictionary: _____

   consent   Guess: _____

                   Dictionary: _____

3. "Whenever any Form of Government becomes destructive of these ends, it is the Right of the People to **alter** or to abolish it, and to institute new Government, laying its foundation on such principles and organizing its powers in such form, as to them shall seem most likely to effect their Safety and Happiness." *(paragraph 2)*

   alter   Guess: _____

                   Dictionary: _____

4. "Prudence, indeed, will dictate that Governments long established should not be changed for light and **transient** causes." *(paragraph 2)*

   transient   Guess: _____

                   Dictionary: _____

B Synonyms

Complete the essay with the words or phrases from the box. Use the synonym in parentheses to help you select the correct word or phrase. Compare answers with a partner.

alter	dissolve	impelled	secure
constrained	endowed with	invariably	transient

In a democratic country, most citizens feel that they are entitled to a minimum

of economic prosperity. However, in a democracy with capitalism as its economic

system, inequality and competition threaten to _____ *dissolve* _____ the ties

1. (break up)

that should bind citizens together. Rich families derive political power from their

wealth while the poor are _____ powerless.

2. (always)

Plato suggested that a government should institute a rule limiting the total

wealth of any citizen. All citizens would have a basic amount of money allowing

them to live a decent life, and then they could make more. But no one would

be allowed to possess more than five times the basic amount. People who

accumulated more than that would be _____ to give up

3. (forced)

the excess, which would be used for the public good. Thus, no family would be

_____ great wealth or political influence, but some people

4. (given)

could have more money than others in return for their work.

To some extent, society has already agreed to _____

5. (modify)

the operation of purely economic laws. Many developed countries have social

security, health benefits, and income tax payments that increase with the amount

of money people earn. In some European countries, for example, political leaders,

_____ by a desire to create greater equality, have proposed

6. (driven)

tax codes that would oblige the wealthy to contribute more than 50% of their income

to taxes in order to help society as a whole. These laws have taken us in the direction

of a more compassionate society, allowing us to _____

7. (obtain)

more protection from _____ or even lasting misfortunes.

8. (short-lived)

Nevertheless, in our society, there are still homeless people sleeping in the streets.

1 Fill in the chart with the correct word forms. Some categories can have more than one form. Use a dictionary if necessary. An **X** indicates there is no form in that category.

	NOUN	VERB	ADJECTIVE	ADVERB
1.	abolition / *abolitionist*	abolish	X	X
2.		alter		X
3.	consent /			
4.	derivation /	derive		X
5.			equal	

2 Complete the sentences with the correct forms of the words from the chart. Each item follows the order in which the words appear in the chart.

1. Many people who wanted to _____ *abolish* _____ slavery joined the

   _____ *Abolitionist* _____ Movement. The _____ *abolition* _____ of

   slavery came only in 1865 at the end of the Civil War with the 13th Amendment to

   the Constitution.

2. After the Civil War, it was necessary to _____ the

   Constitution with three new amendments. These _____

   provided citizenship for former slaves and equal protection under the law for all

   citizens.

3. We have certain social rights and duties that are defined by common

   _____. We _____ to them if we

   believe they will improve our lives.

4. Some people _____ pleasure from dominating others.

   Pleasure _____ in this way can, in the extreme, lead to

   violence and brutality.

5. A society where everyone is _____ is an egalitarian

   society. Most people feel that _____ of opportunity is a

   very important element of a democracy.

CRITICAL THINKING

Discuss the questions in a small group. Be prepared to share your ideas with the class.

1. According to the Declaration of Independence, all men are created equal. Do you think this is true? People are all different; how can they be equal?

2. The French Declaration of the Rights of Man and of the Citizen was written during the French Revolution, thirteen years after the American Declaration of Independence. In it was written: "Men are born free and remain free and equal in rights. . . . The aim of all political association is the preservation of the natural and imprescriptible [cannot be taken away] rights of man. These rights are liberty, property, security, and resistance to oppression." How are these concepts similar to those of the Declaration of Independence? How are they different?

3. The Declaration of Independence insists that people have the right to "the pursuit of happiness." What do you think the document means by this phrase? What does it mean to you?

4. The Declaration of Independence discusses certain rights. Do you think there are other rights that should be recognized, such as the right to an education? Discuss what rights you think are essential today and why.

5. The Declaration of Independence was written by Thomas Jefferson, a slave owner, and many slave owners signed it. Is there a contradiction between theory and practice in this Declaration? How could such a contradiction be resolved? In the United States, the resolution required 100 years of arguing and finally, a bloody Civil War (from 1861 to 1865) to free the slaves in the name of "all men are created equal." In your opinion, does this contradiction destroy the significance of the Declaration?

NOTE-TAKING: Comparing and Contrasting the Ideas of Two Thinkers

1 Work with a partner. Go back to Readings One and Two and read them again. Then fill out the chart with short notes about the ideas of Niccolò Machiavelli and Thomas Jefferson on certain topics.

	TOPIC	MACHIAVELLI'S IDEAS	JEFFERSON'S IDEAS
1.	Human Nature	men are not good: they are liars, deceivers, ungrateful, greedy, unfaithful, cowardly, not very smart	all men are created equal and have the ability to fulfill their needs according to their talents and interests
2.	The Rights of Man		

	TOPIC	MACHIAVELLI'S IDEAS	JEFFERSON'S IDEAS
3.	The Aims of Government		
4.	The Best Type of Leadership		
5.	The Importance of Political Stability		
6.	Other Topic		

2 Working with your partner, use the notes you took to write a summary comparing and contrasting the ideas of Machiavelli and Jefferson. For assistance with this task, review the *Expressions of Similarity and Contrast*. You may use these expressions or others of your choice as many times as you like.

Expressions of Similarity and Contrast

SIMILARITY	CONTRAST
Similarly,	In contrast (to) . . .
Likewise,	On the other hand,
In the same way,	While (+ clause)
Just as (+ clause)	Whereas (+ clause)
Like X,	Unlike X,

EXAMPLES:
- **Like** Machiavelli, Jefferson was concerned about defining the best possible government.
- Machiavelli was very concerned about advising the ruler **while** Jefferson was more concerned about advising the people.
- In Machiavelli's writings, power and control remained with the prince. For Jefferson, **on the other hand**, power belonged to the people.

(continued on next page)

In their writing, both Niccolò Machiavelli and Thomas Jefferson consider the role that government should play in people's lives. Whereas they are both concerned about the need for the best possible government, their loyalties are different. In The Prince, Machiavelli describes ways in which power and control can remain with the prince while, in The Declaration of Independence, Jefferson explains that power should remain in the hands of the people.

LINKING READINGS ONE AND TWO

Read some statements made by Nicolas de Condorcet, an Enlightenment philosopher from France, explaining the new ideas that emerged in the 18th century.

- For philosophers, the rights of man are derived from the fact that man is a thinking being, capable of reasoning and morality.
- Men no longer dare to divide humanity into two races: one destined to rule and the other to obey, one to deceive and the other to be deceived.
- All men have an equal right to be informed about what concerns them. No one who governs them has the right to hide from them one single truth.
- All philosophers embrace *reason*, *tolerance*, and *humanity*. These principles are shared by all those who are neither Machiavellians nor fools.

Now answer the questions in a small group.

1. According to Condorcet, what qualities do human beings have that animals do not? Why do these qualities give them the right to democracy and self-government? Would Machiavelli agree or disagree? Explain your answer.

2. What do you imagine Condorcet thought about Machiavelli?

3. In the Declaration of Independence, Jefferson wrote that it was obvious ("self-evident") that men are equal. How does Condorcet explain the idea of "all men are created equal"? What other ideas in the Declaration of Independence does Condorcet support?

4. According to Condorcet, why is freedom of the press or freedom of information so important to a democracy? What would Machiavelli say?

READING THREE: Two Cheers for Democracy

Ⓐ Warm-Up

Discuss the question in a small group.

For the French philosopher Condorcet, the most important qualities were "reason, tolerance, and humanity." What are the three most important qualities that you respect and admire?

Ⓑ Reading Strategy

Thinking about the Title and Predicting Content

The **title of a text** is the **first contact we have with the author**. It can inspire us to enter into a **dialogue with the author** even before reading one word of the text. It can also help us **predict** (guess) the content of the text.

Work with a partner. Answer the question about the title of the reading: "Two Cheers for Democracy." Write your answer on the line.

In British tradition, people make three cheers for something they like: "Hip Hip Hooray, Hip Hip Hooray, Hip Hip Hooray!"

E. M. Forster gives only two cheers for democracy. Why do you think he does that?

_____

_____

Now read the text to find out if your guess was correct.

Two Cheers for Democracy

By E. M. Forster

E. M. Forster (1879–1970) is an English writer famous for his novels A Room with a View, Howard's End, *and* A Passage to India. *He also wrote a few short biographies, some essays, and literary criticism. Today many people know of him because of the many film adaptations of his work.*

1   **Tolerance**, good temper and sympathy — they are what really matter, and if the human race is not to collapse they must come to the front before long.[1] Where do I start? With personal relationships. They are something comparatively solid in a world full of violence and cruelty. One must be fond of people and trust them if one is not to make a mess of life, and it is therefore essential that they should not **let** one **down**. They often do. The moral of which is that I must, myself, be as reliable as possible, and this I try to be. But reliability is not a matter of contract — that is the main difference between the world of personal relationships and the world of business relationships. It is a matter for the heart, which signs no documents. In other words, reliability is impossible unless there is a natural warmth. Most men possess this warmth, though they often have bad luck and get chilled. Most of them, even when they are politicians, *want* to **keep faith**. And one can, at all events, show one's own little light here, one's own poor little trembling flame, with the knowledge that it is not the only light that is shining in the darkness, and not the only one which the darkness does not comprehend.

2   Personal relations are **despised** today. They are regarded as luxuries, as products of a time of fair weather which is now past, and we are urged to get rid of them, and to dedicate ourselves to some movement or cause instead. I hate the idea of causes, and if I had to choose between betraying my country and betraying my friend, I hope I should have the guts to betray my country. Such a choice may **scandalize** the modern reader, and he may stretch out his patriotic hand to the telephone at once and ring up the police. It would not have shocked Dante,[2] though. Dante places Brutus[3] and Cassius[4] in the lowest circle of Hell because they had chosen to betray their friend Julius Caesar rather than their country, Rome. Probably one will not be asked to make such an agonizing choice. Love and loyalty to an individual can **run counter to** the claims of the State. When they do — down with the State, say I, which means that the State would down me.

---

[1] *they must come to the front before long:* they must start to be given priority (be respected) soon

[2] *Dante:* an Italian poet (1265–1321), also known as Dante Alighieri; wrote *The Divine Comedy*

[3] *Brutus:* Roman politician and military leader (85?–42 B.C.); participated in the assassination of his friend Julius Caesar because he thought Caesar would become a dictator and destroy the Republic

[4] *Cassius:* Roman politician and conspirator (died 42 B.C.); participated in the assassination of Caesar

3　　This brings me along to democracy. Democracy is not a beloved Republic really, and never will be. But it is less hateful than other **contemporary** forms of government, and to that extent it deserves our support. It does start from the **assumption** that the individual is important, and that all types are needed to make a civilization. It does not divide its citizens into the bosses and the bossed — as an efficiency-regime tends to do. The people I admire most are those who are sensitive and want to create something or discover something, and do not see life in terms of power, and such people get more of a chance under a democracy than elsewhere. They found religions, great or small, or they produce literature and art, or they do **disinterested** scientific research, or they may be what is called "ordinary people," who are creative in their private lives, bring up their children decently, for instance, or help their neighbours. All these people need to express themselves; they cannot do so unless society allows them liberty to do so, and the society which allows them most liberty is a democracy.

4　　Democracy has another merit. It allows criticism, and if there is not public criticism, there are **bound to** be hushed-up scandals. That is why I believe in the press, despite all its lies and vulgarity, and why I believe in Parliament.[5] Parliament is often **sneered at** because it is a Talking Shop. I believe in it *because* it is a talking shop. I believe in the Private Member who makes himself a nuisance. He gets snubbed and is told that he is **cranky** or ill-informed, but he does expose abuses which would otherwise never have been mentioned, and very often an abuse gets put right just by being mentioned. Whether Parliament is either a representative body or an efficient one is questionable, but I value it because it criticizes and talks, and because its chatter gets widely reported. So two cheers for Democracy: one because it admits variety and two because it permits criticism. Two cheers are quite enough: there is no occasion to give three.

---

[5] *Parliament:* the main law-making institution in some countries, such as the United Kingdom

COMPREHENSION

Ⓐ　Main Ideas

Work with a partner. Complete the summary of the main ideas in the reading.

Forster admires tolerance, _____ and
　　　　　　　　　　　　　　　　　　1.
_____ rather than violence and cruelty. For him, personal
　　2.
relationships are _____ in life. Because he believes in the
　　　　　　　　　　　　　3.
individual, Forster chooses democracy because it _____ and
　　　　　　　　　　　　　　　　　　　　　　　　　　　　4.
_____. But he has no illusions that it is a perfect system.
　　5.

B Close Reading

Read the quotes from the reading. Circle the statement that best explains each quote. Share your answers with a partner.

1. "In other words, reliability is impossible unless there is a natural warmth. Most men possess this warmth, though they often have bad luck and get chilled." *(paragraph 1)*

   Based on what Forster says, one example of "bad luck" could be . . .

   a. a fatal disease.

   b. the loss of a job.

   c. a betrayal in personal relationships.

2. "And one can, at all events, show one's own little light here, one's own poor little trembling flame, with the knowledge that it is not the only light that is shining in the darkness, and not the only one which the darkness does not comprehend." *(paragraph 1)*

   Forster communicates the idea that . . .

   a. good people are not alone even in the darkness of bad times.

   b. we shouldn't be afraid of the darkness or the light.

   c. darkness and ignorance play a large role in our lives.

3. "Love and loyalty to an individual can run counter to the claims of the State. When they do — down with the State, say I, which means that the State would down me." *(paragraph 2)*

   a. Forster knows the state will agree with him if he is loyal to a friend against the state.

   b. Forster knows the state will punish him if he protects a friend against the state.

   c. Forster always agrees with the state.

4. "[Democracy] does start from the assumption that the individual is important, and that all types are needed to make a civilization." *(paragraph 3)*

   In this statement, "types" refers to . . .

   a. kinds of individuals.

   b. kinds of governments.

   c. kinds of civilizations.

5. "Two cheers [for democracy] are quite enough: there is no occasion to give three." *(paragraph 4)*

   One can infer from this statement that Forster feels . . .

   a. people shouldn't believe democracy is perfect.

   b. people shouldn't choose democracy.

   c. people shouldn't change democracy.

VOCABULARY

A **Synonyms**

Read the sentences. Match each word or phrase in bold with its synonym in the box below. Compare answers with a partner.

__c__ 1. With the pressures of **contemporary** society consuming all our time and energy, we often turn away from thinking about politics.

_____ 2. However, being passive is **bound to** make things worse.

_____ 3. We shouldn't live with the mistaken **assumption** that we will always enjoy the good things we have without any effort.

_____ 4. It's easy to be concerned only with one's own private life, but sometimes this leads to a thoughtless **tolerance** of injustice.

_____ 5. We hope that all politicians will be ethical, fair, and **disinterested** people, concerned to serve the community.

_____ 6. The goals of politicians who think only about having money and power **run counter to** the ethics of government service.

_____ 7. Reading the newspapers, one gets the impression that the country is full of **cranky** citizens who complain about demonstrators and people who try to change society.

_____ 8. The fear of being **sneered at** should not get in the way of protesting against social injustice.

_____ 9. We must **keep faith with** those who depend on our sympathy and need our help.

_____ 10. Since our ability to interact in society is first learned in the home, parents will be **letting** their children **down** if they do not teach them to stand up for what is right.

_____ 11. Children must learn to accept diversity and not **despise** or fear those who are different.

_____ 12. In addition, parents must tell their children about what is going on in the world around them; otherwise, they will never be **scandalized** by injustices and will never do anything to change them.

a. opinion	g. neglecting
b. likely to	h. are incompatible with
c. modern	i. shocked
d. irritable	j. insulted by others
e. hate	k. be loyal to
f. objective	l. acceptance

B Using the Dictionary

Read the dictionary entries for *disinterested* and *uninterested*.

> **disinterested** *adj.* not personally involved in a situation, and therefore able to judge the situation fairly; objective: *a disinterested observer*
>
> **uninterested** *adj.* not interested; i.e., not giving a lot of attention to something: *I was uninterested in traveling when I was young.*

Do the following actions reflect the person's *disinterested* or *uninterested* behavior? Write D or U next to each one. Discuss your answers with a partner.

__D__ **a.** a research scientist evaluating data

_____ **b.** a woman saying no to a man who asks her out on a date

_____ **c.** a judge who doesn't know any of the people involved in his decision

_____ **d.** an employer considering applicants' abilities and not their physical looks

_____ **e.** a person deciding not to try out for the chess team

_____ **f.** a man refusing to watch a romantic movie

GRAMMAR FOR READING: The Dash

The **dash (—)** is a **punctuation mark** that writers use **instead of parentheses**, and sometimes **commas**, when they **want to "isolate" a point** and give it **prominence**. If the point to be "isolated" comes in the **middle** of the sentence, **two dashes** are needed. If it comes at the **end** of the sentence, only **one dash** is needed. The dash **should not be overused**.

EXAMPLES:

Parentheses:
- E. M. Forster's positive view of democracy (that it permits a variety of opinions and people's right to criticize) is defined in "Two Cheers for Democracy."
- Not everyone agrees with E. M. Forster's positive view of democracy (that it permits a variety of opinions and people's right to criticize).

Commas:
- E. M. Forster's positive view of democracy, that it permits a variety of opinions and people's right to criticize, is defined in "Two Cheers for Democracy."
- Not everyone agrees with E. M. Forster's positive view of democracy, that it permits a variety of opinions and people's right to criticize.

Dashes:
- E. M. Forster's positive view of democracy — that it permits a variety of opinions and people's right to criticize — is defined in "Two Cheers for Democracy."
- Not everyone agrees with E. M. Forster's positive view of democracy — that it permits a variety of opinions and people's right to criticize.

1 Go back to the reading and highlight the points that the author isolates with dashes. Compare answers with a partner. Discuss why the use of dashes in these instances is/is not effective.

2 Rewrite these sentences about E. M. Forster's life and art by putting dashes in the appropriate places.

1. E. M. Forster, the English writer known for five wonderful novels (among them, *A Room with a View, Howard's End*, and *A Passage to India*), was born in London in 1879.

_____

_____

_____

2. In a period of 20 years (between 1905 and 1924), he published most of the works for which he is known.

_____

_____

_____

3. Because his father died of consumption soon after he was born, Forster lived with his mother, a difficult and demanding woman, for the first 66 years of life, until his mother's death in 1945.

_____

_____

_____

4. When writing *Howard's End* (his first major success) in 1910, Forster was part of the Bloomsbury group, a circle of British thinkers and writers (among them, Virginia Woolf, John Maynard Keynes, Dora Carrington, and Lytton Strachey).

_____

_____

5. Although Forster believed that novels could not be adapted into stage or film (in his opinion, the individual experience of reading a book could not be captured in another media form), many of the film adaptations of his work were Academy Award winners.

_____

_____

_____

CRITICAL THINKING

Discuss these questions in a small group. Refer to your notes on the readings to support your views. Be prepared to share your answers with the class.

1. Forster says that most men possess a "natural warmth." He goes further to explain that "reliability" is more prominent in personal relationships than in business relationships because in personal relationships, which are nurtured by man's "natural warmth," there are no contracts.

   Do you agree with the distinction Forster makes between personal relationships and business relationships? Why or why not? Would you agree that reliability and man's natural warmth are also essential qualities for successful business relationships? Why or why not?

2. Forster implies that patriotism — the love of one's country — can often get in the way of personal relationships. In this conflict, Forster would choose personal relationships over the demands of the state. What do you think of his choice?

3. Forster says that democracy is the system that best suits the needs of ordinary people. Why? How do "ordinary people" become creative in his opinion? Do you agree?

4. We sometimes say, "The squeaky wheel gets the grease," meaning, the one who complains or protests the loudest gets the most attention. How does this saying apply to what Forster says about parliamentary discussions?

5. If given a choice, some people might prefer living in a dictatorship. Why do you think they would prefer such a system? Is freedom sometimes frightening?

6. Forster gives two cheers for democracy. How many would you give and why?

AFTER YOU READ

BRINGING IT ALL TOGETHER

Divide into three groups and explain in simple language one of the quotes from famous political philosophers of the Enlightenment. Does the quote support or oppose the main ideas in the three readings in this chapter? Refer to specific statements in the readings. Use some of the vocabulary you studied in the chapter (for a complete list, go to page 194).

1. "Nature has made men so equal in the abilities of body and mind that even if one man is sometimes clearly stronger in body or quicker in thought than another, yet when all is taken together, the difference between one man and another is not so great that any man should be entitled to any special privileges."

   —*Thomas Hobbes*, *"Of the Natural Condition of Mankind as concerning their Felicity and Misery," chapter 13 in* Leviathan, *1588–1679*

2. "The freedom of men under government means having laws to live by, common to everyone in the society, and made by the legislature of the society. . . . This freedom from absolute, arbitrary power, is so necessary to, and closely joined with, a man's preservation, that he cannot part with it."

   —*John Locke*, *"Of Slavery," chapter 4 in* An Essay Concerning the True, Original, Extent, and End of Civil Government, *1632–1704*

3. "The people have to obey the laws, so they ought to be the ones who write the laws. The conditions of society ought to be regulated only by those who come together to form it. . . . How can a blind multitude, which often does not know what it wants because it rarely knows what is good for it, carry out so great and difficult a task as a system of laws? . . . This is what makes a legislator necessary."

—*Jean-Jacques Rousseau, "Law," chapter 6 in* The Social Contract, *1712–1778*

WRITING ACTIVITY

Write an essay explaining your opinion about one of the main ideas of the readings.

1. In politics, the ends justify the means.

2. The right to freedom (the right to choose)

3. The pursuit of happiness

Write at least three paragraphs.

- **Introduction:** Express your opinion (thesis statement).
- **Body Paragraphs:** Give information that best supports your opinion.
- **Conclusion:** Summarize your thesis and predict how future situations might confirm it.

Use more than five of the words and idioms you studied in the chapter.

DISCUSSION AND WRITING TOPICS

Discuss these topics in a small group. Choose one of them and write an essay in response. Use the vocabulary from the chapter.

1. Choose a leader who, in your opinion, followed the ideas of Machiavelli (such as *the ends justify the means* and *it is necessary to lie to people and make them afraid*). What kind of government did the person lead? What happened?

2. Compare and contrast the ideas of Machiavelli, Jefferson (as expressed in the Declaration of Independence), and E. M. Forster.

3. We all need to become "leaders" if we want to make life better. Despite your busy schedule, what kind of contribution could you make to your community?

4. President Franklin D. Roosevelt elaborated four freedoms: freedom from fear, freedom from want (poverty), freedom of worship, and freedom of speech. Explain these freedoms. Which is the most important to you? What does freedom mean to you?

5. Many countries have declarations and constitutions. Do you think these documents serve a purpose? Why or why not?

VOCABULARY

Nouns	Verbs	Adjectives	Adverbs
assumption *	abolish	contemporary *	hence *
charity	alter *	cranky	invariably
compassion	confiscate	disinterested	
consent *	constrain *	equal	**Phrases and Idioms**
deceiver	derive *	fickle	bound to
dread	despise	prudent	endow with
hypocrite	dissolve	transient	keep faith
integrity *	impel		let sb down
patrimony	manipulate *		run counter to
tolerance	scandalize		sneer at
	secure *		

* = AWL (Academic Word List) item

SELF-ASSESSMENT

In this chapter you learned to:

○ Skim a text to identify the author's point of view

○ Highlight the important information in a text

○ Think about the title of a text and predict its content

○ Guess the meaning of words from the context

○ Use dictionary entries to learn the meanings of words

○ Understand and use synonyms, different word forms, figurative language, and expressions of similarity and contrast

○ Use a dash or dashes to isolate and emphasize a point

○ Take notes to compare and contrast the ideas of two thinkers

What can you do well? ✓

What do you need to practice more? ✓

<table>
<tr><td>CHAPTER
8</td><td># PSYCHOLOGY:
Aggression and Violence</td></tr>
</table>

CHAPTER

8

PSYCHOLOGY:
Aggression and Violence

PSYCHOLOGY: the systematic, scientific study of behavior and mental processes

OBJECTIVES

To read academic texts, you need to master certain skills.

In this chapter, you will:

- Predict the content of a text from the title or the first paragraph

- Understand the most important idea of a text from the first and last paragraphs

- Guess the meaning of words from the context

- Use dictionary entries to learn the meanings of words

- Understand and use synonyms, phrases and idioms, collocations, and different word forms

- Identify adjective clauses and the reasons for their use

- Take notes to identify the author's assertions and supporting explanations

- Complete outlines to focus on the sequence of events and main discoveries

In psychology and other social sciences, "aggression" refers to behavior between members of the same species that is intended to cause pain or harm.

Ⓐ Consider These Questions

Discuss the questions with a partner.

1. Is aggressive behavior sometimes necessary in a society? In what situations?

2. When is aggression dangerous for society?

3. Do you ever feel that you would like to do violence to something or someone? In what situations? What makes you control yourself?

4. What helps society control violence?

5. Are people naturally violent, or is violence learned through culture?

6. What is the difference between being aggressive and being assertive?

Ⓑ Consider These Quotes

Read the following quotes about aggression and violence. With a partner, discuss what each one means. Which one expresses your feelings on the matter?

1. "If it's natural to kill, how come men have to go into training to learn how?"

   —*Joan Baez, American folk singer and political activist, born 1941*

2. "Violence, naked force has settled more issues in history than has any other factor."

   —*Robert Heinlein, American science fiction writer, 1907–1988*

3. "If we don't end war, war will end us."

   —*H.G. Wells, English science fiction writer, 1866–1946*

4. "I am a violent man who has learned not to be violent and regrets his violence."

   —*John Lennon, English singer and songwriter, member of the Beatles, 1940–1980*

5. "In each of us there is a Mr. Hyde.[1] The point is to prevent the conditions that would allow the monster to emerge."

   —*Amin Maalouf, Lebanese-born French author, born 1949*

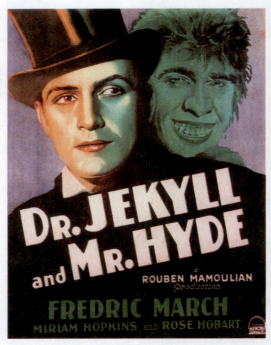

Poster of the 1931 movie based on Robert Louis Stevenson's novel

---

[1] *Mr Hyde:* the embodiment of the dark side of the good Dr. Jekyll; Mr. Hyde is released as an experiment and gradually takes over in Robert Louis Stevenson's *Dr. Jekyll and Mr. Hyde.*

A Warm-Up

Sigmund Freud (1856–1939) was an Austrian medical doctor and neurologist who began seeing patients with emotional problems. He wrote about his patients and about his theory of the unconscious mind, where passions and hidden desires fought for expression. His work in psychoanalysis with the "talking cure" began the modern movement to understand our mind and behavior.

In the years before the outbreak of World War II, Freud wrote *Civilization and Its Discontents*.

Discuss the question with a partner.

Do you think we always make rational and reasonable decisions, or do we sometimes wonder why we do things? Can you give examples of this? Are we often influenced by unconscious desires?

B Reading Strategy

Predicting Content from First Paragraph

Reading the **first paragraph** of a text can help you to **understand the most important idea** of the passage before you read the entire reading.

Read the first paragraph of "Civilization and Its Discontents." Then read each statement and check (✓) *Yes* or *No*.

	YES	NO
1. The reading will say that violence is inborn in human beings.	☐	☐
2. The reading will be optimistic about man's fate in the future.	☐	☐

Now read the text and decide if your answers were correct.

Civilization and Its Discontents

By Sigmund Freud

1   *Homo homini lupus.* [Man is a wolf to man.] Who, in the face of all his experience of life and of history, will have the courage to dispute this **assertion**? As a rule, this cruel aggressiveness waits for some provocation or puts itself at the service of some higher purpose, whose goal might have been reached by milder measures. Anyone who calls to mind the **atrocities** committed during the invasions of the Huns,[1] or by the people known as the Mongols[2] under Genghis Khan and Tamerlane, or at the capture of Jerusalem by the **pious** Crusaders,[3] or even the horrors of the recent World War — anyone who calls these things to mind will have to accept the truth of this view.

2   The existence of this **inclination** to aggression, which we can detect in ourselves and justly assume to be present in others, is the factor which disturbs our relations with our neighbor and which forces civilization into such a high **expenditure** of energy. . . . Civilization has to use its **utmost** efforts in order to set limits to man's aggressive instincts.

3   The meaning of the evolution of civilization is no longer obscure to us. It must present the struggle between Eros and Thanatos,[4] between the instinct of life and the instinct of destruction, as it works itself out in the human species. This struggle is what all life essentially consists of, and the evolution of civilization may therefore be simply described as the struggle for the life of the human species.

4   The **fateful** question for the human species seems to me to be whether and to what extent their cultural development will succeed in **mastering** the disturbance of their communal life by the human instinct of aggression and self-destruction. It may be that in this respect precisely the present time deserves a special interest. Men have gained control over the forces of nature to such an extent that with their help they would have no difficulty in **exterminating** one another to the last man. They know this, and from this comes a large part of their current unrest, their unhappiness and their mood of anxiety. And now it is to be expected that the other of the two "Heavenly Powers," eternal Eros, will make an effort to assert himself in the struggle with his equally immortal **adversary**. But who can foresee with what success and with what result?

---

[1] *Huns:* a group of nomadic people from central Asia who attacked and controlled parts of Europe during the 4th and 5th centuries A.D.

[2] *Mongols:* a group of nomadic people from northeast and central Asia who conquered Asia, the Middle East, and eastern Europe in the 13th and 14th centuries, resulting in a vast Mongol empire under Genghis Khan and a descendant known as Tamerlane.

[3] *Crusaders:* people who took part in the wars fought in the 11th, 12th, and 13th centuries by Christian armies trying to take Palestine from the Muslims; the crusaders' conquest of Jerusalem in 1099 was accompanied by massacres of Muslims and Jews

[4] *Eros* and *Thanatos* were Greek gods — Eros was the god of love, Thanatos the god of death.

COMPREHENSION

A Main Ideas

Complete the sentences based on the main ideas of the reading. Use your own words.

1. According to Freud, people have committed terrible acts of cruelty against other human beings, especially in certain situations, such as _____ _____.

2. Civilization (cultural development) tries very hard to _____ _____.

3. Inside man are two warring instincts, one representing _____ and the other _____.

4. Scientific and technological development have made it possible _____ _____, which makes this a time of potential _____.

B Close Reading

Read the quotes from the reading. Circle the statement that best explains each quote. Share your answers with a partner.

1. "*Homo homini lupus*. [Man is a wolf to man.]" *(paragraph 1)*

   In this saying, . . .

   a. "wolf" is a metaphor for cruelty.

   b. "wolf" is a metaphor for wildness.

2. "As a rule, this cruel aggressiveness waits for some provocation or puts itself at the service of some higher purpose, whose goal might have been reached by milder measures." *(paragraph 1)*

   a. Aggression prevents peaceful conflict resolution.

   b. A higher purpose provokes others into fighting.

3. "The existence of this inclination to aggression, which we can detect in ourselves and justly assume to be present in others, is the factor which disturbs our relations with our neighbor and which forces civilization into such a high expenditure of energy." *(paragraph 2)*

   a. Civilization has to work hard to get us to admit our aggressive instincts.

   b. Civilization has to work hard to control our aggressive instincts.

   (continued on next page)

4. "This struggle is what all life essentially consists of, and the evolution of civilization may therefore be simply described as the struggle for the life of the human species." *(paragraph 3)*

   According to Freud, . . .

   a. civilization evolves in order to give life to the human species.

   b. civilization evolves in order to protect humans from themselves.

5. "The fateful question for the human species seems to me to be whether and to what extent their cultural development will succeed in mastering the disturbance of their communal life by the human instinct of aggression and self-destruction." *(paragraph 4)*

   a. The effort to control aggression will decide man's fate.

   b. Cultural development will master communal life.

6. "And now it is to be expected that the other of the two 'Heavenly Powers,' eternal Eros, will make an effort to assert himself in the struggle with his equally immortal adversary. But who can foresee with what success and with what result?" *(paragraph 4)*

   a. The life instinct will win against the death instinct.

   b. The life instinct and the death instinct will fight it out.

VOCABULARY

Ⓐ Synonyms

1 Cross out the word that is NOT a synonym for the word in bold. Compare answers with a partner.

1. **adversary**	~~supporter~~	foe	opponent
2. **assertion**	statement	claim	controversy
3. **atrocity**	barbarism	cruelty	attack
4. **expenditure**	spending	exposure	exertion
5. **exterminate**	massacre	arrest	kill
6. **fateful**	intense	most important	crucial
7. **inclination**	attraction	tendency	dislike
8. **master**	surrender	control	overcome
9. **pious**	religious	spiritual	content
10. **utmost**	best	better	greatest

2 Complete the sentences with the words from the box. Use the synonym in parentheses to help you select the correct word. Compare answers with a partner.

adversary	expenditure	inclination	pious
assertion	extermination	master	utmost
atrocities	fateful		

1. For Freud, man is divided between the _____inclination_____ to
   (impulse)
   aggression and the need for love.

2. Aggression can lead to self-destruction and even the _____
   (annihilation)
   of the entire human race.

3. Love, a life-giving force, is the _____ of the tendency to
   (enemy)
   violence and destruction.

4. Cruelty and aggressive instincts, according to Freud, have produced many

   _____ in the history of mankind.
   (monstrous actions)

5. Freud's _____ is that mankind's civilized life, cultural
   (belief)
   development, and _____ behavior are all efforts to
   (spiritual)
   _____ the death instinct within.
   (control)

6. The rewards of civilized life justify the enormous _____ of
   (output)
   effort mankind has made.

7. Freud had the _____ respect for his patients, and he used
   (greatest)
   the knowledge gained from their treatment to make the inner workings of the

   mind less obscure to human beings.

8. At the end of his life, he asked a _____ question: Can
   (crucial)
   mankind survive the terrible weapons that their brains, working with their

   aggressive instincts, have invented?

B Collocations

Check (✓) the collocations (words that are often paired together). Discuss your answers with a partner.

☐ **1.** fateful moment   ☐ **3.** master a language   ☐ **5.** a natural inclination

☐ **2.** fateful disaster   ☐ **4.** master a person   ☐ **6.** a false inclination

CRITICAL THINKING

Discuss the questions in a small group. Be prepared to share your answers with the class.

1. Is there anything in the reading that leads you to believe that Freud is pessimistic about the future? What sentences or references in the reading may cause you to draw that conclusion?

2. If a person were motivated mostly by love, what would his or her behavior be? Do we see much of this behavior in everyday life? If so, when?

3. If a person were motivated mostly by aggression and the death wish, what would his or her behavior be? Do we see much of this behavior in everyday life? If so, when?

4. Aggression doesn't always have to be physical. For example, lying about a person's character can be an aggressive act. In what other ways can aggression be manifested in a person's life (e.g., verbally, psychologically, morally, financially, etc.)?

READING TWO: Reflections on Natural History

A Warm-Up

Discuss the question with a partner. Share your answers with the class.

Some people have said that mankind is the most violent species on earth. Do you think they are correct? Why or why not?

B Reading Strategy

Understanding the Most Important Idea from First and Last Paragraphs

Reading the **first (introduction)** and **last (conclusion) paragraphs** of a text **first** is sometimes a very effective way of seeing where the author is going with his story or his argument. It can be very helpful in **understanding the most important idea** of a text.

Read the first and last paragraphs of the reading. Then check (✓) the answer to the question.

Does Stephen Jay Gould agree or disagree with Freud's pessimism about the future of mankind?

☐ Agree

☐ Disagree

Now read the text and find out if you were correct, and in what ways Gould supports his argument.

Reflections on Natural History

By Stephen Jay Gould

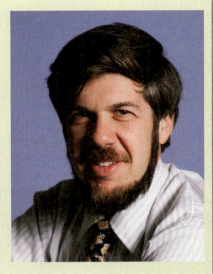

Stephen Jay Gould (1941–2002) was a respected American paleontologist, evolutionary biologist, and historian of science. He taught at Harvard University and New York University and also worked at the American Museum of Natural History. He contributed articles to many academic journals and also wrote, among other books, The Mismeasure of Man, Bully for Brontosaurus, *and* Dinosaur in a Haystack.

1   How often have we been told that man is, by nature, aggressive and selfishly **acquisitive**? Such claims make no sense to me — in a purely empirical way, not as a statement about hope or preferred morality. What do we see on any ordinary day on the streets or in the homes of any American city — even in the subways of New York? Thousands of tiny and insignificant acts of kindness and consideration. We step aside to let someone pass, smile at a child, chat aimlessly with an acquaintance, or even with a stranger. At most moments, on most days, in most places, what do you ever see of the dark side — perhaps a parent slapping a child or a teenager on a skateboard cutting off an old lady? Look, I'm no ivory-tower[1] Pollyanna,[2] and I did grow up on the streets of New York. I understand the unpleasantness and danger of crowded cities. I'm only trying to make a statistical point.

2   Many people are under the impression that daily life is an unending series of unpleasantnesses — that 50 percent or more of human encounters are stressful or aggressive. But think about it seriously for a moment. Such levels of **nastiness** cannot possibly be **sustained**. Society would **devolve** to anarchy in an instant if half our **overtures** to another human being were met with a punch in the nose.

3   No, nearly every encounter with another person is at least neutral and usually pleasant enough. *Homo sapiens*[3] is a remarkably **genial** species. Ethnologists consider other animals relatively peaceful if they see but one or two aggressive encounters while observing an organism for, say, tens of hours. But think of how many millions of hours we can log for most people on most days without noting anything more threatening than a raised third finger[4] once a week or so.

4   Why, then, do most of us have the impression that people are so aggressive, and **intrinsically** so? Unfortunately, one incident of violence can undo a thousand acts

(continued on next page)

---

[1] *ivory tower:* Universities are sometimes referred to as "ivory towers," meaning places that are insulated from the difficulties of ordinary life and therefore, unable to understand them.

[2] *Pollyanna:* an excessively or blindly optimistic person, based on the novel *Pollyanna* by Eleanor Hodgman Porter

[3] *Homo sapiens:* the Latin scientific name for the human species

[4] *raised third finger:* an insulting gesture in many cultures

of kindness, and we easily forget the **predominance** of kindness over aggression by confusing effect with frequency. Kindness is so fragile, so easy to **efface**; violence is so powerful. I am not asserting that humans are either genial or aggressive by inborn biological necessity. Obviously, both kindness and violence lie within the bounds of our nature because we **perpetuate** both, in spades.[5]

5   The central feature of our biological uniqueness also provides the major reason for doubting that our behaviors are directly coded by specific genes. That feature is, of course, our large brain. The increase in our brain added enough neural connections to convert an inflexible and rigidly programmed device into a labile[6] organ. Endowed with sufficient logic and memory, the brain may have substituted non-programmed learning for direct specification as the ground of social behavior. Flexibility may well be the most important **determinant** of human consciousness.

6   Why imagine that specific genes for aggression, dominance, or spite have any importance when we know that the brain's enormous flexibility

---

[5] *in spades:* definitely, unquestionably

[6] *labile:* open to change [in this case, from experience]

permits us to be aggressive or peaceful, dominant or submissive, spiteful or generous? Violence, sexism, and general nastiness *are* biological since they represent one subset of a possible range of behaviors. But peacefulness, equality, and kindness are just as biological — and we may see their influence increase if we can create social structures that permit them to flourish.

7   The long and intense debate surrounding biological determinism[7] has arisen as a function of its social and political message. But I **reiterate** my statement that no evidence exists to support it, that the crude versions of past centuries have been conclusively disproved, and that its continued popularity is a function of social prejudice among those who benefit most from the status quo.[8] We are both similar to and different from other animals. Our biological nature does not stand in the way of social reform.

---

[7] *biological determinism:* the hypothesis that biological factors such as genes (as opposed to social factors or the environment) completely determine how a person behaves or changes over time. Those who believe in biological determinism may not want to help the poor because they feel their situation cannot be changed.

[8] *status quo:* the way things are now

COMPREHENSION

 Main Ideas

Read each statement and check (✓) the ones that are main ideas of the reading.

☐ **1.** Human nature is primarily violent.

☐ **2.** Kindness is statistically more characteristic of relations between people than violence.

☐ **3.** Biology is not destiny for human beings.

☐ **4.** Our biological nature has many aspects, and it's up to us to encourage positive behavior in society.

B Close Reading

Read the quotes from the reading. Circle the statement that best explains each quote. Share your answers with a partner.

1. "Society would devolve to anarchy in an instant if half our overtures to another human being were met with a punch in the nose." *(paragraph 2).*

   a. Social encounters would be impossible with such a high level of violence.

   b. Anarchy would lead to violence.

2. "Unfortunately, one incident of violence can undo a thousand acts of kindness, and we easily forget the predominance of kindness over aggression by confusing effect with frequency." *(paragraph 4)*

   a. Gould is saying that one violent act has a great impact, and we forget that it's not very frequent.

   b. Gould is saying that one violent act has a great impact, and we realize that it's very frequent.

3. "Endowed with sufficient logic and memory, the brain may have substituted non-programmed learning for direct specification as the ground of social behavior." *(paragraph 5)*

   a. The human brain replaced programmed behavior with non-programmed learning.

   b. The human brain replaced non-programmed learning with programmed behavior.

4. "Why imagine that specific genes for aggression, dominance, or spite have any importance when we know that the brain's enormous flexibility permits us to be aggressive or peaceful, dominant or submissive, spiteful or generous?" *(paragraph 6)*

   a. The author agrees with a genetic explanation for behavior.

   b. The author does not agree with a genetic explanation for behavior.

5. "But peacefulness, equality, and kindness are just as biological — and we may see their influence increase if we can create social structures that permit them to flourish." *(paragraph 6)*

   a. Social structure can encourage the expression of positive biological behavior.

   b. Positive behavior is biological.

6. "Our biological nature does not stand in the way of social reform." *(paragraph 7)*

   a. Social reforms won't change anything because biology determines our behavior.

   b. People who don't want social reform cannot use biology as an excuse.

VOCABULARY

A **Guessing from Context**

Read each quote from the reading. Try to guess the meaning of the words in bold from the context. Then consult a dictionary and write the definition.

1. "Many people are under the impression . . . that 50 percent or more of human encounters are stressful or aggressive. But think about it seriously for a moment. Such levels of **nastiness** cannot possibly be **sustained**." *(paragraph 2)*

   nastiness   Guess: _meanness_

   Dictionary: _unpleasantness, spitefulness, cruelty_

   sustain   Guess: _____

   Dictionary: _____

2. "Society would **devolve** to anarchy in an instant if half our **overtures** to another human being were met with a punch in the nose." *(paragraph 2)*

   devolve   Guess: _____

   Dictionary: _____

   overtures   Guess: _____

   Dictionary: _____

3. "Unfortunately, one incident of violence can undo a thousand acts of kindness, and we easily forget the **predominance** of kindness over aggression by confusing effect with frequency." *(paragraph 4)*

   predominance   Guess: _____

   Dictionary: _____

4. "Kindness is so fragile, so easy to **efface**; violence is so powerful." *(paragraph 4)*

   efface   Guess: _____

   Dictionary: _____

5. "Obviously, both kindness and violence lie within the bounds of our nature because we **perpetuate** both, in spades." *(paragraph 4)*

   perpetuate   Guess: _____

   Dictionary: _____

6. "Flexibility may well be the most important **determinant** of human consciousness." *(paragraph 5)*

   determinant   Guess: _____

   Dictionary: _____

B Word Forms

1 Fill in the chart with the correct word forms. Some categories can have more than one form. Use a dictionary if necessary. An **X** indicates there is no form in that category.

	NOUN	VERB	ADJECTIVE	ADVERB
1.	acquisitiveness		acquisitive	X
2.		efface		X
3.		perpetuate		
4.	predominance			
5.		reiterate		X
6.		sustain	sustained /	X

2 Complete the sentences with the correct forms of the words from the chart. The first letter (or letters) of each word has been given to you as a clue. Compare answers with a partner.

1. Gould does not think that human nature is **perpetually** _____

   selfish, **a**_____, and cruel.

2. On the contrary, he **r**_____ several times that most of the

   time, kindness and consideration **pr**_____.

3. For Gould, there is no biological determinism: the brain is so flexible that genetic

   predispositions can be diminished or even **e**_____ by

   experience and learning.

4. In humans, our choices are important; we are

   capable of violence but, if the right conditions can be

   s_____, peace and solidarity

   can **pr**_____ in human relations.

Read the essay about the theories of Albert Bandura. Match each word or phrase in bold with its synonym in the box below. Compare answers with a partner.

The Theories of Albert Bandura

Albert Bandura is a respected psychologist, professor emeritus of social science in psychology at Stanford University. His theories consider that people **acquire** 1. violent behavior by learning it from the people around them in the family, the community, and the wider society. Family influence is a major **determinant** 2. because growing up in a violent or abusive environment can lead to aggressive behavior in the next generation. Violent behavior can then become a **perpetual** 3. vicious cycle.

However, nothing is inevitable. According to Bandura, negative influences can be partially or totally **effaced** 4. by the actions of positive adult role models in school or other areas. Their **sustained** 5. care and attention can allow a child to flourish. A **genial** 6. role model can motivate a young person to control aggressive impulses. In his writings, Bandura **reiterates** 7. that social learning can change behavior and that positive **overtures** 8. must be made to try to reform violent young people.

He refutes the idea that people are **intrinsically** 9. evil. But he puts us on guard against allowing violent videos, games, and movies to **predominate** 10. in a child's life. Although he doesn't believe society will inevitably **devolve** 11. into **nastiness** 12. and chaos, he has done important work warning us against the dehumanizing effects of violence.

____	**a.** erased	____	**g.** take a huge place
____	**b.** cruelty	____	**h.** genetically (inherently)
____	**c.** factor	____	**i.** repeats
_1_	**d.** learn	____	**j.** never-ending
____	**e.** friendly	____	**k.** constant
____	**f.** regress	____	**l.** approaches

NOTE-TAKING: Identifying the Author's Assertions and Explanations

Work with a partner. Go back to the reading and read it again. Then fill in the chart. First, complete Gould's assertions or statements communicating his beliefs. Then take notes on the explanations he gives in support of these assertions.

	GOULD'S ASSERTIONS	GOULD'S EXPLANATIONS
1.	Man is by nature aggressive and _selfishly acquisitive_.	*many acts of kindness in any American city on a given day*
2.	It is impractical to say that 50 percent of human reactions are _stressful_ or _aggressive_.	*such a situation would not be sustainable — would lead to chaos*
3.	Man is a _____ species.	
4.	Humans are both _____ and _____, but we remember _____ more.	
5.	The large human brain allows for more _____.	
6.	The concept of biological determinism has no _____.	

CRITICAL THINKING

Discuss the questions in a small group. Be prepared to share your answers with the class.

1. Freud wrote *Civilization and Its Discontents* in the 1930s, and Gould wrote *Reflections on Natural History* in the 1990s. Would these different time periods have an impact on their assertions? Does the historical context have an influence on our way of viewing man's nature?

2. Why is the flexibility of the brain so important for Gould? Why does it make humans so different from animals?

3. What sentences in Gould's text make you believe Gould is optimistic about the future of mankind?

4. Gould says we can "create social structures" that allow kindness to flourish. What could we do as a society to reduce the despair and violence and help more compassion and generosity to enter our lives?

Work with a partner. Go back to Readings One and Two and read them again. Then read each statement and decide if Freud or Gould would have agreed with it. Write **F/G** if both would have agreed, **F** if only Freud would have agreed, and **G** if only Gould would have agreed.

_____ **1.** The future looks dark.

_____ **2.** We can be optimistic about the future.

_____ **3.** Human beings have an innate potential for violence.

_____ **4.** Kindness predominates in human beings.

_____ **5.** Human behavior can be affected by social structures in a positive way.

READING THREE: A Neuroscientist Uncovers a Dark Secret

Ⓐ Warm-Up

Discuss the question with a partner.

Do you think there is such a thing as a person destined by nature to be a killer?

Ⓑ Reading Strategy

Predicting Content from Title
Predicting or getting some idea of a text before you start reading will help you improve your reading speed and comprehension. The **title** of a text can often help you predict or **guess the author's most important idea** and guide you through the reading with the proper focus.

Examine the title of the reading: "A Neuroscientist Uncovers a Dark Secret."

1 Check (✓) the statements that you think apply.

☐ **a.** This is a dramatic title, probably from the news media.

☐ **b.** The article concerns someone in the medical profession.

☐ **c.** A secret will be revealed in the reading.

2 With a partner, discuss these questions.

1. Do you think this is a pleasant or unpleasant secret?

2. Who do you think the secret is about? About us? About the neuroscientist? About the writer of the article?

Now read the text, taking notes in the margin so that you can follow the sequence of events. Then go back and see if your predictions were correct.

A Neuroscientist Uncovers a Dark Secret

By Barbara Bradley

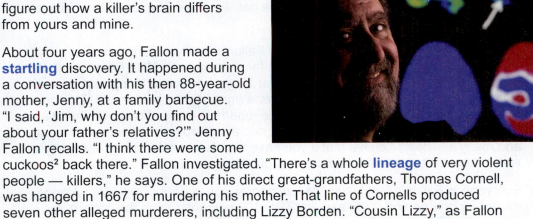

1   The criminal brain has always held a fascination for James Fallon. For nearly 20 years, the neuroscientist at the University of California-Irvine has studied the brains of psychopaths.[1] He studies the biological basis for behavior, and one of his specialties is to try to figure out how a killer's brain differs from yours and mine.

2   About four years ago, Fallon made a **startling** discovery. It happened during a conversation with his then 88-year-old mother, Jenny, at a family barbecue. "I said, 'Jim, why don't you find out about your father's relatives?'" Jenny Fallon recalls. "I think there were some cuckoos[2] back there." Fallon investigated. "There's a whole **lineage** of very violent people — killers," he says. One of his direct great-grandfathers, Thomas Cornell, was hanged in 1667 for murdering his mother. That line of Cornells produced seven other alleged murderers, including Lizzy Borden. "Cousin Lizzy," as Fallon wryly calls her, was accused (and controversially acquitted) of killing her father and stepmother with an axe in Fall River, Massachusetts, in 1882.

3   A little spooked[3] by his ancestry, Fallon set out to see whether anyone in his family possesses the brain of a serial killer. Because he has studied the brains of dozens of psychopaths, he knew precisely what to look for. To demonstrate, he opened his laptop and called up an image of a brain on his computer.

4   "Here is a brain that's not normal," he says. There are patches of yellow and red. Then he points to another section of the brain, in the front part of the brain, just behind the eyes. "Look at that — there's almost nothing here," Fallon says. This is the orbital cortex, the area that Fallon and other scientists believe is involved with ethical behavior, moral decision-making and impulse control. "People with low activity [in the orbital cortex] are either **free-wheeling** types or psychopaths," he says.

5   He's clearly oversimplifying, but Fallon says the orbital cortex **puts a brake on** another part of the brain called the amygdala, which is involved with aggression and appetites. But in some people, there's an imbalance — the orbital cortex isn't doing its job — perhaps because the person had a brain injury or was born that way. "What's left? What takes over?" he asks. "The area of the brain that drives your id-type behaviors,[4] which are rage, violence, eating, sex, drinking."

(continued on next page)

---

[1] *psychopath:* someone who has a personality disorder characterized by a lack of empathy and remorse, shallow emotion, and extremely violent behavior

[2] *cuckoo:* (informal) someone who is mentally ill; crazy or silly

[3] *spooked:* (informal) frightened

[4] *id-type behaviors:* In Freud's theory of the mind, the *id* represents the uncontrolled instincts, the *ego* is the organized, realistic part, and the *superego* is the critical and moralizing part.

6   After learning his violent family history, Fallon persuaded 10 of his close relatives to submit to a PET brain scan[5] and give a blood sample. He examined the images and compared them with the brains of psychopaths. His wife's scan was normal. His mother: normal. His siblings: normal. His children: normal. "And I took a look at my own PET scan and saw something **disturbing** that I did not talk about," he says. What he didn't want to reveal was that *his* orbital cortex looks inactive. "If you look at the PET scan, I look just like one of those killers."

7   Fallon **cautions** that this is a young field. Scientists are just beginning to study this area of the brain — much less the brains of criminals. Still, he says the evidence is accumulating that some people's brains **predispose** them toward violence and that psychopathic tendencies may be passed down from one generation to another.

8   And that brings us to the next part of Jim Fallon's family experiment. Along with brain scans, Fallon also tested each family member's DNA for genes that are associated with violence. He looked at 12 genes related to aggression and violence and **zeroed in on** the MAO-A gene (monoamine oxidase A). This gene, which has been the target of considerable research, is also known as the "warrior gene" because it regulates serotonin in the brain. Serotonin[6] affects your mood and many scientists believe that if you have a certain version of the warrior gene, your brain won't respond to the calming effects of serotonin.

9   Everyone in Fallon's family has the low-aggression variant of the MAO-A gene, except for one person. "You see that? I'm 100 percent. I have the pattern, the risky pattern," he says, then pauses. "In a sense, I'm a born killer." Fallon's being **tongue-in-cheek** — sort of. He doesn't believe his fate or anyone else's is entirely determined by genes. They merely tip you in one direction or another. Brain patterns and genetic makeup are not enough to make anyone a psychopath. You need a third ingredient: abuse or violence in one's childhood.

10 Jim Fallon says he had a terrific childhood; he was **doted on** by his parents and had loving relationships with his brothers and sisters and entire extended family. Significantly, he says this journey through his brain has changed the way he thinks about nature[7] and **nurture**. He once believed that genes and brain function could determine everything about us. But now he thinks his childhood may have made all the difference. "We'll never know, but the way these patterns are looking in the general population, had I been abused, we might not be sitting here today," he says.

11 As for the psychopaths he studies, Fallon feels some compassion for these people who, he says, got "**a bad roll of the dice**." "It's an unlucky day when all of these three things come together in a bad way," he says.

---

[5] *PET brain scan:* Positron Emission Tomography can show images of what is happening inside the brain.

[6] *serotonin:* a neurotransmitter (a natural chemical in the body) carrying impulses between nerve cells

[7] *nature:* biological or genetic influences through heredity as opposed to influences from the individual's experience or environment

COMPREHENSION

A Main Ideas

Read each statement. Decide if it is *True* or *False* according to the reading. Check (✓) the appropriate box. If it is false, change it to make it true. Discuss your answers with a partner.

	TRUE	FALSE
1. The battle between nature and nurture is not an important part of Fallon's discussion.	☐	☐
2. A person's brain patterns and genetic make-up determine whether he will be a criminal or not.	☐	☐
3. Some people may be more naturally inclined to commit violence than others.	☐	☐
4. Current evidence suggests that the tendency to engage in criminal behavior may be passed down from generation to generation.	☐	☐

B Close Reading

Read the quotes from the reading. Circle the statement that best explains each quote. Share your answers with a partner.

1. "He's clearly oversimplifying, but Fallon says the orbital cortex puts a brake on another part of the brain called the amygdala, which is involved with aggression and appetites. But in some people, there's an imbalance — the orbital cortex isn't doing its job." (*paragraph 5*)

   People who are violent have . . .

   a. an overactive orbital cortex.

   b. an overactive amygdala.

2. "But in some people, there's an imbalance — the orbital cortex isn't doing its job — perhaps because the person had a brain injury or was born that way. 'What's left? What takes over?' he asks. 'The area of the brain that drives your id-type behaviors, which are rage, violence, eating, sex, drinking.'" (*paragraph 5*)

   a. Killers have something wrong with their brains due to genetics or injury.

   b. Killers don't have enough id-like behavior.

(continued on next page)

3. "Serotonin affects your mood and many scientists believe that if you have a certain version of the warrior gene, your brain won't respond to the calming effects of serotonin." *(paragraph 8)*

    a. Violent people respond too much to serotonin.

    b. Normal people calm down with serotonin.

4. "'We'll never know, but the way these patterns are looking in the general population, had I been abused, we might not be sitting here today,' he says." *(paragraph 10)*

    a. Childhood abuse activates negative patterns in the brain.

    b. Childhood abuse is not a part of the pattern.

VOCABULARY

A Phrases and Idioms

Read the phrases and idioms found in the reading. Match them with their meaning.

_____ 1. a bad roll of the dice   a. carefree; irresponsible

_____ 2. free-wheeling   b. to slow down

_____ 3. tongue-in-cheek   c. to give something your full attention

_____ 4. zero in on   d. an unlucky occurrence, due to chance

_____ 5. put a brake on   e. to care very much about someone

_____ 6. dote on   f. humorous

B Using the Dictionary

Read the dictionary entry for **disturb**.

> **disturb** *v.* **1** to annoy someone or interrupt what they are doing by making noise, asking a question, etc.: *If she's sleeping, don't disturb her.* **2** to make someone feel worried or upset: *What disturbs you most about this decision?* **3** to do something that changes the position or condition of things, usually in a bad way: *I was careful not to disturb anything in his office.*

Now read each sentence. Decide which meaning of *disturb* is being used. Write the number of the appropriate definition.

_____ a. The results of the tests, which showed that the scientist had the brain patterns and DNA common to most serial killers, **disturbed** him a bit.

_____ b. He kept the information to himself because he did not want to **disturb** his family members with the news.

_____ c. Loud music in the lab **disturbed** the work of the scientists.

_____ d. The discovery about the paternity of the royal child **disturbed** the status of the other people in line to the throne.

C Synonyms

Read the essay about biology and destiny. Match each word or phrase in bold with its synonym in the box below. Compare answers with a partner.

Biology and Destiny

For many centuries people thought that biology was destiny: If, through a **bad roll of the dice** you were born a girl, you were doomed to an inferior life. The
1.
same was true for anyone whose ___lineage___ wasn't noble. An aristocratic birth
2.
meant a **free-wheeling** life of privilege. An inferior birth **put a brake on** a person's
3.   4.
ambition and possible achievement. ___Doting___ parents would **caution** their
5.   6.
children to accept reality because those who went outside traditional roles were

punished.

Then came the **disturbing** rise of capitalism, and traditional society was changed
7.
forever in **startling** ways. In the 19th century, an unknown Corsican rose to become
8.
emperor of the French (Napoleon), and the man who presided over the end of

slavery in America was himself born in a one-room log cabin (Abraham Lincoln). The

old conservative ideas gave way to a new idea: People could make their own destiny.

The debate between nature (genetics) and **nurture** has always been difficult
9.
to decide. Although genes may **predispose** people to some advantages or
10.
disadvantages, the environment they interact with as a child and adult can activate

or deactivate their potential. Today we have **zeroed in on** many aspects of the brain,
11.
but the most important is that it is constantly remodeling itself based on experience.

Without seeming too **tongue-in-cheek**, we can say that "Hope springs eternal."
12.

_____	a. upsetting	_____	g. blocked
_____	b. warn	_____	h. heredity
_____	c. focused on	_____	i. irresponsible
_____	d. upbringing	_1_	j. chance occurrence
_____	e. silly	_____	k. amazing and strange
_____	f. loving	_____	l. make . . . likely to have

An **adjective clause** tells you something about the **noun** or **pronoun** it follows. An adjective clause begins with a word like **who, whom, whose, that, which, when, where, why**.

In academic English, sentences can become long and complicated. It's important to remember that an **adjective clause** describes the noun or pronoun that **comes right before** it.

EXAMPLE:

- He's clearly oversimplifying, but Fallon says the orbital cortex puts a brake on another

                         noun   adjective clause

part of the brain called the **amygdala, *which* is involved with aggression and appetites.**

The word *which* and the entire adjective clause that follows refer to the noun "amygdala." The amygdala is involved with aggression and appetites.

Work with a partner. Read each sentence and identify which noun the adjective clause refers to. Circle the correct answer.

1. "[It is] the area of the brain that drives your id-type behaviors, *which* are rage, violence, eating, sex, drinking." *(paragraph 5)*

   a. id-type behaviors   **b.** brain

2. "Along with brain scans, Fallon also tested each family member's DNA for genes *that* are associated with violence." *(paragraph 8)*

   a. DNA   **b.** genes

3. "As for the psychopaths he studies, Fallon feels some compassion for these people *who*, he says, got 'a bad roll of the dice.'" *(paragraph 11)*

   a. people (psychopaths)   **b.** Fallon

4. "As a rule, this cruel aggressiveness waits for some provocation or puts itself at the service of some higher purpose, *whose* goal might have been reached by milder measures." *(Reading One, paragraph 1)*

   a. aggressiveness   **b.** purpose

5. "The existence of this inclination to aggression, *which* we can detect in ourselves and justly assume to be present in others, is the factor *which* disturbs our relations with our neighbor and *which* forces civilization into such a high expenditure of energy." *(Reading One, paragraph 2)*

   a. inclination   **b.** existence

   a. others   **b.** factor

   a. neighbor   **b.** factor

NOTE-TAKING: Focusing on Sequence of Events and Main Discoveries

1   Sequence of Events

Work with a partner. In each of the boxes below, recapture the sequence of events that led to Fallon's realization about himself and others. Write notes to complete the information in each box.

1. University of California: *for 20 years researching criminal minds and biological basis for behavior* _____

_____

_____

↓

2. About four years ago, his mother . . . _____

_____

_____

_____

↓

3. Fallon found out . . . _____

_____

_____

_____

↓

4. Fallon persuaded 10 close relatives . . . _____

_____

_____

_____

↓

5. The results of the tests were . . . _____

_____

_____

_____

2 Main Discoveries in Brain and Genetic Research

Write notes next to each cue about a discovery in brain and genetic research mentioned in the reading.

1.	Orbital cortex	A low activity in orbital cortex not good — doesn't inhibit activity of amygdala
2.	Amygdala	
3.	Warrior gene	
4.	Serotonin	
5.	Nature and nurture (Fallon's views)	

CRITICAL THINKING

Discuss the questions in a small group. Be prepared to share your answers with the class.

1. How important is childhood in Fallon's opinion? Why? Was he a "natural-born killer"?

2. Can society prevent people from becoming killers?

3. Fallon says he has more compassion today for those who have become psychopaths. Why? Would you?

4. Would you want to know about your brain and your family history to see if you were in the same situation as Fallon? Why or why not?

BRINGING IT ALL TOGETHER

Work in groups of four. Role-play an interview with Sigmund Freud, Stephen Jay Gould, and James Fallon about men's aggressiveness and violence. The journalist will ask questions of the others. Freud, Gould, and Fallon will express their opinions. Use some of the vocabulary you studied in the chapter (for a complete list, go to page 220).

Topic: Men's aggressiveness and violence

ROLES:

- Journalist
- Sigmund Freud
- Stephen Jay Gould
- James Fallon

QUESTIONS:

- Are humans a very violent species?
- Is violence in our genes?
- How can we control and prevent the expression of violence?

WRITING ACTIVITY

Write a three-paragraph essay about how an important event or lesson in childhood shaped your ethical behavior and moral sense. Use more than five of the words or idioms you studied in the chapter.

- **Introduction:** Tell the reader about yourself as a child.
- **Body Paragraph:** Describe the situation and the lesson you learned.
- **Conclusion:** Discuss how it affected your later life.

DISCUSSION AND WRITING TOPICS

Discuss these topics in a small group. Choose one of them and write a paragraph or two about it. Use the vocabulary from the chapter.

1. Why do you think people, even scientists and writers of popular entertainment for movies and TV, are so interested in serial killers: their lack of empathy, fear, or remorse? Is it that they are a lot like us or very much unlike us?

2. What are some ways we can reduce aggression in today's society?

3. Do you think violent movies and video games contribute to violence among young people?

4. "The fault is not in our stars but in ourselves." — *William Shakespeare*

   Do you think the fault is in our genes or in our environment? Is aggression the result of "nature" (inborn qualities) or "nurture" (the result of experience)?

5. How can a belief in biological determinism affect our future and our concept of freedom? Does biological determinism excuse a violent criminal?

VOCABULARY

Nouns	Verbs	Adjectives	Adverb
adversary	caution	acquisitive *	intrinsically *
assertion	devolve	disturbing	
atrocities	efface	fateful	**Phrases and**
determinant	exterminate	genial	**Idioms**
expenditure	master	pious	a bad roll of the
inclination *	perpetuate	startling	dice
lineage	predispose	utmost	free-wheeling
nastiness	reiterate		put a brake on
nurture	sustain *		tongue-in-cheek
overtures			
predominance *	**Phrasal Verbs**		
	dote on		
	zero in on		

* = AWL (Academic Word List) item

SELF-ASSESSMENT

In this chapter you learned to:

○ Predict the content of a text from the title or the first paragraph

○ Understand the most important idea of a text from the first and last paragraphs

○ Guess the meaning of words from the context

○ Use dictionary entries to learn the meanings of words

○ Understand and use synonyms, phrases and idioms, collocations, and different word forms

○ Identify adjective clauses and the reasons for their use

○ Take notes to identify the author's assertions and supporting explanations

○ Complete outlines to focus on the sequence of events and main discoveries

What can you do well? ✓

What do you need to practice more? ✓

CHAPTER 9

ETHICS: Resistance to Evil in the 20th Century

ETHICS: the study of the moral rules and principles of behavior in society, and how they influence the choices people make

OBJECTIVES

To read academic texts, you need to master certain skills.

In this chapter, you will:

- Predict the content of a text from the title or from the subheadings

- Preview a text using an Editor's Insert

- Guess the meaning of words from the context

- Use dictionary entries to learn the meanings of words

- Understand and use synonyms, collocations, and different word forms

- Identify noun clauses and the reasons for their use

- Take notes to identify the main details of the action

- Complete a chart to identify the main points of the author's arguments

Mahatma Gandhi used nonviolent civil disobedience to lead India to independence from Britain in 1947. He inspired the leaders of nonviolent resistance movements across the world.

A Ethical Philosophers

Some famous philosophers have written about morality. Read the short and very simplified summary of their ideas.

Aristotle (384 B.C.–322 B.C.): You should decide what kind of person you want to be. Then you make moral choices based on whether they will help you become that person.

Emmanuel Kant (1724–1804): When you have a moral question, you should ask yourself, "What would happen if everyone behaved this way?" For Kant, morality was an absolute. For example, lying was forbidden in all circumstances because it manipulated people and destroyed their dignity.

Jeremy Bentham (1748–1832): For Bentham, it is the greatest happiness of the greatest number of people that is the measure of right and wrong. Happiness is pleasure rather than pain. Morality is based on consequences and "the greater good."

Now answer the questions. Discuss your answers with a partner.

1. Which philosopher's ideas do you agree with?

2. How would you react . . .

   a. if someone followed Aristotle's idea and decided to be selfish?

   b. if someone followed Kant's idea and refused to lie to save a life?

   c. if someone followed Bentham's idea and harmed a minority of innocent people to help "the greater good" of the majority?

B Consider These Questions

Check (✓) your answers. Then discuss your answers with a partner.

1. How do you decide what is right or wrong?

   ☐ **a.** My feelings tell me what is right or wrong.

   ☐ **b.** My conscience tells me what is right or wrong.

   ☐ **c.** My religious beliefs tell me what is right or wrong.

   ☐ **d.** The law tells me what is right or wrong.

2. Would any of your replies to the above change . . .

   ☐ **a.** if your feelings were anger or fear?

   ☐ **b.** if the law dictated discrimination toward some people?

   ☐ **c.** if your society accepted things you think are wrong?

A Warm-Up

Indira Gandhi (no relation to Mahatma Gandhi) was the first woman prime minister of India. In 1984, she sent troops to invade the Golden Temple, sacred to the Sikh religion, in order to capture rebels hiding there. She was later assassinated by two of her Sikh bodyguards. This act sparked murderous riots of Hindus against any Sikhs they could find. Millions of Sikhs were made homeless, and 5,000 were burned alive according to government figures.

Discuss the questions with a partner.

1. What should we do when we see terrible things happening to others? Something? Nothing?

2. Some people have performed heroic deeds trying to protect others. What do you think motivates such people?

B Reading Strategy

Predicting Content from Subheadings

Reading the **subheadings** in a text can give you a fuller idea of what the text will be about. They can help you **predict or guess its content**.

Read the subheadings in "The Ghosts of Mrs. Gandhi." With a partner, decide if these statements are *True* or *False*. Check (✓) the appropriate box.

	TRUE	FALSE
1. The reading will discuss two separate incidents during the riots.	☐	☐
2. The author was present during both incidents.	☐	☐
3. The author is writing a personal memoir.	☐	☐

Now read the text and decide if your predictions were correct.

The Ghosts of Mrs. Gandhi

By Amitav Ghosh

Amitav Ghosh was born in Calcutta and grew up in India, Bangladesh, and Sri Lanka. He studied in Delhi, Oxford, and Alexandria and is the author of many award-winning novels, including Sea of Poppies *and* River of Smoke, *about the opium trade in India and China.*

First day of the riots — on a bus going home from the university

1   As the bus made its way down New Delhi's broad tree-lined avenues, official-looking cars overtook us, speeding toward the hospital. As we drew nearer, it became evident that a large number of people had gathered there. But this was no ordinary crowd: it seemed to consist of red-eyed young men in half-buttoned shirts. It was now that I noticed that my Sikh[1] fellow passenger was showing signs of increasing anxiety: sometimes standing up to look out, sometimes glancing at the door. It was too late to get off the bus; **thugs** were everywhere.

2   The bands of young men grew more and more **menacing** as we approached the hospital. Some were armed with steel rods and bicycle chains; others had **fanned out** across the busy road and were stopping cars and buses.

3   A stout woman wearing a sari was the first to understand what was going on. Rising to her feet, she gestured urgently at the Sikh, who was sitting hunched in his seat. She hissed at him in Hindi, telling him to get down and keep out of sight.

4   The man **started** in surprise and squeezed himself into the narrow foot-space between the seats. Minutes later, our bus was intercepted by a group of young men dressed in bright, sharp synthetics. Several had bicycle chains wrapped around their wrists. They ran alongside the bus as it slowed to a halt. We heard them call out to the driver through the open door, asking if there were any Sikhs on the bus.

5   The driver shook his head. No, there were no Sikhs on the bus.

6   A few rows ahead of me the crouching, turbaned figure had gone completely still.

7   Outside, some of the young men were jumping up to look through the windows, asking if there were any Sikhs on the bus. There was no anger in their voices; that was the most **chilling** thing of all.

8   No, someone said, and immediately other voices picked up the refrain. Soon all the passengers were shaking their heads and saying, No, no, let us go now, we have to get home.

---

[1] **Sikh:** Sikh men are recognizable by their distinctive turbans (a **turban** is a long piece of cloth that you wind tightly around your head).

9   Eventually, the thugs stepped back and waved us through.

10   Nobody said a word as we sped away down Ring Road.

Second day of the riots — in a march against violence

11   The march headed first for Laipat Nagar, a busy commercial area a mile or so away. We were shouting slogans as we marched: old Gandhian slogans[2] of peace and brotherhood from half a century before. Then, suddenly we were confronted with a **starkly** familiar spectacle, a twentieth-century urban horror: burned-out cars, debris and rubble everywhere. The scene my memory preserved is of a moment when it seemed inevitable that we would be attacked.

12   Rounding a corner, we found ourselves facing a crowd that was larger and more determined-looking than any other crowds we had encountered. On each previous occasion, we had **prevailed** by marching at the thugs and engaging them directly, in dialogues that turned quickly into extended shouting matches. In every instance, we had succeeded in facing them down. But this particular **mob** was **intent on** confrontation. As its members advanced on us, waving knives and steel rods, we stopped. Our voices grew louder as they came toward us. We **braced for** the attack, leaning forward as though into a wind.

_____

[2] *Gandhian slogans:* phrases used by Mahatma Gandhi and his followers during the struggle for independence

13   And then something happened that I have never completely understood. Nothing was said: there was no signal, nor was there any break in the rhythm of our chanting. But suddenly all the women in our group — and the women made up more than half of the group's number — stepped out and surrounded the men; their saris and kameezes[3] became a thin, fluttering barrier, a wall around us. They turned to face the approaching men, challenging them, daring them to attack.

14   The thugs took a few more steps toward us and then **faltered**, confused. A moment later, they were gone.

15   In the next couple of hours, an organization was created, and its work — to bring relief to the injured and the **bereft**, and to shelter the homeless — began the next morning. Food and clothing were needed and camps had to be established to **accommodate** the thousands of people with nowhere to sleep. And by the next day we were overwhelmed — literally. The large compound was crowded with vanloads of blankets, second-hand clothing, shoes, sacks of flour, sugar and tea. Previously unsentimental businessmen sent cars and trucks. There was barely room to move.

_____

[3] *kameeze:* a piece of clothing like a long shirt, worn by many people from the Indian subcontinent

COMPREHENSION

A Main Ideas

Read each statement. Decide if it is *True* or *False* according to the reading. Check (✓) the appropriate box. If it is false, change it to make it true. Discuss your answers with a partner.

	TRUE	FALSE
1. People took a long time to decide to help others.	☐	☐
2. The people who helped victims were policemen.	☐	☐
3. People used nonviolence to try to stop the revenge killings.	☐	☐
4. The Sikh in the bus had killed Indira Gandhi.	☐	☐
5. After the fact, more people made contributions to help the victims.	☐	☐

B Close Reading

Read the quotes from the reading. Circle the statement that best explains each quote. Share your answers with a partner.

1. "But this was no ordinary crowd: it seemed to consist of red-eyed young men in half-buttoned shirts." *(paragraph 1)*

   a. The author is suggesting that these men were half-asleep.

   b. The author is suggesting that these men were dangerous.

2. "Outside, some of the young men were jumping up to look through the windows, asking if there were any Sikhs on the bus. There was no anger in their voices; that was the most chilling thing of all." *(paragraph 7)*

   a. The author is communicating the cold-blooded nature of this violence.

   b. The author is communicating the idea that the mob is moved by emotion.

3. "On each previous occasion, we had prevailed by marching at the thugs and engaging them directly, in dialogues that turned quickly into extended shouting matches. In every instance, we had succeeded in facing them down. But this particular mob was intent on confrontation." *(paragraph 12)*

   a. In other circumstances, the rioters talked with the demonstrators, but not this time.

   b. In other circumstances, the rioters refused to talk with the demonstrators, but now they would.

4. "The large compound was crowded with vanloads of blankets, second-hand clothing, shoes, sacks of flour, sugar and tea. Previously unsentimental businessmen sent cars and trucks." *(paragraph 15)*

   a. People felt bad about what had happened.

   b. People wanted to encourage business.

VOCABULARY

A **Guessing from Context**

Read each quote from the reading. Try to guess the meaning of the words in bold from the context. Write the clues that helped you guess and your guess. Then consult a dictionary and write the definition.

1. "The bands of young men grew more and more **menacing** as we approached the hospital. Some were armed with steel rods and bicycle chains; others had **fanned out** across the busy road and were stopping cars and buses." *(paragraph 2)*

   menacing   Clues: _armed / steel rods / chains_____

                     Guess: _scary_____

                     Dictionary: _threatening, making you expect something bad_

   fan out   Clues: _____

                     Guess: _____

                     Dictionary: _____

2. "On each previous occasion, we had **prevailed** by marching at the thugs and engaging them directly, in dialogues that turned quickly into extended shouting matches. In every instance, we had succeeded in facing them down." *(paragraph 12)*

   prevail   Clues: _____

                     Guess: _____

                     Dictionary: _____

3. "Our voices grew louder as they came toward us. We **braced for** the attack, leaning forward as though into a wind." *(paragraph 12)*

   brace for   Clues: _____

                     Guess: _____

                     Dictionary: _____

4. "Food and clothing were needed and camps had to be established to **accommodate** the thousands of people with nowhere to sleep." *(paragraph 15)*

   accommodate   Clues: _____

                     Guess: _____

                     Dictionary: _____

B Synonyms

Complete the essay with the words or phrases from the box. Use the synonym in parentheses to help you select the correct word or phrase. Compare answers with a partner.

accommodate	chilling	intent on	stark
bereft	faltering	menacing	started
braced for	fanning out	prevail	thugs

More about the Riots

"Throughout the city, Sikh homes were being looted and set on fire, often with their occupants still inside." Ghosh reports the testimony of a Sikh woman, her voice _____ faltering _____ as
1. (stumbling)
she spoke of her husband and three sons burned alive by the mob. They had been hiding in a nearby house. "There was treachery in people's hearts. Someone must have told the crowd they were there." A

_____ survivor, her testimony was a living condemnation of
2. (grief-stricken)
the barbarism of the mobs and a symbol of the thousands of people, overwhelmingly Sikh males, dead in the riots.

Some people were saved by their friends and associates. Ghosh tells the story of a wealthy Sikh couple, who were _____ sitting out the crisis in
3. (set on)
their home. They found it difficult to understand the _____
4. (grim)
reality of the riots. The crowds had become so _____ that
5. (threatening)
their lives were in danger. Yet they kept saying that they had no sympathy with Sikh terrorists and were totally committed to the Indian state. Although they wanted to believe that calm would _____, their friends
6. (be victorious)
finally persuaded them to flee. They were hidden by neighbors in a place that could

_____ all their needs and keep them safe.
7. (take care of)

They left just in time. Minutes after their departure, their cook _____

                                                             8. (jumped)

at the sound of the mob coming down the street. He _____

                                             9. (prepared for)

the inevitable confrontation. The _____ were at the gates

                                  10. (criminals)

of the house, _____ across the garden, holding knives

                          11. (spreading)

and torches. The mob asked him if his employers were Sikhs and whether they

were in the house. They wanted to know who owned the house — Hindus

or Sikhs? The cook told them his employers were Sikhs, but they'd left town.

They were only renting from a Hindu, who owned the house. There was a

_____ silence as he waited to see what would happen. Did

           12. (gravely/disturbing)

they know he was lying? What would be his fate? But the mob believed him.

Of this time, Ghosh writes, "I had witnessed the risks that perfectly ordinary

people were willing to take for one another."

C Using the Dictionary

1 Read the dictionary entries for *crowd* and *mob*.

> **crowd** *n.* a large group of people in a public place: *The crowd cheered.*
>
> **mob** *n.* a large noisy crowd, especially one that is angry and violent: *Police officers fired at the mob of unruly protesters.*

What would you call these people? Decide if they are a *crowd* or a *mob*. Check (✓)
the appropriate box.

	CROWD	MOB
1. a group of peaceful demonstrators	☐	☐
2. a group of people going to the movies	☐	☐
3. a group of people carrying chains and knives	☐	☐
4. a group of people trying to loot a store and take things	☐	☐
5. a group of people registering for a course at the university	☐	☐
6. a group of people threatening the authorities with physical harm	☐	☐
7. a group of people joining the discussion	☐	☐

2 Read the dictionary entries for *start*, *startle*, *startled*, and *startling*.

start *v.* **1** [T*] to begin doing something: *They're starting construction next spring.*
2 [I**] to move your body suddenly, especially because you are surprised or afraid: *A loud knock at the door made her start.*

startle *v.* [T] to make someone feel suddenly surprised or slightly shocked, often so that they make a sudden movement: *A loud knock at the door startled her.*

startled *adj.* feeling suddenly surprised or slightly shocked: *I was startled to see her there. / his startled look*

startling *adj.* very unusual or surprising: *a startling change in attitudes*

*T = **Transitive:** A transitive verb carries action to another noun.

I = **Intransitive: An intransitive verb carries no action; it applies only to the subject.

Now complete each sentence with the correct word: ***start, startled, startling***

1. The _____ city awoke to news of terrible riots.

2. The loud shouts of the rioters as they came down the streets made everyone

   _____ with fear.

3. The committee Ghosh worked with wrote a _____ exposé

   of those responsible for the riots.

4. We hoped that things would _____ to get better after that.

NOTE-TAKING: Identifying Main Details of the Action

Work with a partner. Go back to the reading and read it again. Then fill in the chart with short notes identifying the main details of the action: the dangers and solutions found on the bus and on the street.

Location	Danger	Solution People Found
On the bus	• The Sikh passenger was in danger of being taken by the rioters and killed.	• A woman told him to hide. •
On the street	•	• •

CRITICAL THINKING

Discuss the questions in a small group. Be prepared to share your answers with the class.

1. Do you think the woman on the bus was a hero? Why do you think she tried to save the man? Why did the others go along? If she hadn't spoken up, what might have happened? Did the people also help themselves by hiding the man? Did they risk anything? Why does Ghosh include this incident in his essay?

2. Although the state authorities acted promptly against the violence in some cities, they did not always do so in northern India. In New Delhi, people waited and waited for the army to be called in or for the police to act. Finally, some people decided to march against the rioters themselves in order to try to stop them. Why would they risk their lives to do that? What view of ethical behavior do you think they had?

3. Can you imagine what made the women come forward during the confrontation with the mob?

4. Why do you think the rioters turned away from the women? Ghosh wrote: "When I think of the women staring down the mob, I am not filled with writerly wonder. I am reminded of my gratitude for being saved from injury." What did he mean by that comment?

5. Ghosh has written: "Our organization formed a team to investigate the riots. I thought an investigation would be a waste of time. I was wrong. A document produced by this team — a slim pamphlet entitled 'Who Are the Guilty?' — has become a classic, an indictment of the politicians who encouraged the riots and the police who allowed the rioters to have their way." Why at first did Ghosh think the report would be a waste of time? Do you think such pamphlets are important? Why or why not?

Women in a nonviolent demonstration in India

A **Warm-Up**

Discuss the question with a partner.

In Reading One ("The Ghosts of Mrs. Gandhi"), people had to act alone; their government and police didn't help them or protect the victims.

What do you think could happen if a whole people, including their government, resisted evil orders?

1942, Denmark — Danes overturn a German prison van and release fellow citizens.

B **Reading Strategy**

Previewing Using an Editor's Insert

Reading an **editorial insert** — a preliminary paragraph written by the editor — gives you **important information** that helps you appreciate the **context of the text it precedes**. Reading it where it usually appears, right before the text itself, in the form of a preface, puts you at a great advantage and **prepares you for the challenges of the text**.

Work with a partner. Read the Editor's Insert before the text of "Denmark in World War II" and answer the questions.

1. When did the Germans invade Denmark?

2. What did the Danes do when the Germans announced their plans?

3. What do you think the text will show?

Now read the text and decide if the information provided in the Editor's Insert gave you a good preview of the text.

Denmark in World War II

By Hannah Arendt

Hannah Arendt (1906–1975) was a political scientist and philosopher born in Hanover, Germany. When Hitler came to power, she was forced to leave Germany and came to the United States in 1940. She continued her academic career by lecturing and teaching at various colleges, including The New School for Social Research in New York City. Among the many books she wrote were Eichmann in Jerusalem, On Revolution, *and* The Origins of Totalitarianism.

Editor's Insert

During the Second World War, the Germans invaded Denmark in April, 1940. In the beginning of her essay, Hannah Arendt explains that of the four countries almost completely **immune** to anti-Semitism — Denmark, Sweden, Italy, and Bulgaria — only Denmark challenged its German masters directly. As soon as the German authorities talked about forcing Jews to wear the yellow badge,[1] the Danes replied that all Danish citizens, including the King, would be wearing it the next day if the policy were carried out. In addition, all Danish government officials threatened the German authorities with their immediate **resignation** if the Germans started to implement any anti-Jewish actions. The following excerpt from *Eichmann in Jerusalem* shows how the Danes **sabotaged** the German plan to carry out the mass extermination of the Jews.

---

1   What happened then was truly amazing; compared with what took place in other European countries, everything went topsy-turvy. In August, 1943 — after the German offensive in Russia had failed, the Afrika Korps had surrendered in Tunisia, and the Allies had invaded Italy — the Swedish government canceled its 1940 agreement with Germany which had permitted German troops the right to pass through the country. Thereupon, the Danish workers decided that they could help a bit in hurrying things up; riots broke out in Danish shipyards, where the dock workers refused to repair German ships and then went on strike. The German military commander proclaimed a state of emergency and imposed martial law, and Himmler[2] thought this was the right moment to **tackle** the Jewish

(continued on next page)

---

[1] *yellow badge:* a yellow star that Jews were forced to wear on their clothing to identify themselves as Jews

[2] *Heinrich Himmler* (1900–1945): chief of the German police (including the Gestapo — secret police), and overseer of the concentration camps

question, whose "solution" was long overdue. What he did not **reckon with** was that — quite apart from the Danish resistance — the German officials who had been living in the country for years were no longer the same. Not only did General von Hannecken, the military commander, refuse to put troops at the disposal of the Reich plenipotentiary, Dr. Werner Best;[3] the special S.S. units (*Einsatz-kommandos*) employed in Denmark very frequently objected to "the **measures** they were ordered to carry out by the central agencies" — according to Best's testimony of Nuremberg. And Best himself, an old Gestapo man and former legal adviser to Heydrich,[4] author of a then famous book on the police, who had worked for the military government in Paris to the entire satisfaction of his superiors, could not longer be trusted, although it is doubtful that Berlin ever learned the extent of his unreliability.

2   Best went to Berlin and obtained a promise that all Jews from Denmark would be sent to Theresienstadt[5] regardless of their category — a very important **concession**, from the Nazis' point of view. The night of October 1 was set for their **seizure** and immediate departure — ships were ready in the harbor — and since neither the Danes nor the Jews nor the German troops stationed in Denmark could be relied on to help, police units arrived from Germany for a door-to-door search. At the last moment, Best told them that they were not permitted to break into apartments, because the Danish police might then interfere, and they were not supposed to fight it out with the Danes. Hence they could seize only those Jews who voluntarily opened their doors. They found exactly 477 people,[6] out of a total of more than 7,800, at home and willing to let them in. A few days before the date of doom, a German shipping agent, Georg F. Duckwitz, having probably been **tipped off** by Best himself, had revealed the whole plan to Danish government officials, who, in turn, had hurriedly informed the heads of the Jewish community. They, in marked contrast to Jewish leaders in other countries, had then communicated the news openly in the synagogues on the occasion of the New Year services. The Jews had just time enough to leave their apartments and go into hiding, which was very easy in Denmark, because, in the words of the judgment, "all sections of the Danish people, from the King down to simple citizens," stood ready to receive them.

---

[3] *Dr. Werner Best* (1903–1989) served as civilian administrator of France and Denmark while these countries were under Nazi occupation during World War II. At the Nuremberg trials after the war, Best referred to his complicated "dual role." Although he was extradited to Denmark and originally given the death penalty, he was soon released from prison after an appeal based on the idea that "he had done his best."

[4] *Reinhart Heydrich* was a high-ranking Nazi official during World War II, known as "the hangman." He was one of the main architects of the Holocaust and was assassinated by members of the Czech resistance in 1942.

[5] *Theresienstadt, Czechoslovakia:* a transit camp, in Nazi propaganda billed as a "spa" for elderly Jews. More than 33,000 people were killed there, and 90,000, including children, were sent from there to death camps further east.

[6] These 477 people went to Theresienstadt, and most of them were saved because of the intervention of the Danish government and King Christian, who insisted they be seen by the Red Cross.

COMPREHENSION

A Main Ideas

Read each statement and check (✓) the ones that are main ideas of the reading.

☐ 1. A nation's solidarity in dangerous times can be strengthened when the government takes a courageous action that its citizens willingly follow.

☐ 2. Even when some people do the right thing, it may be difficult to follow their example.

☐ 3. Organized resistance by a people opposed in principle to an evil plan can sometimes influence even their oppressors.

☐ 4. It is important to resist the preparations for persecution as soon as they occur.

B Close Reading

Read the quotes from the reading. Circle the statement that best explains each quote. Share your answers with a partner.

1. "Everything went topsy-turvy. In August, 1943 — after the German offensive in Russia had failed, the Afrika Korps had surrendered in Tunisia, and the Allies had invaded Italy — the Swedish government canceled its 1940 agreement with Germany which had permitted German troops the right to pass through the country." (paragraph 1)

   Based on the description of events given, "everything went topsy-turvy" means that . . .

   a. no one knew what was happening.

   b. things were no longer going well for the Germans.

2. "Thereupon, the Danish workers decided that they could help a bit in hurrying things up; riots broke out in Danish shipyards, where the dock workers refused to repair German ships and then went on strike." (paragraph 1)

   What "things" did the Danish workers want to "help . . . in hurrying . . . up"?

   a. defeating the German military machine

   b. challenging the Danish government

3. "The German officials who had been living in the country for years were no longer the same. Not only did General von Hannecken, the military commander, refuse to put troops at the disposal of the Reich plenipotentiary, Dr. Werner Best; the special S.S. units (Einsatz-kommandos) employed in Denmark very frequently objected to 'the measures they were ordered to carry out by the central agencies' — according to Best's testimony of Nuremberg." (paragraph 1)

   a. Living in Denmark far away from the authorities in Germany had changed the attitude of the German officials in Denmark.

   b. The German officials living in Denmark didn't care about the Danes' objections to German orders.

VOCABULARY

A **Synonyms**

Complete the essay with the words or phrases from the box. Use the synonym in parentheses to help you select the correct word or phrase. Compare answers with a partner.

concessions	reckon with	seizure	tipping off
immune	sabotage	tackled	took measures

The Heroism of an Ordinary Man

Genocide, the systematic killing of everyone in a particular ethnic group or nation, did not stop after World War II. The systematic extermination of people has happened again in several places in the world. It is clear that we humans are not

_____ to repeating the mistakes of the past over and over again.
　　　1. (resistant)

We have to _____ this grim reality when considering the
　　　　　　2. (come to terms with)
tragic events that occurred in Rwanda in 1994. Sadly, these events were ignored by the world community at the time. The film *Hotel Rwanda* discusses an episode from

this period, when one man tried to _____ the murderous
　　　　　　　　　　　　3. (disrupt)
plans of the killers.

The film tells the true story of Paul Rusesabagina, a family man and manager of the Hôtel des Mille Collines, a luxury hotel in Kigali, Rwanda's capital, run by the Belgian company Sabena. On April 6, 1994, when Rwanda's president Habyarumana was assassinated along with the president of Burundi, the Tutsis[1] were blamed

for the assassinations. The government _____ to get rid of
　　　　　　　　　　　　　4. (made preparations)
the Tutsis. From the radio, the only source of communication in the country at the time, words telling Hutus to kill the Tutsi "infestation" blasted 24 hours a day. As a result, in a period of 100 days up to 800,000 Tutsis were killed, with the burning and

_____ of their homes and businesses becoming the norm.
　　5. (taking possession)

_____

[1]The *Tutsis* are the second largest group in Rwanda after the *Hutus*. The two groups share the same language and religion. There are few, if any, basic differences between them.

As manager of the Hôtel des Mille Collines, Mr. Rusesabagina, the son of a Hutu father and a Tutsi mother married to a Tutsi wife, _____ the

6. (dealt with)

problem as best he could by finding ways to convert the hotel into a shelter for more than a thousand refugees escaping persecution. They, like Mr. Rusesabagina and his family, were eventually able to escape from Rwanda. When he found refuge in Belgium in 1996, he resigned from the hotel business.

Mr. Rusesabagina, who now lives in Belgium, was awarded the Lantos Human Rights Award in Washington, D.C., in November 2011, because he had risked his life during the Rwandan genocide to save many others. Although he has been criticized for straddling two worlds and sometimes _____ the Hutu

7. (giving information to)

rebels with blood on their hands, he responds to his critics in his book, *An Ordinary Man*, with the explanation that in order to achieve his results, he sometimes had to take advantage of the influence the hotel business had given him and seek certain

_____ by negotiating with the Hutus.

8. (special agreements)

B **Using the Dictionary**

Read the dictionary entry for *resignation*.

> **resignation** *n.* **1** the act of resigning (officially and permanently leaving your job because you want to), or a written statement to say you are doing this: *a letter of resignation* **2** the act of calmly accepting a bad situation that cannot be changed: *He watched his children argue with resignation.*

Now read each sentence. Decide which meaning of *resignation* is being used. Write the number of the appropriate meaning.

_____ **a.** The lieutenant's **resignation** from his post in the army reflected his lack of faith in the high command's struggle.

_____ **b.** He had thought about the consequences of this **resignation** long before he made it known.

_____ **c.** However, he imagined that remaining in that army position much longer would have made him feel the kind of apathy and **resignation** that brings one closer and closer to a living death.

_____ **d.** To some people, living a life of total **resignation** is a sign of strength, but for him behaving that way would have been a sign of weakness.

C Word Forms

1 Fill in the chart with the correct word forms. Some categories can have more than one form. Use a dictionary if necessary. An *X* indicates there is no form in that category.

	NOUN	VERB	ADJECTIVE	ADVERB
1.	concession	*concede*	X	X
2.	immunity /		immune	X
3.		reckon	X	X
4.	seizure			X
5.	resignation			X

2 Complete the sentences with the correct form of the words from the chart. The first letter of each word has been given to you as a clue. Compare answers with a partner.

1. It's not easy to r_____ with man's potential for evil.

2. Sometimes it emerges as an effort to s_____ other people's goods or take away what is perceived as their privileges.

3. No one is i_____ to prejudice; we can all find someone to dislike, but we need to rise above our worst instincts.

4. Anyone who studies history will readily c_____ that prejudice can be dangerous.

5. Sometimes, as Arendt points out about the Danish government officials, people have to be ready to r_____ from their jobs rather than participate in evil.

D Collocations

Check (✓) the collocations (words that are often paired together). Discuss your answers and the meaning of the collocations with a partner.

☐ **1.** tackle the problem   ☐ **4.** take emergency measures

☐ **2.** tackle the question   ☐ **5.** take drastic measures

☐ **3.** tackle the answer   ☐ **6.** take false measures

GRAMMAR FOR READING: Noun Clauses

> **Noun clauses** function the **same way** that **nouns do** in a sentence: as subjects, objects of verbs, or complements. The following words often introduce noun clauses: **that, what, who, whom, whether, why, where, how, whatever, whoever, whomever, wherever, however.**
>
> ***That* can be omitted** when it introduces an object noun clause or a complement noun clause.
>
> **EXAMPLES:**
> - **What the Danes did during World War II** is the subject of Hannah Arendt's essay.
> - Most people would agree **(that) the Danes were very courageous during World War II.**
>
> Writers use **noun clauses** in order to **introduce a topic**. A noun clause can often be considered as a "frame" or structural device that alerts the reader to information that is to follow. Being aware of noun clauses in a text can therefore help you improve your note-taking skills.
>
> **EXAMPLE:**
> - As we grew nearer, it became evident **that a large number of people had gathered there.** But this was no ordinary crowd: it seemed to consist of red-eyed young men in half-buttoned shirts.
>
> The author tells us that there was a crowd ("the large number of people gathered there"), but then further information is given. It is not an "ordinary crowd," but one with violence on its mind ("red-eyed young men in half-buttoned shirts").

1   Go back to the reading and underline all the noun clauses. Discuss with a partner how these noun clauses contribute to the reading experience.

2   Examine the underlined noun clauses in these sentences from Readings One and Two and explain how they provide a frame (the general idea) for the information that is to follow (the details).

1. "It was now that I noticed that my Sikh fellow passenger was showing signs of increasing anxiety: sometimes standing up to look out, sometimes glancing at the door. It was too late to get off the bus; thugs were everywhere." (*Reading One, paragraph 1*)

_____

_____

(continued on next page)

2. "A stout woman wearing a sari was the first to understand what was going on. Rising to her feet, she gestured urgently at the Sikh, who was sitting hunched in his seat. She hissed at him in Hindi, telling him to get down and keep out of sight." (*Reading One, paragraph 3*)

_____

_____

_____

3. "Himmler thought [that] this was the right moment to tackle the Jewish question, whose "solution" was long overdue. What he did not reckon with was that — quite apart from the Danish resistance — the German officials who had been living in the country for years were no longer the same. Not only did General von Hannecken, the military commander, refuse to put troops at the disposal of the Reich plenipotentiary, Dr. Werner Best; the special S.S. units (*Einsatz-kommandos*) employed in Denmark very frequently objected to 'the measures they were ordered to carry out by the central agencies' — according to Best's testimony of Nuremberg." (*Reading Two, paragraph 1*)

_____

_____

_____

CRITICAL THINKING

Discuss the questions in a small group. Be prepared to share your answers with the class.

1. Do you believe Dr. Werner Best was a hero? Why or why not?

2. Why do you think Hannah Arendt tells this story about Denmark? What is her aim? In this narrative, who showed ethical behavior?

3. The Nazis considered the Danes and other Scandinavians a part of their "racially superior" Europe. Does this view play any role in explaining why the German command in Denmark was so sensitive to Danish concerns? Would they have felt the same way about moral opposition in other countries in Europe? Was it important that this opposition was mainly nonviolent and that it was supported by the vast majority of people?

4. As Arendt shows, the Danes were unique in their heroism during World War II. Despite the danger, they worked in concert with one another to defy the Germans. Is there any way to prepare people to be so united that they take actions that are potentially at their own risk? If so, what kind of education is needed in order to cultivate ethical behavior in the citizens of a nation?

LINKING READINGS ONE AND TWO

1 Work with a partner. Compare and contrast the content of Readings One and Two by answering the questions in the chart.

	QUESTIONS	READING ONE	READING TWO
1.	What are the victims being threatened with?	Death	Death
2.	Are the threats carried out?		
3.	What role do the authorities play?		
4.	What kind of success is enjoyed?		

2 Discuss with a partner if people in both readings demonstrated an understanding of ethics. Did their respect for ethical behavior contribute to their resistance to evil?

READING THREE: Three Ways to Meet Oppression

A Warm-Up

Discuss the questions with a partner.

1. What are the advantages and disadvantages of fighting for your rights without using violence?

2. Is it important to you to fight in an ethical way? Could circumstances make it necessary to use violence?

B Reading Strategy

Predicting Content from Title

Predicting or getting some idea of a text before you start reading it will help you improve your reading speed and comprehension. The **title** of a text can often help you predict or **guess the author's most important idea** and guide you through the reading with the proper focus.

Work with a partner. Look at the title of Reading Three—"Three Ways to Meet Oppression" — and guess what the three ways to deal with oppression are.

Now read the essay to find out if your guesses were correct.

Three Ways to Meet Oppression

By Martin Luther King, Jr.

Martin Luther King, Jr. (1929–1968) was an American clergyman, activist, and leader of the American civil rights movement. He became a proponent of nonviolence through his experience with the Montgomery bus boycott and his readings of Mahatma Gandhi, Henry David Thoreau, and others. He received the Nobel Peace Prize in 1964 because of his work to end racial segregation and racial discrimination through civil disobedience. At the time of his assassination in Memphis, Tennessee, on April 4, 1968, he was working tirelessly to put an end to poverty and the U.S. involvement in the Vietnam War. He was awarded the Presidential Medal of Freedom posthumously in 1977 and the Congressional Gold Medal in 2004. His birthday, January 15th, was established as a U.S. federal holiday in 1986. The reading comes from Stride toward Freedom, *King's first book.*

1   Oppressed people deal with their oppression in three characteristic ways. One way is **acquiescence**: the oppressed resign themselves to their doom. They **tacitly** adjust themselves to oppression and thereby become **conditioned** to it.

2   There is such a thing as the freedom of exhaustion. Some people are so worn down by oppression that they give up. A few years ago in the **slum** areas of Atlanta, a Negro guitarist used to sing almost daily: "Been down so long that down don't bother me." This is the type of negative freedom and resignation that often **engulfs** the life of the oppressed.

3   But this is not the way out. To accept passively an unjust system is to cooperate with that system; thereby the oppressed become as evil as the oppressor. Non-cooperation with evil is as much a moral obligation as is cooperation with good. The oppressed must never allow the conscience of the oppressor to **slumber**.

4   A second way that oppressed people sometimes deal with oppression is to **resort to** physical violence and **corroding** hatred. Violence often brings about momentary results. Nations have frequently won their independence in battle. But in spite of temporary victories, violence never brings permanent peace. It solves no social problem; it merely creates new and more complicated ones.

5   Violence is immoral because it **thrives** on hatred rather than love. It destroys community and makes brotherhood impossible. It leaves society in monologue rather than dialogue. Violence ends by defeating itself. It creates bitterness in the survivors and brutality in the destroyers. Violence is not the way.

6   The third way open to oppressed people in their **quest** for freedom is the way of nonviolent resistance. The nonviolent resister agrees with the person who acquiesces that one should not be physically aggressive toward his opponent; but he balances the equation by agreeing with the person of violence that evil must be resisted. He avoids the nonresistance of the former and the violent resistance of the latter. With nonviolent resistance, no individual or group need **submit to** any wrong, nor need anyone resort to violence in order to right a wrong.

7   By nonviolent resistance, the Negro can also enlist all men of good will in his struggle for equality. The problem is not a purely racial one, with Negroes set against whites. In the end, it is not a struggle between people at all, but a tension between justice and injustice. Nonviolent resistance is not aimed against oppressors but against oppression. Under its banner consciences, not racial groups, are enlisted.

Photos: (left) *Martin Luther King giving his "I have a dream" speech at the March on Washington (1963);* (above) *leading the March from Selma to Montgomery (1965)*

COMPREHENSION

A Main Ideas

Read each statement. Decide if it is *True* or *False* according to the reading. Check (✓) the appropriate box. If it is false, change it to make it true. Discuss your answers with a partner.

	TRUE	FALSE
1. The author cannot understand how the oppressed can resign themselves to their fate.	☐	☐
2. The author sees nothing good about violence.	☐	☐
3. Nonviolence allows the oppressed minority to appeal to the majority's moral conscience.	☐	☐
4. Violence leaves a chance for the oppressors to change their minds and see the error of their ways.	☐	☐
5. According to the author, hatred is part of the struggle to change society.	☐	☐

B Close Reading

Read the quotes from the reading. Circle the statement that best explains each quote. Share your answers with a partner.

1. "A few years ago in the slum areas of Atlanta, a Negro guitarist used to sing almost daily: 'Been down so long that down don't bother me.'" *(paragraph 2)*

The guitarist could have said these words:

   a. "I've become so used to my poverty that it doesn't upset me anymore."

   b. "My poverty is not as bad as it seems."

2. "The oppressed must never allow the conscience of the oppressor to slumber." *(paragraph 3)*

   a. The oppressed must not let the oppressors trouble their conscience.

   b. The oppressed must make the oppressors ashamed of what is being done.

3. "[Violence] leaves society in monologue rather than dialogue." *(paragraph 5)*

   a. With violence, there is no discussion or exchange of ideas.

   b. No one listens when violence speaks.

4. "Nonviolent resistance is not aimed against oppressors but against oppression. Under its banner consciences, not racial groups, are enlisted." *(paragraph 7)*

   a. With nonviolent resistance, there is a moral outcome.

   b. Racial consciousness remains strongest with nonviolence.

VOCABULARY

(A) Guessing from Context

Read each quote from the reading. Try to guess the meaning of the words in bold from the context. Write your guess. Then consult a dictionary and write the definition.

1. "Oppressed people deal with their oppression in three characteristic ways. One way is **acquiescence**: the oppressed resign themselves to their doom." *(paragraph 1)*

   acquiescence   Guess: _agreement_____

   Dictionary: _the quality of being too ready to agree with_____

   _someone or do what they want without arguing or_____

   _complaining_____

2. "They tacitly adjust themselves to oppression and thereby become **conditioned** to it." *(paragraph 1)*

   conditioned   Guess: _____

   Dictionary: _____

3. "A few years ago in the **slum** areas of Atlanta, a Negro guitarist used to sing almost daily: 'Been down so long that down don't bother me.'" *(paragraph 2)*

   slum   Guess: _____

   Dictionary: _____

4. "This is the type of negative freedom and resignation that often **engulfs** the life of the oppressed." *(paragraph 2)*

   engulf   Guess: _____

   Dictionary: _____

5. "Violence is immoral because it **thrives** on hatred rather than love." *(paragraph 5)*

   thrive   Guess: _____

   Dictionary: _____

6. "The third way open to oppressed people in their **quest** for freedom is the way of nonviolent resistance." *(paragraph 6)*

   quest   Guess: _____

   Dictionary: _____

Read the essay. Match each word or phrase in bold with its synonym in the box below. Compare answers with a partner.

Rosa Parks and Martin Luther King

In the days when black people were forced to __submit to__ the power of the white supremacist system whose unfair practices totally __conditioned__ their
1.
                                    2.
lives, Rosa Parks refused to give up her seat to a white man on a Montgomery, Alabama, bus. Her action began a mass movement that made the nation rethink its ____tacit____ acceptance of racial injustice.
3.

When she was a child, Parks's family had sent her to the Industrial School for Girls run by two white women reformers from the North for black girls ages 5 to 14. The school had a difficult relationship with the southern white community and had been burned twice by arsonists. Despite the __corroding__ influence of segregation,[1]
                                                              4.
Parks later obtained a high school diploma, encouraged by her husband. Together the couple followed the ____quest____ for their rights by joining the NAACP.[2] When
                           5.
World War II __engulfed__ the world, Parks worked at Maxwell Air Force base,
              6.
a federal area where racial discrimination was not allowed. She wrote that this experience opened her eyes to the wider world. Later, she attended the Highlander Folk School in Tennessee, a place that trained people who wanted to lead their community to freedom. She ____thrived____ there; in her *Autobiography*, she said it was
                               7.
the first time she had been at meetings where black people and white people worked together as equals.

---

[1] *segregation:* a system of legalized separation of the races that began in the defeated southern states after the Civil War (1861–1865) and lasted until the 1960s

[2] *NAACP:* The National Association for the Advancement of Colored People, an integrated organization of black and white people, begun in 1909, to gain equal rights for all Americans

Rosa Parks was a well-known and respected member of her church and the civil rights organizations in her community. She was not just the stubborn dressmaker the policeman saw on the bus when he __resorted to__ arresting her like a common

8.
criminal on December 1, 1955. The women of her church and the Montgomery Women's Political Council were shocked. They worked all night making leaflets calling people to refuse to go on the buses. They described how they stayed by their windows in the morning and watched as the buses went by empty. They were themselves amazed that the moment had come when people awoke from their __slumber__ — "people just weren't going to take it any more." That night the

9.
Reverend Martin Luther King, Jr., the new minister in town, made his first speech to encourage the continuation of a bus boycott he had no part in planning or foreseeing. As he himself said, the people were leading him.[3]

As a younger man, he had wondered how America would ever change without violence, even though as a clergyman, he could not __acquiesce__ to such a solution.

10.
But in Montgomery he realized that ordinary people fighting for their rights could change a nation. The boycott continued for more than a year. On December 20, 1956, the Supreme Court declared that the law requiring segregated buses was unconstitutional.[4] All that King had learned about the power of mass movement and nonviolence he took everywhere in the country, from the farms to the cities, from the __slums__ to the nation's capital, working for the disenfranchised, joining the

11.
antiwar movement, and fighting for economic equality.

_____	a. destructive	_____	e. poorest neighborhoods	_____	i. was successful
_____	b. agree	_____	f. determined	_____	j. overwhelmed
_____	c. unspoken	_____	g. struggle	_____	k. inactivity
_1_	d. give in to	_____	h. ended up		

_____

[3] King's mature philosophy included civil disobedience, the refusal to obey unjust laws, just as Rosa Parks had refused to obey the law on segregation of the buses. Disobeying the law often meant arrest and jail for King and his followers, but they practiced self-control so that they would never respond to violence with violence.

[4] This decision was a major blow to the segregation system that was officially ended in 1964.

NOTE-TAKING: Identifying Main Points of Author's Argument

Work with a partner. Go back to the reading and read it again. Then fill out the chart with short notes identifying Martin Luther King's attitudes toward the three ways of dealing with oppression. For each way, check whether King accepts or rejects it. Then give his reasons for doing so.

THREE WAYS OF DEALING WITH OPPRESSION	MARTIN LUTHER KING'S REASONS FOR ACCEPTING OR REJECTING THIS APPROACH
1. Acquiescence	☐ **Accepts**　　☐ **Rejects** a. passive acceptance of injustice makes you complicit in the system b. c.
2. Violence	☐ **Accepts**　　☐ **Rejects** a. no permanent peace b. c.
3. Nonviolent resistance	☐ **Accepts**　　☐ **Rejects** a. no physical harm to anyone b. c.

Now discuss these questions.

According to Martin Luther King:

1. What's good about violence?

2. What's better about nonviolence?

3. Do you agree? Why or why not?

CRITICAL THINKING

Discuss the questions in a small group. Be prepared to share your answers with the class.

1. The civil rights movement wasn't a fight just for black people's rights but for the rights of all Americans. How does King explain this in the reading?

2. The poet Emma Lazarus, whose poem, "The New Colossus," is on the Statue of Liberty, wrote: "Until we are all free, we are none of us free." What does this statement mean? How does the freedom or lack of freedom of others affect us? Why is it important to resist any discrimination against other people as soon as it begins?

3. African Americans are a minority (about 11% of the population) in the United States. How is a nonviolent struggle more suited to winning allies in the majority? Why is it easier to involve large numbers of ordinary people in a nonviolent movement than in a violent struggle?

AFTER YOU READ

BRINGING IT ALL TOGETHER

Work in groups of four. Role-play an interview with the three authors in this chapter about resisting evil. The journalist will ask questions of the others about some of the issues listed below. Ghosh, Arendt, and King will express their opinions and give examples. Use some of the vocabulary you studied in the chapter (for a complete list, go to page 251).

Topic: Resisting evil

ROLES:

- Journalist
- Amitav Ghosh
- Hannah Arendt
- Martin Luther King, Jr.

ISSUES:

- how to counter violence
- how to help and protect people
- how to fight with dignity
- how to get people over to one's side
- how to live a good life

WRITING ACTIVITY

Write a three-paragraph essay about a time when you or your family were caught up in a political or historical event of some importance. Use more than five of the words or idioms you studied in the chapter.

- **Introduction:** Give a general portrait of your family.
- **Body Paragraph:** Explain what historical events influenced you or your family and what the consequences were for your lives.
- **Conclusion:** Tell what lessons can be learned.

DISCUSSION AND WRITING TOPICS

Discuss these topics in a small group. Choose one of them and write a paragraph or two about it. Use the vocabulary from the chapter.

1. Give examples of nonviolent change (the fall of the Berlin Wall and the end of the Soviet bloc, for example). When can nonviolence work? Does it work in democratic regimes? In dictatorial regimes?

2. Comment on these quotes about ethical behavior, using the information from this chapter or from your own experience or reading.
   - "You can't let people be treated in an inhuman way around you. Otherwise you start to become inhuman." —*Hetty Voûte*
   - "The heart has reasons that reason knows not of." —*Blaise Pascal*
   - "We need to know people who have made choices that we, too, can make to turn us into human beings." —*Richard Bach*

3. According to Philip Zimbardo, a social psychologist at Stanford University, we have to tell our children that ordinary everyday people can do the right thing in difficult situations. In this sense, comic book heroes are not good role models for children because their "superpowers" allow them to do good deeds. Zimbardo believes that we must teach children to be heroes waiting for a chance to act. "One day you will be in a new situation. Path one, you're going to be a perpetrator of evil. You're going to steal, cheat, allow bullying. Path two, you become guilty of the evil of passive inaction. Path three, you become a hero. The point is, are we ready to take the path to celebrating ordinary heroes, waiting for the right situation to come along to put heroic imagination into action?"

   Do you think this is a good way to educate our children? Why or why not?

4. Amitav Ghosh's story is a personal narrative while Hannah Arendt's work is not. Which style has more of an impact on you? Why?

5. Martin Luther King, Jr., said that violence "leaves society in monologue rather than dialogue." In his autobiography, *An Ordinary Man*, Paul Rusesabagina says: "If anybody tried to threaten me, I would simply look him in the eye and ask him in a firm but friendly voice, 'Why?' The bully would have no choice but to engage me verbally, and this made violence next to impossible. I learned that it is very difficult to fight someone with whom you are already talking."

   Do you think we can do something to encourage nonviolence in interpersonal relationships? Why or why not?

VOCABULARY

Nouns
acquiescence
concession
measures
mob
quest
resignation
seizure
slum
thug

Verbs
accommodate *
engulf
falter
prevail
sabotage
slumber
start
tackle
thrive

Phrasal Verbs
fan out
reckon with
resort to
tip off

Adjectives
bereft
chilling
conditioned
corroding
immune
menacing

Adverbs
starkly
tacitly

Phrases and Idioms
be intent on
brace for
submit to *

* = AWL (Academic Word List) item

SELF-ASSESSMENT

In this chapter you learned to:

○ Predict the content of a text from the title or from the subheadings

○ Preview a text using an Editor's Insert

○ Guess the meaning of words from the context

○ Use dictionary entries to learn the meanings of words

○ Understand and use synonyms, collocations, and different word forms

○ Identify noun clauses and the reasons for their use

○ Take notes to identify the main details of the action

○ Complete a chart to identify the main points of the author's arguments

What can you do well? ✓

What do you need to practice more? ✓

Ethics: *Resistance to Evil in the 20th Century*   **251**

CHAPTER 10

WOMEN'S STUDIES:
Reaching for Equality

WOMEN'S STUDIES: academic courses in sociology, history, literature, and psychology that focus on the roles, experiences, and achievements of women in society

OBJECTIVES

To read academic texts, you need to master certain skills.

In this chapter, you will:

- Predict the content of a text from the first two paragraphs

- Use paraphrasing to identify the main ideas of a text

- Scan a text for dates to understand the sequence of events

- Guess the meaning of words from the context

- Use dictionary entries to learn the meanings of words

- Understand and use synonyms, collocations, phrasal verbs, and different word forms

- Recognize the use of repetition for emphasis in speeches

- Fill out an organizer and a timeline with notes describing details, reactions, or events

A Famous Women

Many men have become famous in history. Here is a very partial list of some women who have achieved fame for their work. Match the names with their achievements and the century in which they lived. See answers below.

_____ 1. Florence Nightingale

_____ 2. Georgia O'Keefe

_____ 3. Lady Murasaki Shikibu

_____ 4. Charlotte Brontë

_____ 5. Margaret Thatcher

_____ 6. Marie Curie

_____ 7. Queen Elizabeth I

_____ 8. Jane Austen

_____ 9. Maria Montessori

_____ 10. Sojourner Truth
(Isabella Baumfree)

a. 19th-century author of *Jane Eyre*

b. 20th-century prime minister of Britain

c. 20th-century American painter

d. 19th-century author of *Pride and Prejudice*

e. 16th-century queen of England

f. 11th-century member of Japanese nobility; wrote *Tale of Genji*, the world's first novel

g. 19th-century nurse and administrator; established nursing as a profession

h. 20th-century scientist; received two Nobel prizes, for physics and chemistry

i. 20th-century Italian physician and educator of children

j. 19th-century abolitionist; first black woman to speak out against slavery

B Consider These Questions

1 What conclusions can you draw from the above list of names? Check (✓) all the possible conclusions.

☐ **a.** Before the 19th century, the only women to achieve fame were from aristocratic families.

☐ **b.** In certain very limited circumstances, women born into royal families were allowed to rule.

☐ **c.** Women begin to appear in the historical record in considerable numbers in the 19th century.

2 Discuss the questions with a partner.

1. Why did many women start to appear in literature, art, and the professions only in the 19th century? What had changed?

2. If women were so absent from history before the 19th century, do you think this was because they were inferior, or because they were not allowed to participate?

Famous Women Answers:
1. g   2. c   3. f   4. a   5. b   6. h   7. e   8. d   9. i   10. j

A Warm-Up

During the French Revolution, the Declaration of the Rights of Man was passed in 1789. In 1790 Nicolas de Condorcet and Etta Palm d'Aelders unsuccessfully called on the National Assembly to extend civil and political rights to women. Condorcet declared that "whoever votes against the right of another, whatever the religion, color, or sex of that other, has henceforth given up his own rights."

However, the French Revolution did not lead to a recognition of women's rights, and this prompted Olympe de Gouges to publish the Declaration of the Rights of Woman and the Female Citizen in early 1791.

Discuss the questions with a partner.

1. The Declaration of the Rights of Man began: "Men are born free and remain free and equal in right." How do you think de Gouges began her Declaration?

2. In the United States, Elizabeth Cady Stanton modeled her Declaration of Sentiments after the Declaration of Independence. How do you think her Declaration began?

B Reading Strategy

Predicting Content from First Two Paragraphs

The **first two paragraphs** of a text often **summarize the main points** of the text. By reading the beginning of a text and taking a moment to think about it, the reader can become **familiar with the topic** and begin to **predict what will follow**.

Read the first two paragraphs of the reading. Then check (✓) the appropriate answers to the question.

What rights do you think women wanted in 1848?

☐ the right to divorce

☐ the right to own property

☐ the right to vote

☐ the right to an education

Now read the rest of the text to find out if your predictions were correct.

Elizabeth Cady Stanton

The Declaration of Sentiments (1848)
By Elizabeth Cady Stanton

Elizabeth Cady Stanton (1815–1902) was an American social activist. With her husband and seven children, she worked as an abolitionist against slavery and became a leading figure of the early women's rights movement. The first women's rights convention in the United States was held in Seneca Falls, New York, in July, 1848. The Declaration of Sentiments, *asking for the vote and full rights for women, was read at the convention.*

1   When, in the course of human events, it becomes necessary for one portion of the family of man to assume among the people of the earth a position different from that which they have hitherto occupied, but one to which the laws of nature and of nature's God entitle them, a decent respect to the opinions of mankind requires that they should declare the causes that impel them to such a course.

2   We hold these truths to be self-evident: that all men and women are created equal.

3   The history of mankind is a history of repeated injuries on the part of man toward woman, establishing an absolute tyranny over her. To prove this, let facts be **submitted** to a **candid** world.

4   Having **deprived** her **of** the elective franchise,[1] the first right of a citizen, he has oppressed her on all sides.

5   He has made her, if married, civilly dead in the eyes of the law. He has taken from her all right to any property, even to the wages she earns.

6   In the **covenant** of marriage, she is **compelled to** promise obedience to her husband, he becoming, to all intents and purposes, her master — the law giving him power to deprive her of her liberty, and to administer punishment.

7   He has monopolized nearly all the profitable employments, and from those she is permitted to follow, she receives very little **remuneration**. He closes against her all the careers that lead to wealth and **distinction**. As a teacher of theology, medicine, or law, she is not known.

8   He has denied her any way of **obtaining** a **thorough** education, all colleges being closed against her.

9   He has given the world a different code of morals for men and for women. Moral failures which **exclude** women from society are not only tolerated, but considered of little importance in man.

10   He has tried, in every way that he could, to destroy her confidence in her own powers, to lessen her self-respect, and to make her willing to lead a dependent and **abject** life.

11   Now, in view of this complete disenfranchisement of one-half the people of this country and in view of the unjust laws above mentioned, and because women do feel themselves **aggrieved**, oppressed, and **fraudulently** deprived of their most sacred rights, we insist that they have immediate admission to all the rights and privileges which belong to them as citizens of the United States.

---

[1] *franchise:* the legal right to vote in your country's elections

COMPREHENSION

(A) Main Ideas

Read each statement. Decide if it is *True* or *False* according to the reading. Check (✓) the appropriate box. If it is false, change it to make it true. Discuss your answers with a partner.

		TRUE	FALSE
1.	According to Stanton, marriage is a contract that was unfavorable to women.	☐	☐
2.	According to the Declaration, women at this time were not allowed to work outside the home.	☐	☐
3.	Women were not allowed to learn to read and write.	☐	☐
4.	Men profited from the dependency of women.	☐	☐
5.	Women enjoyed the rights of American citizens.	☐	☐

(B) Close Reading

Read the quotes from the reading. Circle the statement that best explains each quote. Share your answers with a partner.

1. "He has made her, if married, civilly dead in the eye of the law. He has taken from her all right to any property, even to the wages she earns." (*paragraph 5*)

   a. Married women have more rights than single women.

   b. All the property and money of a married woman belong to her husband.

2. "In the covenant of marriage, she is compelled to promise obedience to her husband, he becoming, to all intents and purposes, her master." (*paragraph 6*)

   a. Traditional marriage is conceived as an equal partnership.

   b. Traditional marriage gives men power over women.

3. "He has monopolized nearly all the profitable employments, and from those she is permitted to follow, she receives very little remuneration. He closes against her all the careers that lead to wealth and distinction." (*paragraph 7*)

   a. Women are excluded from most careers, especially professional careers.

   b. Women cannot work at all outside of the home.

4. "He has tried, in every way that he could, to destroy her confidence in her own powers, to lessen her self-respect, and to make her willing to lead a dependent and abject life." (*paragraph 10*)

   a. Men have tried to undermine women's desire for independence.

   b. Men have tried to undermine women's respect.

VOCABULARY

A Word Forms

1 Fill in the chart with the correct word forms. Some categories can have more than one form. Use a dictionary if necessary. An *X* indicates there is no form in that category.

	NOUN	VERB	ADJECTIVE	ADVERB
1.	compulsion		compelled / compelling /	
2.		deprive		X
3.		exclude		X
4.				fraudulently
5.	remuneration			X

2 Complete the sentences with the correct form of the words from the chart. The first letter of each word has been given to you as a clue. Compare answers with a partner.

1. In traditional societies, most women were c ompelled _____ to

    remain in the home in order to do the work the family needed.

2. Their e _____ from society was explained by the need for

    someone to take care of the house, cook, wash, and raise the children.

3. But as the Industrial Revolution changed the context of the family with

    department stores, washing machines, plentiful food, and easier transportation

    and communication, confining women to the home was increasingly seen as

    d _____ them of their rights.

4. Women were particularly active in education, leading to c _____

    education laws for both boys and girls.

5. It became clear that women needed to have just r _____ for

    their work outside the home.

6. People gradually realized that a husband's appropriation of his wife's property

    was a f _____ interpretation of the marriage contract.

7. However, very few divorces were granted in the first part of the 19th century,

    and custody of the children was given to the husband. Being d _____

    of their children was agonizing for women who wanted to be free.

B Synonyms

Complete each paragraph with the words or phrases from the box. Use the synonym in parentheses to help you select the correct word or phrase. Compare answers with a partner.

compelled	covenant	deprived of	exclude

In the 19th century, marriage was viewed as a _____ _covenant_ _____

1. (contract)

between two people that was not supposed to be broken. Although women could

not be _____ to marry, it was the only way to have a family

2. (forced)

and be accepted by society. Unmarried women could own property, but when they

married, they were _____ this right. All property, real estate,

3. (kept from having)

and wages belonged to their husband. The husband, on the other hand, had to

support his wife and, in some states, could not _____ her

4. (bar)

from inheriting one-third of his property after his death.

abject	aggrieved	distinction	remunerated

Although women in the United States were not kept in _____

5. (hopeless)

ignorance, they were not able to pursue university degrees until well into the second

half of the 19th century. Women were _____ by this exclusion,

6. (angered)

which prevented them from embarking on careers of _____.

7. (importance)

The first colleges for women were teaching seminaries; some of the first

_____ jobs for women were as teachers. Most of the well-

8. (paid)

known women's colleges opened in the 1870s and 1880s.

candid	fraudulently	obtain	submitted	thorough

Elizabeth Blackwell was an exception to almost every rule. She was

very _____ about her desire to study medicine. She

9. (frank)

_____ her application to the admissions committees of

10. (gave)

seventeen schools for their consideration. Sixteen schools rejected her before she found a place. She endured the teasing and meanness of the other students, who

believed she was _____ taking up a place designed for a man.

11. (dishonestly)

Against all odds, she was the first woman to graduate from

medical school in the United States in 1849. Blackwell joined

the antislavery movement and the women's rights movement.

She opened a school for women doctors, where women could

_____ a _____

12. (get)   **13. (rigorous)**

medical education. She eventually founded a hospital for

women and children staffed by female doctors in New York.

Stamp issued to honor Elizabeth Blackwell

CRITICAL THINKING

Discuss the questions in a small group. Be prepared to share your answers with the class.

1. Was it a good idea to make a declaration asking for the vote and full rights for women, as Stanton did in the Declaration of Sentiments? Why or why not?

2. What do you think Stanton might have meant when she said men undermined women's confidence?

3. The great women novelists of the 19th century began writing either anonymously, like Jane Austen, or under male pseudonyms. Charlotte Bronte wrote as Currer Bell; her sister Emily, the author of *Wuthering Heights*, wrote as Ellis Bell; Amandine Lucie Aurore Dupin used the name George Sand, and Mary Ann Evans wrote as George Eliot.

   It was not illegal for women to publish books. Nevertheless, what might have been their reasons for choosing male names?

4. Do you think things have changed for women today? In what ways? Why? What would Elizabeth Stanton think if she came back today?

5. Have women asked for too much? Is the vote important, or is economic and educational opportunity more important? Do women lose their femininity when they ask to be equal?

A Warm-Up

Work with a partner. Read the quote by Margaret Mead, a famous anthropologist who lived in the 20th century, and the quote by Abraham Lincoln, 16th president of the United States, who served during the Civil War. Then discuss the questions.

Every time we liberate a woman, we liberate a man. —*Margaret Mead*

All are free or none are free. —*Abraham Lincoln*

What do these quotes mean? Lincoln wrote about slaves and free men; Mead wrote about women and men. How are these two ideas similar?

B Reading Strategy

Paraphrasing to Identify Main Ideas

A **paraphrase** is a statement that expresses in a shorter way something someone has said or written. When a text is difficult, stopping to think after each paragraph may be useful on the first or second reading. It may be useful also to write a **one-sentence paraphrase for each paragraph**. It will help you **identify the main ideas**.

Example Paragraph:

   I have been thinking of the scene presented forty years ago at the Seneca Falls convention, and the manner in which this organized suffrage movement was born. It was a very small thing then. Few of those who saw it had any notion that the little thing would live.

Example Paraphrase:

   It is hard to imagine that the women's suffrage movement has grown so much since it began at the Seneca Falls convention 40 years ago.

Work with a partner. Read the paragraph and write a one-sentence paraphrase for it.

It was a great thing for the friends of peace to organize in opposition to war; it was a great thing for humane people to organize in opposition to slavery; but it was a much greater thing, in view of all the circumstances, for woman to organize herself in opposition to her exclusion from participation in government. Men took for granted all that could be said against war and slavery. But no such advantage was found in the beginning of the cause of suffrage for women. On the contrary.

_____

_____

As you read the text, write a one-sentence paraphrase in the margin next to each paragraph, starting with paragraph 3.

Speech on Women's Rights (1888)

By Frederick Douglass

Frederick Douglass (1818–1895) was an American social reformer. He was born a slave, escaped to freedom, and became a leader in the abolitionist movement. Douglass was one of the few men present at the first women's rights convention, held at Seneca Falls, New York, in July 1848. He remained a champion of the right of women to vote. In April 1888, in a speech before the International Council of Women, in Washington, D.C., Douglass recalls his role at the Seneca Falls convention, although he insists that women rather than men should be the primary spokespersons for the movement.

1   I have been thinking of the scene presented forty years ago at the Seneca Falls convention, and the manner in which this organized suffrage[1] movement was born. It was a very small thing then. Few of those who saw it had any notion that the little thing would live.

2   It was a great thing for the friends of peace to organize in opposition to war; it was a great thing for **humane** people to organize in opposition to slavery; but it was a much greater thing, in view of all the circumstances, for woman to organize herself in opposition to her exclusion from participation in government. Men took for granted all that could be said against war and slavery. But no such advantage was found in the beginning of the cause of suffrage for women. On the contrary.

3   Everything in her condition was supposed to be lovely, just as it should be. She floated along on the tide of life as her mother and grandmother had done before her, as in a dream of Paradise. It required a daring voice and a determined hand to awake her from this delightful dream and **call** the nation **to account** for the rights and opportunities of which it was depriving her. It was well understood at the beginning that woman would not thank us for disturbing her by this call to duty, and it was well known that man would **denounce** and scorn us for such a daring innovation upon the established order of things.

(continued on next page)

---

[1] *suffrage:* the right to vote in the democratic process

4   Then who were we, for I count myself in, who did this thing? We were few in numbers, moderate in resources, and very little known in the world. There are few facts in my **humble** history to which I look back with more satisfaction than to the fact, recorded in the history of the woman-suffrage movement, that I was sufficiently **enlightened** at that early day, and when only a few years from slavery, to support your resolution for woman suffrage. When I ran away from slavery, it was for myself; when I **advocated** emancipation, it was for my people; but when I stood up for the rights of woman, self was out of the question, and I found a little nobility in the act.

5   Time is a **conservative** power — a very conservative power. Man has been so long the king and woman the subject — man has been so long accustomed to command and woman to obey — that both parties to the relation have been hardened into their respective places, and thus has been piled up a mountain of iron against woman's enfranchisement.

6   The universality of man's rule over woman is another factor in the resistance to the woman-suffrage movement. We are pointed to the fact that men have not only always ruled over women, but that they do so everywhere, and they easily think that a thing that is done everywhere must be right. Though the **fallacy** of this reasoning is too transparent to need refutation, it still exerts a powerful influence.

7   All good causes are mutually helpful. The benefits **accruing** from this movement for the equal rights of woman are not confined or limited to woman only. They will be shared by every effort to **promote** the progress and welfare of mankind everywhere and in all ages.

8   I do not forget the thoughtful remark of our president in the opening address to this International Council, reminding us of the incompleteness of our work. The remark was wise and timely. But, however this may be and whatever the future may have in store for us, one thing is certain — this new revolution in human thought will never go backward. When a great truth once gets abroad in the world, no power on earth can imprison it, or prescribe its limits, or **suppress** it. It is bound to go on till it becomes the thought of the world. Such a truth is woman's right to equal liberty with man. She was born with it. It was hers before she comprehended it. It is inscribed upon all the powers and **faculties** of her soul, and no custom, law or usage can ever destroy it. Now that it has gotten fairly fixed in the minds of the few, it is bound to become fixed in the minds of the many, and be supported at last by a great cloud of witnesses[2] which no man can number and no power can withstand.[3]

---

[2] *cloud of witnesses:* from the Bible; witnesses to the faith

[3] Although Douglass's support of women's rights never wavered, in 1869 he publicly disagreed with Elizabeth Cady Stanton and Susan B. Anthony. Douglass urged the acceptance of the post-Civil War Fifteenth Amendment to the Constitution, giving black men the right to vote, even though he agreed with Stanton and Anthony that the amendment unfairly excluded white and black women.

COMPREHENSION

A **Main Ideas**

1 Work with a partner. Compare the paraphrases you have written in the margin of the text. Then, for paragraphs 2 through 4, circle the best paraphrase.

PARAGRAPH 2:

a. For women to demand equality for themselves was more difficult than speaking out in favor of antislavery or antiwar causes.

b. It was a worthier goal for women to ask for their freedom than for people to campaign against war and slavery.

PARAGRAPH 3:

a. People were disturbed by the women's movement because it tried to change the established order in society.

b. It was very difficult to convince many women that they deserved more in life because they had been told for centuries that whatever they had was all they needed.

PARAGRAPH 4:

a. Douglass felt that all slaves should support the women's movement.

b. To Douglass, standing up for the rights of women was a selfless and noble act.

2 Now, for paragraphs 5 through 8, write your paraphrases on the lines.

PARAGRAPH 5:

_____

_____

PARAGRAPH 6:

_____

_____

PARAGRAPH 7:

_____

_____

PARAGRAPH 8:

_____

_____

B Close Reading

Read the quotes from the reading. Circle the statement that best explains each quote. Share your answers with a partner.

1. "Few of those who saw it had any notion that the little thing would live." *(paragraph 1)*

   a. Not enough people were at the convention to give life to the idea.

   b. The idea took hold despite the few people who supported it at first.

2. "Everything in her condition was supposed to be lovely, just as it should be. She floated along on the tide of life as her mother and grandmother had done before her, as in a dream of Paradise. It required a daring voice and a determined hand to awake her from this delightful dream and call the nation to account for the rights and opportunities of which it was depriving her." *(paragraph 3)*

   a. Women were fooled into thinking their lives were perfect.

   b. The nation realized that women were being deprived of their rights.

3. "Then who were we, for I count myself in, who did this thing? We were few in numbers, moderate in resources, and very little known in the world." *(paragraph 4)*

   a. The few people who started the movement were not very rich but famous.

   b. The few people who started the movement were unknown and not very rich.

4. "Though the fallacy of this reasoning is too transparent to need refutation, it still exerts a powerful influence." *(paragraph 6)*

   a. Although it is clear that the reasoning is sound, it doesn't exert much influence.

   b. Although it is clear that the reasoning is not sound, many people believe it.

5. "I do not forget the thoughtful remark of our president in the opening address to this International Council, reminding us of the incompleteness of our work. The remark was wise and timely. But, however this may be and whatever the future may have in store for us, one thing is certain — this new revolution in human thought will never go backward." *(paragraph 8)*

   a. The president is right in thinking that our work is not done, but we should take courage that victory will come.

   b. The president made a wise and timely statement in her opening speech, and we still have a long way to go.

6. "Such a truth is woman's right to equal liberty with man. She was born with it. It was hers before she comprehended it. It is inscribed upon all the powers and faculties of her soul, and no custom, law or usage can ever destroy it." *(paragraph 8)*

   a. Women, like men, have a natural right to be free even if they don't realize it at a certain moment.

   b. Women have the right to change the customs and laws of society.

VOCABULARY

A **Guessing from Context**

Read each quote from the reading. Try to guess the meaning of the words in bold from the context. Write your guess. Then consult a dictionary and write the definition.

1. "It was a great thing for the friends of peace to organize in opposition to war; it was a great thing for **humane** people to organize in opposition to slavery; but it was a much greater thing, in view of all the circumstances, for woman to organize herself in opposition to her exclusion from participation in government." *(paragraph 2)*

   humane   Guess: _kind, generous_____

   Dictionary: _treating people or animals in a way that is kind_____

2. "It was well understood at the beginning that woman would not thank us for disturbing her by this call to duty, and it was well known that man would **denounce** and scorn us for such a daring innovation upon the established order of things." *(paragraph 3)*

   denounce   Guess: _____

   Dictionary: _____

3. "There are few facts in my humble history to which I look back with more satisfaction than to the fact, recorded in the history of the woman-suffrage movement, that I was sufficiently **enlightened** at that early day, and when only a few years from slavery, to support your resolution for woman suffrage. When I ran away from slavery, it was for myself; when I **advocated** emancipation, it was for my people; but when I stood up for the rights of woman, self was out of the question, and I found a little nobility in the act." *(paragraph 4)*

   enlightened Guess: _____

   Dictionary: _____

   advocate   Guess: _____

   Dictionary: _____

4. "They will be shared by every effort to **promote** the progress and welfare of mankind everywhere and in all ages." *(paragraph 7)*

   promote   Guess: _____

   Dictionary: _____

5. "When a great truth once gets abroad in the world, no power on earth can imprison it, or prescribe its limits, or **suppress** it." *(paragraph 8)*

   suppress   Guess: _____

   Dictionary: _____

1 Read the paragraph. Match each word or phrase in bold with its synonym in the box below. Compare answers with a partner.

World Anti-Slavery Convention

History proves that the efforts devoted to the enfranchisement of one group often lend energy to other groups' struggles for social justice. Famous women's rights activists Lucretia Mott and Elizabeth Cady Stanton first discussed organizing a women's rights convention when they met in London, England in 1840, at the World Anti-Slavery Convention. Just before the conference began, it was decided that the six American women delegates __advocating__ an end to slavery would be excluded
1.
from participating and would have to sit in a separate area. Antislavery leaders were afraid that the women's rights issue would take attention away from their cause of ending slavery worldwide. Wasn't there a ___fallacy___ in their reasoning? Weren't
2.
both groups fighting to end a kind of slavery that was manifested in different forms? Along with several other men attending the convention, William Lloyd Garrison, the prominent abolitionist and founder of the American Anti-Slavery Society, __denounced__ the women's exclusion and sat with them in the segregated area. For
3.
Garrison and his colleagues to ally themselves with the women in such a way at that period of time was truly a refutation of everything people said about the inferiority of women. This was a courageous and necessary stand against the __conservative__
4.
thinking that had prevailed in society for too many years.

_1_ **a.** publicly supporting
____ **b.** publicly expressed disapproval of
____ **c.** preferring to keep things the way they are
____ **d.** error

2 Complete each paragraph with the words or phrases from the box. Use the synonym in parentheses to help you select the correct word or phrase. Compare answers with a partner.

called . . . to account	promote	suppress

The Seneca Falls convention was not only the first public women's rights meeting

in the United States, but also the first time that women and men came together to

_____promote_____ women's right to vote. Among the participants at
　　　　1. (support)

this meeting, which was organized by members of a radical Quaker group in Seneca

Falls, were Lucretia Mott, Elizabeth Cady Stanton, and Frederick Douglass.

After two days of discussions, the group produced the Declaration of Sentiments,

which _____ the nation _____ for women's
　　2. (made . . . responsible)

lack of rights in many areas of life. At first, Lucretia Mott and others wanted to

avoid talking about the right to vote for women because they were afraid that such

a radical idea would lead to demands to _____ the whole
　　　　　　　　3. (put an end to)

movement. However, the suffrage resolution remained in the document after

Frederick Douglass spoke eloquently in support of it.

accrued	enlightened	faculties	humane	humble

Frederick Douglass was an American social reformer, statesman, writer,

and orator, who was born into slavery in the South of the United States. This

eloquent, cultured, and _____ individual, coming from
　　　　　　　　4. (wise)

a _____ background, realized that education was the
　　5. (lowly)

"pathway to freedom" when he taught himself to read as a child. The most important

benefit _____ from his ability to read was the knowledge
　　6. (gained)

of the abolitionist movement in the North fighting against slavery. This knowledge

allowed him to escape from the South and pursue a life in which he would have

the opportunity to develop all his _____ . One of these was
　　　　　　　　7. (abilities)

compassion for the suffering of others. In his view, all human beings deserved to

receive the most _____ treatment.
　　　　8. (kind-hearted)

C Using the Dictionary

Read the dictionary entry for *faculty*.

> **faculty** *n. plural* **faculties** **1** all the teachers in a particular school or college, or in a particular department of a school or college: *Both students and faculty have protested.* / *faculty members* / *the Faculty of Social Sciences* **2** a particular skill that someone has + **for** *She has a great faculty for absorbing information.* **3** a natural ability, such as the ability to see, hear, or think clearly: *the patient's mental faculties* / + **of** *the faculty of hearing* / *Mrs. Darwin is no longer in full possession of all her faculties.*

1 Now read each sentence. Decide which meaning of *faculty* is being used. Write the number of the appropriate definition.

_____ a. The **faculty** of the women's studies program encourage both men and women to take their courses.

_____ b. Learning that there are women with an inborn **faculty** of thinking mathematically and men with an inborn **faculty** of writing poetically is an important lesson.

_____ c. Our individual **faculties** should not be defined according to gender stereotypes.

_____ d. The ninety-five-year-old man was still in the possession of all his **faculties**, and it was fascinating to hear his detailed accounts of his childhood in the segregated South.

_____ e. The **faculty** of the history department invited him to come speak at its seminar on the civil rights movement.

_____ f. A young student with a **faculty** for looking at a reading passage once and remembering everything in it was one of the few students who was able to keep up with the heavy reading load.

2 Complete the sentences with the words *faculty* or *faculties*.

1. Freedom cannot be fully enjoyed in a society unless the majority of people are

   given the opportunity to develop their _____.

2. That is why the _____ of our college are so special.

3. Only teachers with a great _____ for inspiring students

   will succeed in this college.

4. The interdisciplinary focus of the first-year curriculum allows students to take a

   variety of courses in the _____ of liberal arts, education,

   and engineering.

GRAMMAR FOR READING: Repetition for Emphasis in Speeches

> Both Readings One (**declaration**) and Two (**speech**) were written to be delivered **orally**. Their authors intended not only to **move the audience** but to **persuade listeners** to adopt their point of view. Stanton and especially Douglass were good **orators** — they were skilled at making powerful speeches.
>
> One way you can make powerful speeches that move and persuade your audience is to **use repetition for emphasis**. For example, you can use the following techniques:
>
> 1. Repeat words.
> 2. Focus on "gradations of intensity" of words (like *great, greater, greatest* or *few, fewer, fewest*).
> 3. Repeat phrases in well-constructed sentences.
> 4. Use parallel structures.
>
> Good writers use these techniques as well in their writing.
>
> **EXAMPLE:**
>
> Now, **in view of** this complete disenfranchisement of one-half the people of this country and **in view of** the unjust laws above mentioned, and **because** women do feel themselves **aggrieved**, **oppressed**, and fraudulently **deprived** of their most sacred rights, we insist that they have immediate admission to all the rights and privileges which belong to them as citizens of the United States.
>
> This is the concluding sentence of Stanton's Declaration of Sentiments (Reading One). "In view of" is repeated (technique #1) and, with "because," explains why equal rights are needed. The three-part construction at the beginning of the sentence (technique #3 — yellow highlight) is echoed in the three adjectives (technique #4 — blue highlight) that follow.

1 Frederick Douglass was a master at using repetition for emphasis in speeches. Go back to his "Speech on Women's Rights" and highlight at least five places where you see repetition of words and structures.

2 Work with a partner. Examine these passages of Douglass's speech and discuss which techniques he used. Write the number of the technique(s) on the line (#1, 2, 3, or 4).

_____ **a.** "It was a very small thing then. Few of those who saw it had any notion that the little thing would live.

It was a great thing for the friends of peace to organize in opposition to war; it was a great thing for humane people to organize in opposition to slavery; but it was a much greater thing, in view of all the circumstances, for woman to organize herself in opposition to her exclusion from participation in government." (*paragraphs 1 and 2*)

_____ **b.** "When I ran away from slavery, it was for myself; when I advocated emancipation, it was for my people; but when I stood up for the rights of woman, self was out of the question, and I found a little nobility in the act." (*paragraph 4*)

NOTE-TAKING: From Main Ideas to Support to Reaction

Go back to the reading and read it again. Then fill out the organizer. Next to the main idea for each paragraph, write down the details that support the main idea. Then give your reaction: write why you agree or disagree with the author's argument.

PARAGRAPH	MAIN IDEA	SUPPORT	YOUR REACTION
2	Women's movement had a difficult start	few people agreed — harder to fight for women than for peace or the antislavery cause	
3	Women didn't realize the truth of their situation	women asleep through centuries — fooled — hard to convince women to fight and men to agree	
4	For Douglass, it was an unselfish effort		
5/6	It is hard to convince society to change		
7	Freedom movements intersect		

Now work with a partner. Make an oral summary of Douglass's main ideas and discuss which points you agree with and which points you disagree with.

CRITICAL THINKING

Discuss the questions in a small group. Be prepared to share your points of view with the class.

1. Douglass says that when he "stood up for the rights of woman, self was out of the question, and [he] found a little nobility in the act." Why did he think this was noble? Can you think of other examples of this kind of nobility?

2. There is optimism in Douglass's remark that once a good idea is expressed, "it is bound to become fixed in the minds of the many" and eventually be embraced. Are there changes in history that you know of that support his assertion?

3. The women's suffrage movement was connected to the antislavery movement. Do you agree with Douglass that "all good causes are mutually helpful"? Why or why not? You may want to refer to issues in modern times to defend your point of view.

4. Douglass explains that in "time" (a long tradition) and "space" (all countries in the world), women had always been deprived of their rights. What did he mean? How do you think women could eventually win their emancipation?

5. Douglass is being ironic when he says, "Everything in her condition was supposed to be lovely, just as it should be. She floated along on the tide of life as her mother and grandmother had done before her, as in a dream of Paradise." Were women's lives really "lovely"? Why was it difficult to change women's minds about fighting for their rights?

LINKING READINGS ONE AND TWO

Work with a partner. Go back to Readings One and Two, and read them again. Then read each imaginary statement and decide if Stanton or Douglass could have made it. Write *S/D* if both could have made it, *S* if only Stanton could have made it, and *D* if only Douglass could have made it.

_____ 1. The list I have written points to the specific abuses that women have suffered.

_____ 2. History pervades my writing because I refer to historical texts and events.

_____ 3. I would like to explain why the progress of the women's movement has been so slow.

_____ 4. I want women to have the right to vote and to be men's equals in every respect.

_____ 5. Women feel oppressed and angry about their status in society.

_____ 6. Faulty thinking, despite its apparent lack of logic, can often shape human attitudes.

_____ 7. This is the beginning of the women's suffrage movement.

A **Warm-Up**

There had to be a constitutional amendment for women to obtain the vote in the United States. Reading Three tells the story of the final struggle to get the vote, 62 years after the Seneca Falls convention.

Discuss the questions with a partner.

1. Why do you think "the vote" was so important to the women's movement?

2. Why do you think it took so long to achieve the vote for women?

Women suffragists picketing in front of the White House (1917)

B **Reading Strategy**

Scanning for Dates to Understand Sequence
Some texts are **organized by dates** and the respective events associated with them. Scanning such a text for dates allows you to **understand the sequence (order) of events** it describes. It can also help you **get an overview** of the development of the main idea of the text.

Scan the reading for dates and answer the questions.

1. What is the earliest date mentioned? _____

2. What is the latest date mentioned? _____

Now read the text to find out what happened between these two dates.

The Day the Women Got the Vote

By George Sullivan

Suffragists marching in New York (1913)

1   During the early 1900s, a new generation of **feminists** launched a final push for women's suffrage. The struggle they **waged** eventually led to the passage of the Nineteenth Amendment to the Constitution in 1920, giving women voting rights equal to men.

2   These women were inspired at least in part by what was happening in state legislatures in the West. Between 1910 and 1914, the states of Washington, California, Oregon, Arizona, Kansas, Montana, Nevada, Illinois, and the territory of Alaska passed legislation granting women suffrage. In 1916, Carrie Chapman Catt took over the presidency of the National American Woman Suffrage Association and developed what she called her "Winning Plan," which was intended to win **ratification** of the suffrage amendment by 1920.

3   Other women, including Alice Paul and Harriet Stanton Blatch, the daughter of Elizabeth Cady Stanton, were influenced by Emmeline Pankhurst and the British suffragists who did not hesitate to use extreme methods to achieve their goals.[1] Blatch organized suffrage parades in New York City, the first demonstrations by American suffragists. After the United States entered World War I in 1917, Alice Paul and the Women's party **stepped up** their campaign. They stood in silent **vigil** in front of the White House and outside President Wilson's Washington home. Their signs accused the president of terrible deceit in fighting a war that was supposed to secure democratic principles in foreign lands, while at the same time denying democratic rights to American women.

4   After the protesting and picketing[2] had gone on for several months, police began **cracking down** and making arrests. At first the women were released without being sentenced. But **subsequently** when they returned to the picket line, they were arrested again. This time they were found guilty of blocking the sidewalk traffic and given prison sentences.

(continued on next page)

---

[1] *Emmeline Pankhurst* (1858–1928): a leader of the British suffragist movement along with her daughters Christabel, Sylvia, and Adela. In 1908, 500,000 women marched for the vote in London. Faced with the indifference of the government and the abusive tactics of the police, the Women's Social and Political Union resorted to breaking windows and attacking policemen; it was even accused of setting fires.

[2] *picketing:* a group of people, usually with signs, stationed outside a location in order to protest

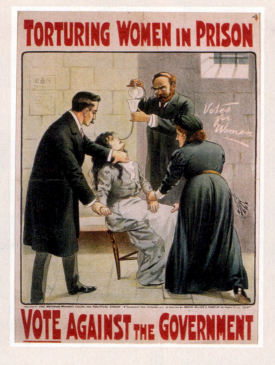

TORTURING WOMEN IN PRISON

Votes for Women

VOTE AGAINST THE GOVERNMENT

5   In prison, many of the women joined in a hunger strike. The authorities tried to force-feed them.[3] The public, horrified at this harsh treatment, began to look with sympathy on the cause of suffrage. When Paul and others were eventually released from prison, they were greeted as heroes.

6   The dramatic demonstrations staged by Alice Paul and the Women's party combined with Catt's hard work to win the support of the **rank and file** of ordinary people paid off. On January 10, 1918, Jeannette Rankin of Montana, who, when elected to the House of Representatives in 1916, had become the first female member of Congress, introduced the suffrage amendment on the floor of the House. One Congressman left his wife's death bed — **at her behest** — to vote for the amendment. Another Congressman was brought in on a stretcher. The final vote was 274 in favor of the amendment and 136 opposed. The amendment had passed by one vote more than the majority required.[4]

7   It took another year and a half for the amendment to win passage in the Senate. In June 1919, the amendment was submitted to the states for ratification. On August 26, 1920, after Tennessee had delivered the last needed vote, the Nineteenth Amendment became a part of the Constitution.

8   In the years that followed, the Women's party **set a** new **goal**: full equality for women under the law. The organization began **campaigning for** an Equal Rights Amendment to the Constitution. The struggle to win passage of *that* amendment continues to this day.[5]

---

[3] *force-feeding:* When the women protested their harsh treatment in prison by going on hunger strikes, feeding tubes were pushed down their throats or up their noses, causing great pain and vomiting, and pneumonia and pleurisy if the vomit was aspirated. Sylvia Pankhurst described being held down with a steel gag in her mouth until her gums bled. Her mother described the screams of the women in Holloway prison in Britain. This practice was stopped in 1913.

[4] *amendment:* All 27 amendments to the U.S. Constitution were ratified after two-thirds of the House of Representatives and two-thirds of the Senate approved of each amendment and sent it to the states; three-quarters of the states had to ratify each amendment.

[5] The *Equal Rights Amendment (ERA)* called for equality for women in all aspects of life, not just voting. It was approved by the House and Senate in 1972 but was not ratified by three-quarters of the states.

COMPREHENSION

A Main Ideas

Check (✓) the main ideas of the reading. Compare answers with a partner.

☐ **1.** Men overwhelmingly supported women's right to vote.

☐ **2.** If you want your rights, you have to fight for them.

☐ **3.** Different tactics helped bring the cause to the attention of the public.

☐ **4.** The effort for equal rights is not over.

B Close Reading

Read the quotes from the reading. Circle the statement that best explains each quote. Share your answers with a partner.

1. "The struggle they waged eventually led to the passage of the Nineteenth Amendment to the Constitution in 1920, giving women voting rights equal to men." *(paragraph 1)*

   a. Women achieved equal rights in 1920.

   b. Women were able to vote in 1920.

2. "Their signs accused the president of terrible deceit in fighting a war that was supposed to secure democratic principles in foreign lands, while at the same time denying democratic rights to American women." *(paragraph 3)*

   a. To the women, the president was a hypocrite.

   b. To the women, the president was the leader of the free world.

3. "One Congressman left his wife's death bed — at her behest — to vote for the amendment. Another Congressman was brought in on a stretcher." *(paragraph 6)*

   a. These men knew the vote was going to be a close one.

   b. These men knew the amendment would win.

4. "The organization began campaigning for an Equal Rights Amendment to the Constitution. The struggle to win passage of *that* amendment continues to this day." *(paragraph 8)*

   a. Women are still fighting for the vote.

   b. Women are still fighting for full equality.

VOCABULARY

A **Guessing from Context**

Read each quote from the reading. Try to guess the meaning of the words in bold from the context. Write your guess. Then consult a dictionary and write the definition.

1. "The struggle they **waged** eventually led to the passage of the Nineteenth Amendment to the Constitution in 1920, giving women voting rights equal to men." (*paragraph 1*)

   wage   Guess: _participate in_

                     Dictionary: _to be actively involved in a war, struggle, or fight_

2. "In 1916, Carrie Chapman Catt took over the presidency of the National American Woman Suffrage Association and developed what she called her "Winning Plan," which was intended to win **ratification** of the suffrage amendment by 1920." (*paragraph 2*)

   ratification   Guess: _____

                     Dictionary: _____

3. "They stood in silent **vigil** in front of the White House and outside President Wilson's Washington home." (*paragraph 3*)

   vigil   Guess: _____

                     Dictionary: _____

4. "After the protesting and picketing had gone on for several months, police began **cracking down** and making arrests." (*paragraph 4*)

   crack down   Guess: _____

                     Dictionary: _____

5. "At first the women were released without being sentenced. But **subsequently** when they returned to the picket line, they were arrested again." (*paragraph 4*)

   subsequently   Guess: _____

                     Dictionary: _____

6. "In the years that followed, the Women's party **set a** new **goal**: full equality for women under the law. The organization began **campaigning for** an Equal Rights Amendment to the Constitution." (*paragraph 8*)

   set a goal   Guess: _____

                     Dictionary: _____

   campaign for   Guess: _____

                     Dictionary: _____

B Synonyms

Complete the paragraph with the words or phrases from the box. Use the synonym in parentheses to help you select the correct word or phrase. Compare answers with a partner.

behest	feminists	set their goals	vigils
campaigned	rank and file	step up	waged
cracked down on	ratification	subsequently	

The "Angel" in the House

It's clear that men have to change in order to accept equal rights for women.

But despite what some extreme _____feminists_____ believe, women, too
1. (advocates of women's rights)

must change. As Mary Wollstonecraft wrote in the 18th century, women have got to

_____ and give up the fluttery childish persona they have
2. (accept responsibility)

often adopted at the _____ of men. In the early part of the
3. (request)

20th century, Virginia Woolf metaphorically _____ the "Angel
4. (attacked)

of the House." The "Angel" was completely unselfish, thought only of securing the

happiness of others in the family, and never contradicted a man. "Be sympathetic,

flatter, deceive, use all the arts and wiles of our sex," whispers the Angel into the ears

of women. But if women _____ based on this traditional
5. (established their future objectives)

version of womanhood, they would never be free to think for themselves. In her

essay "Professions for Women," Woolf _____ to kill the
6. (made a public effort)

Angel in herself whenever she appeared, and called on other women to be real and

express their true thoughts. _____, in the 1960s, Simone
7. (Later)

de Beauvoir also wrote about how women must free themselves from the false

notions of femininity that make it impossible for the _____
8. (majority)

of women to express their true faculties. Women picketed, participated in

_____ and _____ a struggle
9. (silent night protests) **10. (engaged in)**

for three generations and more than 70 years until they could get the

_____ of their right to equal citizenship. The effort to make
11. (passage)

men and women understand each other, respect each other, and help each other as

equals still goes on.

C Phrasal Verbs with *crack* and *step*

Read the dictionary entries of phrasal verbs with *crack* and *step*.

crack down *phr. v.* to become more strict in dealing with a problem and punishing the people involved: *We have to crack down on software pirates.*

crack up *phr. v.* INFORMAL **1 crack sb up** to laugh a lot at something or to make someone laugh a lot: *That joke still cracks me up.* **2** to have a mental breakdown: *If I don't get some time off soon, I'll crack up.* **3 sth's not all it's cracked up to be** something is not as good as people say it is: *The movie was OK, but it's not all it's cracked up to be.*

step down *phr. v.* to leave your job or official position, to resign: **+ as** *Arnez is stepping down as chairman.* / **+ from** *She's stepping down from the committee.*

step in *phr. v.* to become involved in a discussion, disagreement, etc., especially in order to stop trouble: *The police stepped in to break up the fight.*

step up *phr. v.* **1 step sth up** to increase the amount of an activity or the speed of a process in order to improve a situation: *They have stepped up security at the airport.* **2 step up (to the plate)** to agree to help someone or to be responsible for doing something: *Residents will have to step up if they want to rid this area of crime.*

Now complete each sentence with the correct form of the appropriate phrasal verb.

1. The women _____ the pressure on the White House during World War I because they hoped they would finally get the vote.

2. Many men _____ at the ridiculous idea that women would ever be able to participate in the political process.

3. However, some men _____ and did what they could to support women's rights.

4. Carrie Chapman Catt _____ as president of the National American Woman Suffrage Association before the war but resumed its leadership in 1917.

5. She _____ to resolve the arguments about tactics.

6. The police _____ on the demonstrators and arrested them because they wouldn't move.

7. Although the demonstrations were always peaceful, the police _____ security at future events.

8. In order for the women's rights movement to be successful, men as well as women needed to _____ and show their support.

D Collocations

Check (✓) the words that are often paired together. Discuss your answer with a partner and the meaning of the collocations.

☐ 1. wage a struggle   ☐ 5. set an example

☐ 2. wage a war   ☐ 6. set a task

☐ 3. wage a possibility   ☐ 7. set an agenda

☐ 4. wage a campaign   ☐ 8. set an accomplishment

NOTE-TAKING: Filling Out a Timeline

Go back to the reading and read it again. Then fill out the timeline with your notes detailing the event(s) for each date.

Date(s)	What Happened
1910–1914	Western states gave the vote to women
1916	
1917	
1918	
1919	
1920	

CRITICAL THINKING

Discuss the questions in a small group. Be prepared to share your answers with the class.

1. What factors do you think contributed to women being granted the vote after World War I in most European countries? The war? The desire for change? The women's own struggle?

2. Why do you think women were given the vote in the new western states of the United States before they got the vote in the old eastern states? Is it relevant that the first countries to grant women the vote were New Zealand in 1893 and South Australia in 1894? In what ways were these countries similar to the West in the United States?

3. In Britain in 1918 the Representation of the People Act eliminated property restrictions for men and, at the same time, granted the right to vote only to women over 30 (the voting age for men was 21) who owned property or were married to a man who owned property. Why do you think only women over 30 were given the vote?

4. When you change laws, do you really change attitudes? Did women get more respect when they got the vote? Did men change their minds?

BRINGING IT ALL TOGETHER

Work in groups of four. Role-play a discussion about women's rights between Elizabeth Cady Stanton, Frederick Douglass, a woman or man living in 1919, and someone living today.

Topic: Looking back on the struggle for women's rights in the past and evaluating what has been achieved

ROLES:
- Elizabeth Cady Stanton
- Frederick Douglass
- Man/woman living in 1919
- Man/woman living today

QUESTIONS:
- Was the struggle for women's rights worth it?
- Are men and women better off now? Why or why not?
- What still needs to be done?
- Has too much been done for women?

Each person in your group asks one of the questions. The others try to answer, expressing opinions Stanton, Douglass, and people living in 1919 or today might have had. Use some of the vocabulary you studied in the chapter (for a complete list, go to page 282).

WRITING ACTIVITY

Write a three-paragraph essay about something you had to fight for — a time when you had to struggle to gain recognition for yourself and your abilities. Use more than five of the words or idioms you studied in the chapter.
- **Introduction:** Explain what you wanted to achieve.
- **Body Paragraph:** Tell the reader how you finally achieved it (or didn't).
- **Conclusion:** Describe what effect the effort had on you.

DISCUSSION AND WRITING TOPICS

Discuss these topics in a small group. Choose one of them and write a paragraph or two about it. Use the vocabulary from the chapter.

1. Comment on these quotes. What do they mean? Do you agree or disagree?

   - "Never let the hand you hold hold you down."
     —*Author Unknown*

   - "I do not wish women to have power over men, but over themselves."
     —*Mary Wollstonecraft, early defender of women's rights (18th century)*

   - "And here I believe is the clue to the feelings of those men who have a real antipathy to the equal freedom of women. I believe they are afraid not that women should be unwilling to marry, but that they should insist that marriage should be on equal conditions; that all women of spirit and capacity should prefer doing almost anything else not in their own eyes degrading, rather than marry, when marrying is giving themselves a master."
     —*John Stuart Mill,* On the Subjection of Women, *British philosopher (19th century)*

   - "It was we, the people; not we, the white male citizens; nor yet we, the male citizens; but we, the whole people, who formed the Union. . . . Men, their rights and nothing more; women, their rights and nothing less."
     —*Susan B. Anthony, leader of the women's movement in the U.S. (19th century)*

   - "Any woman born with a great gift in the sixteenth century would certainly have gone crazed, shot herself, or ended her days in some lonely cottage outside the village, half witch, half wizard, feared and mocked at. For it needs little skill in psychology to be sure that a highly gifted girl who had tried to use her gift for poetry would have been so thwarted and hindered by other people, so tortured and pulled apart by her own contrary instincts, that she must have lost her health and sanity to a certainty."
     —*Virginia Woolf,* A Room of One's Own, *British novelist and essayist (20th century)*

2. In your opinion, what still needs to be done to make men and women equal? Eliminate differences in pay? Offer more affordable child care? Grant paternity leave for fathers of new babies? Other points?

VOCABULARY

Nouns
covenant
distinction
faculties
fallacy
feminist
rank and file
ratification
remuneration
vigil

Verbs
accrue
advocate *
denounce
exclude *
obtain *
promote *
submit
suppress
wage

Phrasal Verbs
crack down
deprive sb of
step up

Adjectives
abject
aggrieved
candid
enlightened
humane
humble
thorough

Adverbs
fraudulently
subsequently *

Phrases and Idioms
at the behest of sb
be compelled to
call sb to account
campaign for
set a goal

* = AWL (Academic Word List) item

SELF-ASSESSMENT

In this chapter you learned to:

○ Predict the content of a text from the first two paragraphs

○ Use paraphrasing to identify the main ideas of a text

○ Scan a text for dates to understand the sequence of events

○ Guess the meaning of words from the context

○ Use dictionary entries to learn the meanings of words

○ Understand and use synonyms, collocations, phrasal verbs, and different word forms

○ Recognize the use of repetition for emphasis in speeches

○ Fill out an organizer and a timeline with notes describing details, reactions, or events

What can you do well? ✓

What do you need to practice more? ✓

VOCABULARY INDEX

The number following each entry is the page where the word, phrase, or idiom first appears. Words followed by an asterisk (*) are on the Academic Word List (AWL). The AWL is a list of the highest-frequency words found in academic texts.

prevail 225
proliferation 94
promote* 262
prospect* 94
prosper 16
prudent 169
prune 17
push 76
put a brake on 211

Q
quest 243

R
raise expectations 102
rank and file 274
ratification 273
reciprocate 160
reckless 45
reckon with 234
reconstitute 122
refute 149
reinvigorate 35
reiterate 204
relinquish 103
remedy 17
remuneration 255
resemble 122
resignation 233
resort to 243
resource* 16
restraint* 35
restricted* 122
resurrect 59
retain* 128
retrieve 122
rummage 8
run counter to 186

S
sabotage 233
scandalize 186

scratch the surface 45
secure* 176
seizure 234
self-governance 159
set a goal 274
sever 113
shelter 9
shift* 17
shrewd 29
simultaneously 86
skeptic 142
slaughter 76
slum 242
slumber 242
sneer at 187
soaring 59
solidarity 103
sorting 122
span 103
starkly 225
start 224
startling 211
step up 273
strain 35
submit 255
submit to* 243
subsequently* 273
subtle 141
suppress 262
sustain* 203
sway 85
swift 68

T
tacitly 242
tackle 233
tariff 29
team up with 44
therapeutic 95
thorough 255
thrive 243
thug 224
tip 59
tip off 234

tolerance 186
tongue-in-cheek 212
trace* 141
transient 176
transmission* 113
traumatic 113
trend* 59

U
ubiquitous 141
ultimate 113
undermine 86
unimpaired 128
uniquely* 149
upheaval 103
uphold 28
urge 35
utmost 198
utter 142

V
vigil 273
visceral 76
vivid 129

W
wage 273
wane 59
what it comes down to 45
withstand 95

Y
yearn for 129

Z
zero in on 212

CREDITS

Page 224 "The Ghosts of Mrs. Gandhi," by Amitav Ghosh. Copyright © 1995 by Amitav Ghosh. Originally published in *The New Yorker*. Reproduced by permission of The Karpfinger Agency; Page 233 "Deportations from Western Europe", from *Eichmann In Jerusalem* by Hannah Arendt, copyright © 1963, 1964 by Hannah Arendt, copyright renewed © 1991, 1992 by Lotte Kohler. Used by permission of Viking Penguin, a division of Penguin Group (USA) Inc.; Page 242 Martin Luther King, Jr., "Three Ways of Meeting Oppression," from *Strive Toward Freedom.* New York: Harper & Row, Publishers. 1958; Page 254 Elizabeth Cady Stanton, "The Declaration of Sentiments"; Page 261 Frederick Douglass, "Speech On Women's Rights"; Page 273 George Sullivan, "The Day the Women Got the Vote" Copyright 1994 by George Sullivan; Dictionary Entries From *Longman Advanced American Dictionary* 2nd Ed Paper and CD ROM Pack. Copyright © Pearson Education. Reprinted with permission. All rights reserved.

PHOTO CREDITS

Page 1 David Papazian/Corbis/Glow Images; p. 3 AP Images/Associated Press; p. 8 David Grossman/Alamy; p. 15 ZUMA Press, Inc./Alamy; p. 16 David Grossman/Alamy; p. 25 Everett Collection Inc/Alamy; p. 28 (left) Everett Collection Inc/Alamy, (right) Everett Collection Historical/Alamy; p. 29 Pictorial Press Ltd/Alamy; p. 34 Everett Collection Inc/Alamy; p. 35 Everett Collection Inc/Alamy; p. 39 Buyenlarge/Getty Images; p. 44 David Grossman/Alamy; p. 56 Pictorial Press Ltd/Alamy; p. 58 Marilyn K. Yee/New York Times Co./Getty Images; p. 59 Everett Collection/Everett Collection; p. 67 CBW/Alamy; p. 68 ITAR-TASS Photo Agency/Alamy; p. 75 AP Images/Fa Zhi/Color China Photo; p. 83 Ryan McVay/Getty Images; p. 85 carlos castilla/Fotolia; p. 94 NetPics/Alamy; p. 102 Megapress/Alamy; p. 110 pixologic/Fotolia; p. 112 Henrik Montgomery/epa/Newscom; p. 121 (top) adimas/Fotolia, (left) Peter Gardiner/Science Source, (right) Peter Gardiner/Science Source; p. 127 Kathy deWitt/Alamy; p. 128 Ros Drinkwater/Alamy; p. 139 imagebroker/Alamy; p. 142 pwollinga/Fotolia; p. 150 Frans Lanting Studio/Alamy; p. 159 catolla/Fotolia; p. 165 MasterLu/Fotolia; p. 168 (left) INTERFOTO/Alamy, (right) Erich Lessing/Art Resource, NY; p. 175 lawcain/Fotolia; p. 176 Lebrecht Music and Arts Photo Library/Alamy; p. 186 Pictorial Press Ltd/Alamy; p. 195 igorigorevich/Fotolia; p. 196 AF archive/Alamy; p. 197 Mary Evans Picture Library/Alamy; p. 203 Wally McNamee/Corbis; p. 207 Gina Sanders/Fotolia; p. 211 Courtesy of the University of California, Irvine; p. 221 INTERFOTO/Alamy; p. 223 Keystone Pictures USA/Alamy; p. 228 Jacques Langevin/Sygma/Corbis; p. 231 NOAH SEELAM/AFP/Getty Images/Newscom; p. 232 Corbis; p. 233 Pictorial Press Ltd/Alamy; p. 242 UPI Photo Service/Newscom; p. 243 akg-images/Newscom; p. 246 Underwood Archives/Getty Images; p. 252 Everett Collection Inc/Alamy; p. 254 Napoleon Sarony/Picture History/Newscom; p. 259 air/Fotolia; p. 261 AP Images/Associated Press; p. 272 Everett Collection Historical/Alamy; p. 273 Everett Collection Inc/Alamy; p. 274 Mary Evans Picture Library/Alamy.